TRADE REGIME AND ECONOMIC GROWTH

Dedication
Charles Chanthunya: to Nifa Francisca Sandalamu
Victor Murinde: to Philo and Makarios

Trade Regime and Economic Growth

CHARLES L. CHANTHUNYA
CLC Consulting Services
Blantyre, Malawi

VICTOR MURINDE
The Birmingham Business School
The University of Birmingham

Ashgate

Aldershot • Brookfield USA • Singapore • Sydney

Published by
Ashgate Publishing Ltd
Gower House
Croft Road
Aldershot
Hants GU11 3HR
England

Ashgate Publishing Company
Old Post Road
Brookfield
Vermont 05036
USA

British Library Cataloguing in Publication Data
Chanthunya, Charles L.
  Trade regime and economic growth
  1. Trade regulation - Africa 2. Africa - Economic policy
  3. Africa - Commerce
  I. Title II. Murinde, Victor
  382.3'096

Library of Congress Catalog Card Number: 97-76946

ISBN 1 85628 624 X

Printed and bound by Athenaeum Press, Ltd.,
Gateshead, Tyne & Wear.

Contents

List of figures

List of tables

About the authors

Dr Charles Chanthunya was, until 1994, a Senior Monetary Expert with the main regional trading block in Sub-Saharan Africa, the Preferential Trade Area for Eastern and Southern African States (PTA), now the Common Market for Eastern and Southern African States (COMESA). He is currently Executive Director of CLC Consulting Services and serves as an economic consultant and a part-time Lecturer on the Masters degree in Policy Studies programme sponsored by the Southern African Institute for Policy Studies in Harare, Zimbabwe.

Dr Victor Murinde is Senior Lecturer in Finance and Director of Development Finance Programmes at the Birmingham Business School, the University of Birmingham. He is the author of *Macroeconomic Policy Modelling for Developing Countries* (Avebury, 1993; Reprinted 1995), *Development Banking and Finance* (Avebury, 1996; Reprinted 1997), and co-editor (with John Doukas and Clas Wihlborg) of *Financial Sector Reform and Privatization in Transition Economies* (Elsevier Science Publishers B. V., 1998). He has also contributed to economics and finance literature in many leading journals.

Preface and acknowledgements

The relationship between trade regime and economic growth is a topical policy issue today. For example, African countries have, since the 1970's, continued to face economic downturn; most of the countries are poorer now than they were at the time of political independence. Singular among the widely held explanations of Africa's economic problems is that, in the post-independence era, the countries got wrong the nexus between trade policy and development strategy. The main two competing approaches were whether the countries should adopt import substitution strategies and build their industrial base just as Europe had done, or whether they should heed advice from the Bretton Woods institutions (mainly the World Bank and International Monetary Fund) and the World Trade Organisation (WTO) to pursue export promotion and free trade strategies.

This book therefore focuses on one of the controversial questions in the emerging paradigm on "international trade and economic development", namely the relationship between trade policy and economic growth. The question, asked is: which trade regime is appropriate for promoting economic growth in developing countries? The most extant theoretical and empirical aspects of the question are integrated smoothly with institutional and policy issues. The analysis is illustrated through examples from a sample of ten African countries, with special reference to Malawi and Zambia. The book concludes by discussing the appropriate strategy for African countries. It is hoped that this book will make a timely contribution on this paradigm and on African countries; the work is comprehensive in coverage and attempts to strike a balance between the theory, evidence and policy issues.

In the academic arena, most economics departments in modern universities have introduced a course titled International Trade and Development. In the majority of cases, the course supplants two traditional courses titled International Trade, covering the pure theory of international trade, and Development Economics, covering traditional economics of development; these two courses used to be taught separately. Most lecturers for the new course largely rely on a collection of material from journal articles, numerous books and data sources, notwithstanding the fact that International Trade and Development is increasingly becoming an attractive area for teaching at both the undergraduate and postgraduate levels.

This book is therefore motivated to contribute to the academic and policy contexts of the relationship between the trade regime and economic growth. The book is expected to have its widest appeal to faculty members and students on undergraduate programmes in International Trade and Development, Development Economics, International Trade, and International Economics in Universities in Europe, particularly UK, as well as overseas universities especially in developing countries, particularly Africa. Practitioners in international organisations (UN, EC, IMF, World Bank), who are involved in trade and development policy issues, as well as practitioners in developing countries, particularly Africa, should find the book relevant and worthwhile. A peripheral readership will consist of postgraduate students and researchers in this subject area.

The book is structured to unfold in a systematic manner. A brief introduction offers the motivation of the study and an outline of the contents of the book. The rest of the work is structured into seven neatly divided, but thematically linked, chapters. Notes and appendices are given at the end of each chapter. The book ends with a bibliography of useful literature, including text references, and an author-cum-subject index.

It should be pointed out that this work has had a long gestation period; it has its origins in an unpublished doctoral thesis by the first author, successfully defended at the University of Wales in 1991. The research benefited immensely from constructive comments and criticisms from numerous people; special mention must be made of Lynn Mainwaring of the University of Wales at Swansea; Patrick J. O'Sullivan of the University Wales at Cardiff; Gervase Maipose of the University of Botswana; Bax D. Nomvete and Bingu Mutharika, former holders of the post of Secretary General of the Preferential Trade Area for Eastern and Southern African States (now Common Market for Eastern and Southern Africa, COMESA), respectively.

Preface and acknowledgements

Useful research material was kindly provided by the staff of the library and information services departments at the University of Zambia, the University of Wales at Cardiff and the University of Birmingham.

Some parts of the book, especially the empirical evidence on Africa as well as the theoretical (and diagrammatic) exposition, have been put to the test in a University teaching environment. Successive cohorts of Victor's undergraduate students in International Trade and Development at Cardiff Business School, in the period October 1991 - June 1996, read and discussed in seminars the raw materials that were used to write up some parts of the book. Their queries for further clarification, and contributions about their experience elsewhere, significantly influenced us in writing and revising the manuscript for this book.

We owe a special debt to Heather Rowlands for competently accomplishing the painstaking exercise of giving this book a perfect finish. The staff at Ashgate Publishing Limited, especially Anne Keirby and Rachel Hedges deserve a lot of thanks for their patience and support during the long gestation period for this final product.

We could really do without a final caveat, but in the usual tradition we accept responsibility for all errors and omissions in the book.

Charles L. Chanthunya, PhD
Blantyre

Victor Murinde, PhD
Birmingham

October 1997

1 Introduction

1.1 Backdrop

The attainment of political independence brought much hope and expectation to the people of Africa. It was widely believed that the new era would enable African countries to control and direct their political and economic destinies and thereby generate self-sustaining growth and development and improve the standards of living of the people. However, as we write, this cherished dream is not yet within striking distance. Indeed, the most glaring fact about Africa is that the continent is still the poorest in the world with the majority of its citizens still living in absolute poverty. Africa's economic and social conditions began to deteriorate in the 1970s. According to World Bank (1996), Africa's Gross Domestic Product (GDP) grew at an average rate of 3.6 per cent a year between 1970 and 1980, but fell every year thereafter. With a population growth of over 3 per cent a year, Africa's per capita income in 1983 was estimated to be about 4 per cent below its 1970 level and the GDP per capita is now said to be even much lower. The United Nations Economic Commission for Africa (UNECA) has estimated that during the period 1980 to 1987, Africa's GDP grew at an average annual growth rate of only 0.4 per cent and that per capita income steadily declined by about 2.6 per cent per annum over the same period (see UNECA, 1989). In addition to increasing poverty, the productive and infrastructural facilities have disintegrated. Agricultural output per capita continues to decline and food imports continue to increase.

Much industrial capacity stands idle. The physical infrastructure built during the immediate post-independence era has deteriorated considerably due to poor maintenance and lack of renovation; and social services and welfare, particularly education, public health and sanitation, housing and portable water, have deteriorated rapidly.

The economic crisis continues unabated despite the fact that most African countries have undertaken policy reforms which have essentially involved economic and trade liberalisation as well as stabilisation measures. This has led some pessimists to predict that Africa's per capita income will continue to fall and that by the turn of the century, sub-Saharan Africa will become irrelevant to the world economy - an economic backwater in irreversible decline.[1] This dismal picture of Africa's economic situation is widely believed to have originated from the development strategies and policies that most African countries pursued upon attaining political independence, particularly import-substitution industrialisation (ISI) strategies which are criticised as having been based on the idea that the rules of orthodox economics do not hold in developing countries. The trouble with import-substitution is said to have arisen not so much from the pursuit of the strategy as such but mainly from the policies that were normally adopted in support of such a strategy. In this connection, it is asserted that the administrative controls which were normally adopted in pursuit of import substitution did not enable the realisation of optimum conditions which make it possible for an economy to operate with maximum efficiency. It is often pointed out that administrative controls introduced distortions in the economic system and interfered with the operation of free market forces and efficient allocation of resources.

It is, however, useful to note that African economies became particularly vulnerable during the ISI stage due to the adverse exogenous forces, in particular the oil price shocks of 1979 and the breakdown of fixed exchange rates. It is, therefore, often argued that African countries should liberalise their trade regimes so as to remove the distortions that were introduced in their economic systems through government intervention. It is also often pointed out that the role of the government should simply be to establish an economic environment in which market forces would realise the efficient allocation of resources and that the appropriate instruments for creating such an environment are prices and price-denominated policies. In this regard, it is argued that governments should rationalise and liberalise economic policy around the price system which would allow the free play of market forces. In addition, tariffs and quotas should be eliminated or reduced substantially and any over-valued exchange rates should be devalued. Such policies are expected to bring a country's productive structure in line with comparative advantage and pave the way for an outward-looking strategy and promote economic growth.

2

However, some evidence from the experience of African countries which have recently undertaken economic and trade liberalisation policy reforms and from the results of other studies which have been undertaken recently on the relationship between trade regime and economic growth have cast some doubt on the efficacy of trade liberalisation in fostering economic growth and development. Brown and Tiffen (1992) present a powerful critique of the export-led growth strategy (hereafter, EGS) for Africa, within the context of the literature on trade policy and economic development. Taking a political economy approach, they argue that EGS is imposed on African countries by the International Monetary Fund (IMF) and the World Bank in the belief that trade liberalization facilitates increases in export earnings and the countries would thus be able to finance economic development and repay their debts. Case studies of the markets for major African exports are used to reveal that the prospects for EGS are poor because there are a number of impediments to free trade between Africa and the industrial world. It is concluded that alternative trade policies and development strategies must be developed to reverse Africa's economic decline. In a foreword to the Brown and Tiffen book, Susan George develops some sort of "conspiracy theory" linking the General Agreement on Trade and Tariffs (GATT), the IMF and the World Bank. She argues that there is an international division of labour in which GATT makes the rules for trade; the IMF finances trade (or balance of payments support); and the World Bank keeps trade *in situ* by insisting that developing countries should implement EGS as an essential part of their structural adjustment programmes. Susan George could have added that African governments have no political or economic clout on the policy decisions made at the Bretton Woods institutions.

It is further shown that while the continent is heavily indebted, export performance has deteriorated in the face of falling commodity prices and adverse terms of trade. Amid all this, almost all African countries have experienced war and drought. As part of the general official response to Africa's crisis, the World Bank and IMF have responded by suggesting structural adjustment. This has mainly involved currency devaluation, freeing of prices, high interest rates and credit squeeze, import liberalization and privatization of state enterprises. The inspiration for these policies is often drawn from Pacific Basin economies; in particular, Korea and Taiwan are quoted as success stories which could be emulated by African countries. This is notwithstanding the fact that Korea pursued a version of EGS which departed from the prescription of the World Bank. Moreover, Africa's factor endowment, according to neoclassical trade theory, should play a central role in EGS. Unlike the Asian "dragons", Africa is rich in resources. However, African economies lack a large and unified market; the economies are

3

characterized by high export concentration ratios as well as foreign trade dependence. It is questionable whether, given that African countries determine neither the prices nor the quantities in international trade, the EGS will work. This argument therefore challenges formal models of the Heckscher-Ohlin variety which predict gains from trade for Africa based on her factor endowment. In addition, these problems persist even when we consider the performance of export crops. In Brown and Tiffen (1992) a comprehensive data base is used to show that the export crops which historically supported economic growth in Africa are facing a declining market and their prices are falling. The terms of trade of these commodities have deteriorated against those of manufactured goods dating as far back as 1870. In addition, Africa's exports have bleak prospects as a result of competing substitutes from biotechnology which uses genetic engineering to produce crops. Further, the industrial world's income elasticity of demand for Africa's coffee, cotton, sugar, and cocoa has generally fallen. This critique is generally consistent with the Singer-Prebisch hypothesis (SPH); it concludes that the EGS for Africa cannot do the trick. This is notwithstanding the fact that there is much controversy on this hypothesis in general; see, for example, Hogendorn (1992). However, the impediments to successful EGS for Africa seem to go beyond the predictions of SPH. Analysis of Africa's export prospects, commodity-by-commodity for the main exports, shows that Africa's agricultural exports have become more concentrated; with nearly 60 percent in coffee and cocoa (Murinde, 1993). Not only has the basket of export commodities generally narrowed, but also the products are generally over-dependent on the vagaries of a few international market and trading systems. Hardly are there any significant new markets given that Africa's exports face market resistance. However, the analysis in this chapter falls short of some forecasts in terms of volume and price for each commodity analysed. Even an "export diversification" strategy for Africa is not promising. Africa's falling share of the world market for minerals may be partly attributed to civil wars and transportation difficulties. Export concentrations for African minerals are greater than for agricultural commodities (Murinde, 1993). It would therefore appear that an EGS based on the minerals sector is mistaken: mineral exploitation opportunities in the former Soviet Union are bound to attract direct foreign investment away from Africa; in addition, biotechnology will generate cheaper minerals at a time when mineral use in industrial production is falling. The analysis of production, demand and pricing aspects for copper, diamonds, gold, aluminium from bauxite, iron and steel, and some "exotic" minerals which form the mineral wealth of Africa - in general, the structure of ownership and the determination of demand and pricing of minerals - suggest that little

4

benefit accrues to African producer countries. It is also questionable whether Africa's fuel and energy resources can be a basis for EGS. Oil is by far the most important fuel and energy resource in Africa. However, it is not fully refined within Africa in order to leave behind some value-added. Indeed, for Nigeria and most other African producers, there is a clash of interests between the government and the international oil campanies. However, it may well be argued that if Africa expands its industrial sector, the demand for locally produced oil will exceed supply.

Perhaps, the key question is "what does Africa get out of its trade?". The exports from Sub-Saharan Africa leave behind only very little value-added; the main beneficiaries are seen to be transnational companies (TNCs). To illustrate this argument, it is useful to note that for the main five Sub-Saharan African agricultural products, namely sugar, cocoa, coffee, tea, and tobacco, nearly 85 percent of the final retail price for these exports is retained in the consuming country. In addition, the processing and marketing of minerals is also dominated by TNCs, with the attendant transfer-pricing problems. Four case studies of transfer pricing abuses by TNCs cited in Brown and Tiffen (1992) show that billions of dollars of revenue are lost to African governments every year, most often with collaboration of corrupt government officials. Given the bleak prospects for primary exports, it is reasonable to consider the possibility of switching to manufactured exports: this amounts to an export substitution industrialisation (ESI) strategy. The experience of the Asian Newly Industrialising Countries (NICs) could be used as a guide. However, Murinde (1993) has argued that, unlike the NICs, Africa lacks target markets and is also engaged in agriculture-allied manufacturing rather than the chemical-based manufacturing of the NICs. Brown and Tiffen (1992) undertake a case by case review of African export commodities which could become the basis for ESI, namely oil, coffee, copper, diamonds, cocoa, timber, cane sugar, cotton and iron ore. It is concluded that there are two serious impediments to ESI in Africa: foreign investors are not interested in ESI; protectionism against ESI products in the markets of industrial countries. Finally, it is useful to consider the export-led growth argument in the context of African politics. Existing literature seems to attack the belief by the World Bank that Africa's main problems are internal and derive from poor economic policies and rent seeking activities by governments (Brown and Tiffen, 1992). The literature, therefore, questions the basis and the political compatibility of the World Bank recommendation for structural adjustment in general and export-led growth in particular. The evidence generated by the UNECA and the Overseas Development Institute (ODA) shows that the World Bank structural adjustment effort has been counterproductive in African economies (Murinde, 1993). Thus, a political

5

economy approach seems to challenge the EGS advocated by those Bretton Woods institutions which profess themselves quite committed to Third World development. Moreover, in a neo-classical setting, some formal modern models of international trade show much the same result: there is no concensus that EGS is tenable in Africa amid market imperfections. Nonetheless, there are some ongoing attempts to remove the market imperfections and to rationalize some of the impediments; for example, the Uruguay Round and the EEC-ACP Lome Convention. Therefore, there is need to examine the difference which the set of trade policies chosen by a developing country makes to its rate of economic growth so as to assess the superiority or otherwise of trade liberalisation in fostering economic growth.

1.2   The motivation and methodology of the book

This book is motivated to contribute to existing knowledge of the theoretical, empirical and policy issues regarding the relationship between trade regime and economic growth. A survey of the literature regarding import substitution and export promotion is conducted, and specifically brings out the theoretical underpinnings of these two dominant trade regimes. Reference is made to the experience of the NICs in order to uncover the factors that underpinned their spectacular economic growth. In addition, a rigorous econometric test of the relationship between trade regime and economic growth is carried out for a sample of 10 Sub-Saharan African countries. For the country-specific experience of Zambia and Malawi, we call upon the method used in the National Bureau of Economic Research (NBER) project as detailed in Bruno (1978). In the application of this method, we bear in mind the structural features and policy experience of the two economies. Specifically, Zambia adopted an import substitution industrialisation strategy upon attaining political independence and also experimented with liberalisation attempts when her economy came to experience difficulties. In contrast, Malawi adopted an outward-looking strategy and persistently pursued this strategy, although her economy also came to experience difficulties which led her to undertake policy reforms aimed at further liberalisation.

The method emphasises the "phases" approach in respect of trade and payments controls which, according to the NBER project, countries tend to pass through in their historical trade and payments experience. Broadly, there are five phases of trade and payments regimes which countries tend to go through in their historical experience. A clear description of these phases is given by Bruno (1978) as follows:

Phase 1: Significant imposition of quantitative restrictions (QRs) on imports in a rather "crude" and "unsophisticated" manner.

Phase 2: QRs still reign but the control mechanism becomes very complex and differentiated with supplementary price measures, tariffs, export rebates. Even when there are export subsidies, the effective exchange rate on exports is always lower than that on imports, which are highly protected.

Phase 3: There are tidying up operations, rationalization of import tariffs; some tariff subsidies are replaced by formal parity changes. It may take the form of a package of devaluation and liberalization accompanied by external grants to facilitate expansion of (liberalised) imports.

Phase 4: This is a successful culmination of Phase 3 liberalisation efforts. There is much greater uniformity of incentives. Inter alia, the effective exchange rate on exports is equated to that on imports.

Phase 5: There is full convertibility on current account; no quantitative restrictions are employed to regulate the balance of payments. Pegged exchange rate is in equilibrium or else a flexible rate regime operates. Monetary and fiscal policies are employed as instruments to achieve payments balance instead of reliance on an exchange control mechanism.

These phases need not be followed in a given historical order. In the NBER project, for example, Phase 5 is not only the culmination of a potential cycle of change, but it is also the typical starting point from which Phase 1 departs. Specifically, Phase 1 might start in response to an unsustainable payments deficit resulting from prior inflationary pressure at a fixed exchange rate - perhaps due to the initiation of a large-scale development plan. Alternatively, it could result from a sharp drop in the price of some major export, or unexpected capital flight that runs down foreign exchange reserves. With no immediate protectionist intent, the government in this phase often imposes rules of thumb such as (i) current year's imports in every identifiable category can only be 80 percent of last year's, or (ii) exporters must convert 90 percent of all foreign-currency receipts into the domestic currency within thirty days. Across-the-board tariffs, which usually require cumbersome legislative or parliamentary approval, are typically too slow or too uncertain to offset the macro-economic impact of the initiating disturbance to balance of payments equilibrium.

The hallmark of Phase 2 is the proliferation of detailed regulations, administered by a large bureaucracy, to differentiate among alternative end uses of imports. Priorities are established to keep plants from closing down due to lack of spare parts or industrial raw materials, and possibly to maintain supplies of basic foodstuffs for consumption. Import licenses are distinguished according to origin and destination, e.g. between wholesalers and final users, and according to very detailed type - capital goods, intermediate goods, and consumer goods. Goods deemed "essential" by the bureaucrats come in at relatively low prices (relative to those prevailing in the domestic market) with large economic rents accruing to fortunate licensees; whereas inessential goods are kept out, thus increasing their domestic prices so as to provide enormous protection to "inessential" import-substitution industries. At this point, the administration of licensing procedures can become more sophisticated in the sense that taxes or special customs duties are often levied to soak up some of the economic rents accruing to particular import licensees, although others in the same commodity categories may be exempted. Moreover, specific exporters may get special subsidies to offset the overvalued domestic currency. While Phase 2 has been virtually a stationary equilibrium for years in some African countries, in others foreign exchange shortages become, from time to time, too severe (because of disincentives given to exporters) or too many obvious anomalies develop in the pricing and allocation of imports. Thus, pressure develops to devalue the currency and undertake further policy reforms.

Accompanying Phase 3 are discrete devaluations of the domestic currency. However, the degree of rationalization accompanying devaluation can vary enormously. Some countries use devaluation primarily to simplify the administration of foreign trade: exchange controls can be relaxed, and more or less equivalent subsidies for exporters and surcharges on imports can be eliminated. In other cases, the intent is to push the real devaluation much further in order to increase the export orientation of the economy and to reduce net incentives for import substitution by actually eliminating import QRs. Further still, the devaluation may be part of a comprehensive package to secure financial stability in the economy.

Phase 4 is a period of continued liberalization efforts. In this latter case, QRs are greatly reduced and/or replaced by formal tariffs so that relative prices become more important in determining what is actually imported. The average premium on import licenses falls, and the dispersion in incentives to deviate from world trade prices is reduced.

Finally, Phase 5 involves full currency convertibility on current account with quantitative restrictions on foreign trade not employed as a significant means of regulating the balance of payments. The pegged exchange rate is at its equilibrium level, and monetary and fiscal policies are consciously employed to maintain external balance. However, Phase 5 could be associated with high tariffs and thus still be biased against exports. Also substantial detailed controls on capital account, necessitating (implicitly) a pegged exchange rate, might still be retained in Phase 5. In the process of economic development, free currency convertibility seems to be either very hard to attain or not a highly regarded objective on the part of the authorities in poor countries.

The NBER "phases" approach has been criticised on two counts. Keesing (1979) has pointed out that one of the defects of the NBER classification of phases is that it looks almost wholly at trade regimes heavily dependent on QRs and that there is no subdivision of trade regimes that have few or no QRs: all are lumped together as Phase 5 regimes. As a minimum, in regard to trade regimes that rely on prices and exchange rates rather than on QRs and exchange controls, one would probably want to draw a distinction between those strongly biased against exports (through high tariff protection and lack of attention to the treatment of imported inputs) and those designed to promote exports along with industrial development for the home market. The second criticism is that the NBER phases approach focuses more on the use of QRs and exchange controls than on the hidden biases against exports in the resulting trade regimes. As part of this shortcoming it pays little attention to differences in the treatment of inputs in general and imported inputs into manufactured exports. Countries are classified as in Phase 4 or Phase 5 based on exchange rate regimes alone, without taking into account that inputs remain overpriced as a result of protection, labour policies, and neglect of the needs of exports. In this regard, Streeten (1990) has suggested that it may be useful to draw a distinction between trade policies that concentrate on raising the rewards to outputs and those that concentrate on reducing the costs of inputs.

In spite of these criticisms, the analyses of the experiences of Zambia and Malawi reported in this book are carried out within the context of the "phases" approach as described in the NBER project. There are two reasons for this. The first reason is that the method still provides a convenient framework of analysis in examining the relationship between trade regime and economic growth; moreover, the method encompasses techniques which are reasonably satisfactory for analysing the other elements that impinge on economic growth in order to assess the general impact of trade regime on the growth process. The second reason is that the NBER stages framework of analysis for trade regimes fits fairly closely the actual pattern of trade regimes in Zambia and Malawi.

From the description of the "phases", one observes that Phases 1 and 2 are the periods in which the government employs a variety of QRs to control economic activity through international trade. Bhagwati (1978) has systematized the bewildering variety of QRs categories that accompany these phases, particularly Phase 2, as follows:

1. regulation of imports by source;

2. regulation of imports by commodity composition;

3. regulation of imports by end use;

4. regulation of imports by payments conditions; and

5. additional *ad hoc* regulations regarding surcharges (or multiple exchange rates) that determine the cost or usefulness of a license to import.

Whatever the origin of these QRs may be, their application is said to have adverse consequences on static and dynamic allocative efficiency and, therefore, on economic performance in general. Because of these adverse effects, and the nature of the QRs that are employed, Phases 1 and 2 can be lumped together as constituting "inward-looking" or "import substituting" industrialisation. Therefore, Phases 1 and 2 would be expected to be associated with poor general economic performance, according to the critics of inward-looking industrialisation. Phases 4 and 5 are periods of liberalisation and can, therefore, be lumped together as constituting "outward-looking" or "export-promoting" industrialisation. These phases would, therefore, be expected to be associated with good general economic performance, according to the proponents of outward-orientation industrialisation. With Phase 1 and 2 on one extreme, and Phases 4 and 5 on the other, Phase 3 can be regarded as an intermediate stage for an economy in transition from inward-looking to outward-looking industrialisation.

In the light of the above, the study reported in this book applies the "phases" approach to the experiences of Zambia and Malawi, following the logical sequence used in the NBER project. First, the study identifies the different phases of trade restrictions which the two countries have gone through since the time of attaining political independence; this period provides a convenient date of departure. It then examines how the economy of each country performed during each of these phases with respect to growth of real GDP, domestic savings, use of investment resources, manufacturing output, real growth of exports, foreign exchange reserves and price stability. The analysis is supplemented by statistical testing of the relationship between trade regime and economic growth, focusing on the relationship between manufacturing activities and economic growth.

Note

1. Max D. Nomvete made reference to this in his speech which he delivered to the Council of Ministers of the Preferential Trade Area (PTA) for Eastern and Southern African States at its Fourth Meeting held in Harare, Zimbabwe, in June 1984 when he was Secretary General of the PTA.

2 Import substitution versus export promotion

2.1 Introduction

The choice of trade regime, as a development strategy, occupies a dominant position in economic policy-making in much of the developing world (see Krueger, 1997). The orthodox view is that outward-orientation, or export promotion, is the most promising strategy, and that the competing strategy of import-substitution or inward-looking industrialisation is detrimental to economic growth. This view is supported by the success of the NICs from the mid-1960s to the end of the 1970s. As a result many developing countries are being encouraged to adopt outward oriented policies by the multilateral aid agencies such as the World Bank and the IMF.

Import-substitution industrialisation strategy was originally proposed as the way out of the state of underdevelopment. Nowadays, the strategy is increasingly being abandoned and has reached the point of almost being forgotten as a spent force. However, as Schmitz (1984) has argued, there is evidence which shows that the success of the NICs took place behind a favourable international economic environment which included full employment in the major advanced economies, high rates of industrial growth and fast growth of world trade. Moreover, the NICs did not really give market forces such a free hand to reign over economic decisions. Schmitz (1984) has also argued that import substitution played a significant role in the economic development of many countries and still offers prospects for rapid economic transformation of the present developing countries, which can be pursued as

13

part of a long term strategy aimed at laying a firm foundation for future export success (see also Chanthunya, 1991).

This chapter aims to give an account of the origin and arguments made for and against each type of trade regime. It traces the theoretical developments, in an historical perspective, of each of the two types of trade regime and the current economic context for industrialisation. It also examines some of the practical problems of outward orientation as well as the need for industrialisation in developing countries, with special reference to Africa. Finally, it draws lessons for future economic policy-making in African countries and elsewhere in the developing world.

2.2   Trade regime bias in Africa in the context of the pure theory of international trade

In broad terms, the relationship between trade regime tenets and economic growth may be explored in the context of the pure theory of international trade. The standard textbook explanations of international trade include mercantilism (as a starting point), absolute advantage, comparative advantage, the Heckscher-Ohlin (H-O) model and its extensions, alternatives to the new-classical thinking, and intra-industry trade. The extensions of the H-O model include the Heckscher-Ohlin-Samuelson model (H-O-S) or factor-price equalization theorem, monopoly considerations, changing factor endowments (or the Rybczynski theorem), footloose industries and intermediate goods, and demand differences. The alternatives to the neo-classical model in explaining international trade include economies of scale, technological gaps and product cycle theories, and the Linder thesis. In their standard forms, these theories offer different implications for the nature of trade regime. For example, the theories predict the economic welfare conditions that may obtain under an autarkical trade regime (no international trade) and those that are associated with a free trade regime. In what follows, we highlight each of the theories.

The mercantilist school, which was popularised during the second half of the eighteenth century, argued that trade offered an opportunity to earn a surplus in the balance of payments. The idea was to encourage exports in order to earn precious metals, gold and silver. In this context, the policy advice was to encourage exports using state support and subsidies. Imports would be discouraged using protectionist measures such as high tariff barriers. In the context of African economies the trade regime advocated by the mercantilist school would mean that commercial policy by African countries should consist of high tariffs and non-tariff barriers, quotas and import controls in order to implement an import substitution industrialization

14

strategy; however, exports would enjoy a subsidy in order to achieve an increase in foreign exchange earnings. In the spirit of mercantilism, high foreign exchange earnings would imply high welfare and prosperity. However, the main limitation of this school of thought and its policy prescription is that the whole purpose of international trade is to benefit all trading partners; the scenario of expanding exports and restricting imports is not sustainable in the long run in the sense that if all countries tried to adopt it, there would not be any trade at all. Thus, no single country can enjoy high prosperity forever.

Given the limitations of the mercantilist school, the theory of absolute advantage may be used to throw some light on the question of trade regime more meaningfully. The theory that was developed to cope with the limitations of the mercantilist school is the theory of absolute advantage. Put forward by Adam Smith, the theory assumes two countries, H (the home country) and W (the rest of the world), and only one factor of production (labour). It is held that W has an absolute advantage in the production of a manufactured good (m), rather than a primary product (x), if the input-output coefficients are related in such a way that:

$$l_m^* \langle l_m \tag{2.1}$$

where l_m^* = the quantity of labour required to produce a unit of output in the foreign country W; l_m = the quantity of labour required to produce a unit of output in the home country H. It is also held that country H has an absolute advantage in the production of x if:

$$l_x^* \langle l_x \tag{2.2}$$

where l_x and l_x^* are the labour units available in the home country H and foreign country W, respectively. The trading possibilities between the two countries are illustrated in Figure 2.1.

Under a trade regime that is completely inward looking on both the demand as well as the supply side, there are no exports and imports and production is purely for the domestic market. This is when the economy operates under autarky conditions as represented at point P at equilibrium. When the economy opens to international trade, and moves towards an outward-oriented trade regime, the economy produces and consumes along PC, where the optimal point for production is P but higher consumption levels are attained as the economy moves, through trading, to point C. Compared to the consumption level at P on indifference curve I_0 under autarky, point C on indifference curve I_1 is higher.

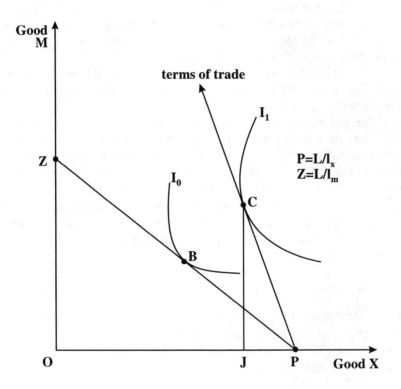

**Figure 2.1 From autarky to trade according to the
theory of absolute advantage**

However, contrary to equations (2.1) and (2.2), it is possible to have:

$$l_x^* \rangle l_x \text{ and } l_m^* \rangle l_m \qquad (2.3)$$

This suggests that home country H has an absolute advantage in the
production of both goods x and m. Or it could be equally possible to have:

$$l_x^* \langle l_x \text{ and } l_m^* \langle l_m \qquad (2.4)$$

This suggests that H has an absolute disadvantage in the production of both
goods. In the context of the trade regime debate, the theory of absolute

advantage would imply that African economies should operate as producers of the primary product x. The countries would adopt an export-led growth strategy and encourage free trade thus moving to point C on the indifference curve I_1. As we argue later in this book, there are serious shortcomings with characterization of African production and trade opportunities based on primary products.

David Ricardo improved on Adam Smith's absolute advantage and argued that it is not absolute advantage that determines the possibilities for international trade, but rather it is comparative advantage. According to Ricardo, to home country H has a comparative advantage in the production of good x given that:

$$(l_x^* / l_m^*) \rangle (l_x / l_m) \tag{2.5}$$

A trade regime of autarky would occur if:

$$(l_x^* / l_m^*) = (l_x / l_m) \tag{2.6}$$

Thus, in Figure 2.1, the trade opportunity line PC would coincide with the line PZ. In this context, the theories of absolute advantage and comparative advantage suggest that if an African economy opens up its trade regime, it should be able to attain higher consumption levels (from P to C) and enjoy higher economic prosperity. However, this result rests on the assumption that the terms of trade (line PC) are favourable (higher than PZ) to African countries so that they can produce at P and consume C. As argued in this book, the question of terms of trade for African countries (and other developing countries) has been hotly debated in the literature, with an overall verdict that runs counter to the predictions of this model.

But it was the contribution of Eli Heckscher and Bertil Ohlin that provided a more refined form of the theory of comparative advantage. The Heckscher-Ohlin (hereafter, H-O) model is explained in a 2x2x2 framework i.e. two factors of production, labour (L) and capital (K); two goods, m and x; and two countries H and W. The fundamental proposition of the H-O model is the Heckscher-Ohlin theorem. The theorem states that the key determinant of the pattern of trade is the relative endowment of the factors of production of a given country; if the country has an abundant supply of labour relative to capital, it will export labour-intensive goods, and vice-versa. The main implication of the H-O model for African countries is that it would be advisable if the countries adopted an open trade regime, if they specialised in production and export of the goods that are consistent with the countries' factor endowment. The production, import and export possibilities of an African country within a H-O setting are presented in Figure 2.2.

In Figure 2.2, trade occurs along the terms-of-trade line CP. Producers of *x* increase their output from *E* to *P* at the expense of the production of *m*. Consumers consume at point *C*. Hence trade equilibrium is (P, C) which is higher than (E, E), suggesting that trade equilibrium is consistent with higher economic welfare for the trading country.

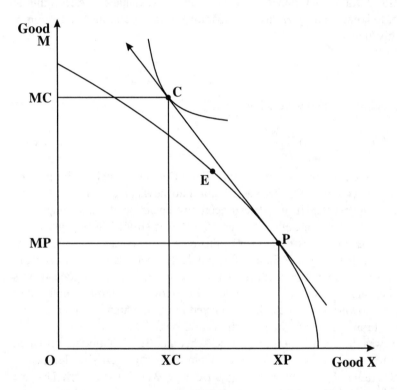

Figure 2.2 Trade possibilities for an African country according to the Hecksher-Ohlin model

It is also shown that exports arise simply as the excess of the production over the consumption of *x*; the excess of consumption over production of *m* yields imports. However, in the context of African economies, the H-O model is subject to the same criticisms as the theory of comparative advantage. The terms of trade line CP is not consistent with the argument that the terms of trade are adverse for African economies. This, if according to the H-O, African countries specialised in primary products and imported manufactured goods, they would not reap any long-run gains from trade.

The H-O is extended theoretically by relaxing some of its basic assumptions. By relaxing the assumption of perfect competition, trade theory explores the implications for international trade under a monopolistic market structure in the home country, *H*. It is argued that monopoly may cause either over-specialisation or under-specialisation in the activity of comparative advantage. If the monopolised sector produces the export good *x*, the monopolist will only exploit higher profits on the domestic market. A move towards an open trade regime implies that product *x* will compete with imports on the domestic market and will also have to compete with other goods in the international market. This extension of the H-O has important implications for African economies in the sense that it implies that an open trade regime breaks down national monopolies and introduces competition; this scenario would not otherwise occur under a very restrictive inward-oriented trade regime.

In addition, under an open trade regime, by relaxing the assumption of fixed factor endowments in the H-O model, the neo-classical model is extended to allow for changing factor endowments. It is predicted that an increase in the endowment of one factor will reduce the production of goods intensive in the other factor: this is known as the Rybczynski theorem. In the context of African economies, this theorem may be illustrated with an example of a population influx, caused for example by unskilled workers moving to a neighbouring country (say from some Southern African countries to South Africa). In this case, an increase in the endowment of unskilled labour in South Africa will reduce the production of capital intensive goods. In addition, by relaxing the assumption that factor endowments are fixed and thereby allowing for changing factor endowments we could be able to argue that if African economies achieved an increase in their capital endowments, through capital mobility and international transfer of technology, they would be able to export manufactured goods. This point is consistent with the recent experience of the emergence of newly industrialised countries as exporters of manufactured goods under an open trade regime.

The H-O model can also be extended by changing the basic assumptions to allow for factor accumulation. For example, multinational companies tend to move capital from country to country, and they may be in a position to change the factor accumulation of some countries. In the process, it becomes possible for trade in intermediate products to take place; the countries thereby acquire a comparative advantage in higher stage products. In the context of African economies, the presence of footloose industries and trade in intermediate goods would enable the countries to acquire relative factor endowments to facilitate trade with developed industrial countries in addition to boosting intra-African trade.

But more specifically for intra-African trade, it would appear that these countries have similar relative factor endowments i.e. they are generally producers of primary products in the agricultural and mining sectors. For intra-African trade, this feature of African economies would tend to fly in the face of the conventional tenets of comparative advantage and the generic H-O model. What appears to be useful in this case is to extend the standard H-O model (which is based on the supply-side) to incorporate the demand side; specifically, we introduce demand-side differences between African countries into the model. Demand dissimilarity would therefore be the main explanation of trade. However, while this extension of the H-O model may be helpful in explaining trade between African countries and the rest of the world, it may be limited in explaining intra-African trade because overall demand and supply characteristics in African countries have remained similar for about three decades now. On the basis of the foregoing, it would appear that the implications of the trade regime of African countries could be further explored by going beyond the H-O model and its extensions, including the H-O-S model or the factor price equalization theorem. In this context, it would be useful to consider alternative explanations of international trade, focussing on those theories that depart from the technological assumptions of neo-classical models.

In an extension of the above analysis it is argued that international trade can be explained by economies of scale. The idea is that if increasing returns to scale occur, they provide an additional factor of trade between two countries (say H and W) even if the countries have identical tastes (homothetic preferences) and technology. However, in the context of the trade regime for African countries, this theory implies that trade cannot be based on perfect competition; rather one of the trading partners has to have some considerable market power in order to enjoy the increasing returns to scale. The implication of market power by one trading power is that the benefits of international trade are distributed asymmetrically. This may well be the case of the trade between African countries and their trading partners in Europe, USA and Japan. To shed more light on this assertion, empirical research is necessary to test the "economies of scale" explanation of Africa's trading relationship with her trading partners; the findings should be able to shed further light on the preferable trade regime for African countries.

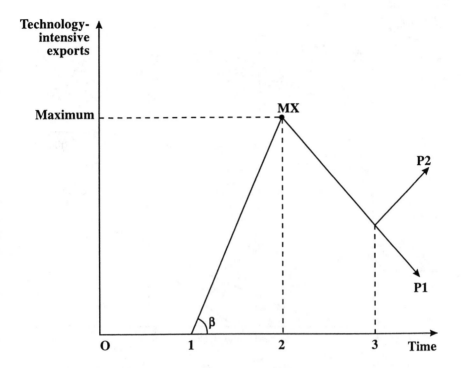

**Figure 2.3 The technology gap theorem in the context of the
trade regime of African economies**

It is also argued, as a departure from the technological assumptions of the
H-O model, that differences in technology partly underlie international trade.
This argument, encapsulated in the technology-theorem, is due to Michael
Posner. African economies seem to be disadvantaged in the sense that
technological changes and their geographical locations, which fashion the
dynamic pattern of comparative advantage, are based outside the African
continent. The technology gap theorem is illustrated in Figure 2.3.

A new technology is conceived at time t_0 (corresponding to 0 on the time
scale in Figure 2.3). The technology facilitates the production of a new good,
which is available for export at time t_1. Exports will expand until the foreign
country is able to imitate the new technology and produce the good under a
trade regime that partially represents import substitution industrialization.
Between t_2 and t_3, the import substitution industrialization is progressing and
therefore exports are falling.

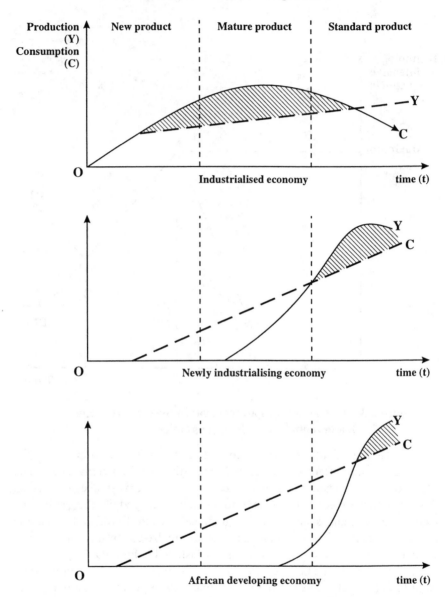

Note: Y and C relationships are indicated by exports (shaded area)
or imports (unshaded).

**Figure 2.4 Vernon's (1966) product-cycle model in the context
of African economies**

There are many examples to illustrate this theory worldwide; for example in the motor-car industry, the manufacture of motor-cycles (UK versus Japan) and in the manufacture of bicycles (UK versus China). In the context of trade regimes for African economies, this theory suggests that African economies would imitate the technological content of their imports at time t_1; however, they would not be in position to implement the technology until time t_2. Import substitution industrialization would then begin, perhaps facilitated by some form of protectionism of the infant industries, until time t_3, when an open trade regime is adopted and domestically produced goods would be able to compete with imports.

In this case, after t_3, exports will expand (Route 1) if the domestically produced good (imitating the technology) is inferior in quality relative to the imports (exports of the technological innovating country); if the domestically produced goods are superior to the imports, the exports of the technologically innovative country will fall to zero (Route 2), in an open trade regime. While the model tells us how African economies could catch up and reduce the technology gaps that exist between her and the rest of the world, the model neither identifies the factors that determine the location of the new technology, nor explains how long the gap may exist (i.e. the time span between t_1 and t_2; and between t_2 and t_3).

All the above considerations of scale economies, technological change and factor endowments are integrated into the product-cycle model put forward by Vernon (1966). A useful exposition of this model and the evidence are given by Tharakan (1985); the basics of the model are presented in Figure 2.4.

It is shown in the diagram that product stage and factor (capital and labour) endowments are inter-related and continue to change throughout the product cycle. There are three types of economies: the capital-rich and high-wage economy, as exemplified by the developed industrial economies; the capital-rich and medium-wage economy, as characterised by the newly industrializing economies; and the capital-poor and low-wage economy, as represented by most African economies and other developing countries. Each product metamorphoses through three stages: a new product, a mature product and a standardised product. The punch-line of the model is that technological know-how is one of the most important factors in explaining cross-country variations in export performance through time. What is interesting for African countries, which tend to adopt an open trade regime, is that in the ultimate (bottom) portion of the diagram, it is shown that the capital-poor and low-wage (African prototype) economy has now acquired the comparative advantage and actually exports the good in its standardized form to the capital-rich and high-wage economy (who are now importers of the good they originally produced).

It is useful, however, to recognise that African countries are not strictly homogenous; the economies are heterogeneous in structure, and differ in their growth rates, inflation rates and external sector performance. In this context, a particularly distinct theory explains international trade by distinguishing between primary products and manufactured products, thus deriving special relevance to African economies in their different stages of growth. The theory, put forward by Linder (1961) stipulates that while trade in primary products is determined on the basis of factor endowments, trade in manufactured goods is determined by the structure of demand as reflected in per capita incomes. Broadly, the Linder thesis incorporates demand similarity, scale economies and trade. Specifically, the thesis has great implications for intra-industry trade. While the theory in intra-industry trade is interesting in its own right (see seminal work by Helpman and Krugman, 1985), this type of explanation for trade is best served by examples from developed countries than from Africa.

Strictly, trade regime is part of development strategy. The existing literature identifies three alternative development strategies: balanced growth (and unbalanced growth); export promotion (or outward-looking strategy); and import substitution (or inward-looking strategy). The last two comprise alternative trade regimes; these are discussed further in the following section.

2.3   The genesis of import substitution and export substitution industrialisation

As countries attained independence in both Asia and Africa, during and immediately after the Second World War, they aimed at accelerated transformation of their economies in order to achieve economic independence without which political independence could not be sustained. Since the new nations did not have the necessary resources, they mobilised support from the international community. The United Nations Charter had, among its objectives, the promotion of higher standards of living, full employment, and conditions of economic and social progress and development. The major capitalist countries were concerned that if the former colonies achieved only very limited social progress, they could fall under communist domination, and that investment opportunities, markets and sources of raw materials would diminish. Moreover, war-time propaganda reinforced egalitarian and humanitarian tendencies for economic assistance. As Meier (1995) observes, all these mechanisms led to the emergence of a political basis for large-scale financial and technical aid from the rich countries to developing countries and many economists began to fashion tools for analyzing the problems of underdevelopment.

To most economists of the time, industrialisation held the key to development (see Chathunya, 1991). It was commonly agreed that the agricultural rural sector, which comprised the majority of the population, suffered from low productivity due to lack of industrialisation. An important problem they had to tackle, however, was "how to support the process of industrialisation". Two main schools of thought emerged on how this could be done. One school advocated export promotion and the second school argued for the development of a self-sufficient economy, based on the home market (see also Krueger, 1997).

The export promotion school   The export promotion school initially started with arguments for an export-drive in agricultural or mineral commodities (Ambler, Cardia and Farazli, 1996); the idea was to encourage developing countries to sustain their development plans. For instance, drawing from Adam Smith's "vent for surplus", it was argued that since the developing countries had surplus productive capacity in the form of surplus land and unskilled labour, they needed to expand production of their agricultural output in order to export the surplus production above domestic consumption (Chanthunya, 1991). He pointed out that this would give these countries a virtually "costless" means of acquiring imports which did not require a withdrawal of resources from domestic production but merely a fuller employment for their semi-idle labour. It was also argued that the export of agricultural or mineral products would enable the developing countries to pay for the larger part of the cost of their economic plans aiming either at greater national self-sufficiency or at the export of manufactured goods, earn the foreign exchange needed for the execution of these development plans, and pursue their development plans successfully.

Arguments against the export-drive school   However, two arguments were levelled against the agricultural or mineral export strategy. The terms of trade argument contended that there was a chronic tendency for the terms of trade to move against primary commodity producing countries and in favour of exporters of manufactured products. According to this argument, contrary to classical trade theory which asserts that all countries benefit from international trade through the equalisation of commodity and factor prices, specialisation of developing countries in the export of food and raw materials to developed countries was unfortunate for the developing countries in a number of important respects (see Chanthunya, 1991). As argued in the seminal papers by Prebisch (1950) and Singer (1950), the result of this was that the rich countries had become richer while the poor countries had become poorer (see Sarkar and Singer, 1991). The Prebisch-Singer hypothesis predicted that two main factors were responsible for this outcome. On the one hand, technical progress which took place in the centre did not result in the lowering of prices of industrial goods exported to the periphery countries. On the contrary, the prices of manufactured goods imported by the periphery countries from the centre went up. On the other hand, technical progress which occurred in the periphery countries resulted in the lowering of prices of primary commodities exported to the rich countries. The fall in the prices of primary commodities was said to have been exacerbated by two other factors, namely, the low elasticity of demand for primary commodities and technical progress in the developed countries which resulted in the reduction of raw materials used per unit of output and reduced the demand for primary commodities in the developed countries. In contrast, manufactured goods faced a high income demand elasticity which always kept their prices buoyant. The inevitable consequence was a maldistribution of gains.

This argument was criticised by the proponents of the agricultural or mineral export strategy (see Chanthunya, 1991) who argued that the assertion that international market forces had transferred income from the poor to rich countries through the deterioration of the terms of trade of the developing countries was flawed on both theoretical and empirical grounds. It was pointed out that the argument was based on wrong inferences drawn from the United Kingdom's commodity terms of trade or the terms of trade between primary products and manufactured products. It was argued that this did not provide a sufficiently strong statistical foundation for any adequate generalisation about the terms of trade of poor countries, that the import price index concealed the heterogeneous price movements within and among the broad categories of foodstuffs, raw materials, and minerals and that no allowance was made for changes in the quality of exports and imports and new commodities, besides the fact that the recorded terms of trade were not corrected for the substantial decline in transportation costs. Moreover, the introduction of new products and qualitative improvements had been greater in manufactured than in primary products, and a large proportion of the fall in British prices of primary products could be attributed to the greater decline in inward freight rates. It was, therefore, concluded that the simple use of the "inverse" of the United Kingdom's terms of trade to indicate the terms of trade of primary producing countries involved a systematic bias which made changes appear more unfavourable to the primary exporting countries than they actually were.

Furthermore, it was argued that even if the developing countries had indeed suffered a secular deterioration in their commodity terms of trade, this did not necessarily present a significant obstacle to their development; it was pointed out that what was crucial was what caused the deterioration. If the deterioration in the commodity terms was due to increased productivity in the export sector, the single-factor terms of trade (commodity terms corrected for changes in productivity in producing exports) could improve at the same time and, as long as productivity in its export industries was increasing more rapidly than export prices were falling, the country's real income could rise, despite the deterioration in the commodity terms of trade. If its factor terms improve, the country benefits from the ability to obtain a greater quantity of imports per unit of factors embodied in its exports. Also possible was an improvement in the country's income terms of trade (commodity terms multiplied by quantity of exports) at the same time as its commodity terms deteriorated. The country's capacity to import would then be greater, and this would ease development efforts. It was also argued that when due weight was given to the increase in productivity in export production and the rise in export volume, the single-factoral terms and income terms of trade actually improved for many poor countries, notwithstanding any possible deterioration in their commodity terms of trade.

In apparent recognition of the weaknesses of relying on primary commodity exports pointed out by the proponents of inward-orientation, the champions of the outward-orientation school, such as Bhagwati (1978) and Krueger (1978), later turned to advocating the export of manufactures. It was argued that this was superior to import-substitution in a number of respects. Firstly, while it is true that in terms of relaxing a country's foreign exchange constraint a unit of foreign exchange saved by import-substitution is equivalent to a unit of foreign exchange earned by export, the domestic resource cost of earning a unit of foreign exchange tends to be less than the domestic resource cost of saving a unit of foreign exchange. This means that the resources used in import-substitution earn a greater amount of foreign exchange through export expansion than the foreign exchange saved through import-substitution that relies on high rates of effective protection. Secondly, since it relies on exogenous world demand, the process of industrialisation through export expansion is not constrained by the narrow domestic market and benefits from economies of scale and efficiency derived from competition on the world market. Thirdly, foreign investment which is essential in the capital poor developing countries has more beneficial effects in export expansion in that it tends to have more linkages to agriculture by the processing of primary products. In addition to upgrading labour skills involved in the production of labour-intensive semi-manufactures, export-substitution contributes more than does import-substitution to the objectives of greater employment and improvement in the distribution of income. As it is labour-intensive in production techniques and dependent on exogenous demand, export-substitution tends to absorb more labour than import replacement and also tends to reduce the cost of employment in terms of complementary use of scarce factors of capital and inputs. Moreover, the export-substitution process uses the surplus factor of labour more intensively than does the import-substitution process and allows the scarce complementary factors to be more productive. Last but not least, export-substitution indirectly aids employment creation in the urban-industrial sector by avoiding an agricultural bottleneck that can otherwise handicap urban-industrial employment. By exporting manufactures and semi-manufactures, the developing countries are enabled to import agricultural goods and thereby keep the real wage low in terms of industrial goods. In contrast, if there is a slow growth of agricultural production and the price of agricultural goods rises relative to that of industrial goods, the real wage in terms of industrial goods rises. This in turn induces a substitution of capital for labour, and reduces profit margins, thereby causing savings to decline and the rate of capital formation to decrease. This harms industrial employment.

However, the shifting of the argument to the promotion of manufactured products is still questionable as the important question is the whole issue of whether the terms of trade of the developing countries vis-à-vis the industrialised countries have not also suffered a secular decline. The first evidence that this, too, is a possibility was provided by Kindleberger (1958) when he observed that during 1913-52, the net barter terms of trade of Western Europe improved by 50 percent vis-à-vis the developing areas of the world. More recently, such evidence has been provided by Sarkar and Singer (1991) who examined the behaviour of the terms of trade of manufactured goods exported by the developing countries to the industrialised countries vis-à-vis manufactured goods exported by the industrialised countries to the developing countries. The Sarkar-Singer study found that although the incomes terms of trade of the developing countries rose unambiguously at an average annual rate of 10 percent due to the tremendous growth in manufactured exports from the developing countries, compared to 6 percent per annum from the industrialised countries, the barter terms of trade for manufactured goods and the double factor terms of trade of the developing countries declined significantly due to a much slower growth rate of labour productivity in the developing countries than in the industrialised countries (0.4 percent compared to 2.3 percent per annum over the 1970-80 period). Therefore, the increasing diversification of exports of developing countries out of primary commodities into manufactured products did not provide a real escape from the deteriorating terms of trade with the industrialised countries of the centre. This finding also puts into doubt the claim that is often made that outward-orientation leads to productivity gains; in general, the whole value of the viability of such a strategy becomes questionable.

The outward-orientation school has also been attacked on other grounds. Some critics argue that the promotion of labour-intensive processes and component manufacturing is no more than the replacement of a nineteenth-century "plantation society" with the twentieth-century creation of a "branch plant society", which involves undue bargaining power in favour of foreign enterprises and which results in an unequal international distribution of the gains from trade and investment (see Chanthunya, 1991). For instance, Helleiner (1973) argued that export-oriented labour-intensive industries selling to multinational firms, and totally unintegrated with the rest of the economies in which they were located, combined some of the most disagreeable features of outward orientation and foreign investment. In particular, where there were "export processing zones", the manufacturing export sector merely became an "enclave" - an "outpost of the mother country." Moreover, these disagreeable features combined in a way that left the host country with a minimum of bargaining advantage. The export manufacturing activity was not only extraordinarily "foot-loose", dependent as it was on neither local resources nor local markets, but also bound the host country both to sources of inputs and to market outlets over which it had virtually no control. The fundamental problem with this dependency relationship was that continuation or further development in the field of these manufactured exports was subject to the decisions of foreign firms over which the host countries had extraordinarily little influence on decisions over plant location, new product development, choice of techniques, market allocations, etc.

Some earlier authors, for example Vaitos (1974), also attacked the outward-orientation strategy as being only "shallow development" (see Chanthunya, 1991). This is because in export activities of processed goods, transnational enterprises become important suppliers of unskilled-labour-intensive know-how and as the type of labour utilised is generally the weakest and less organised part of the labour class; this limits the possibilities for increasing returns to labour, unless a general shortage takes place in the country, in which case opportunity cost considerations arise for the host economy. If wages increase, foreign investors tend to shift to other countries since their locational interests stem from the existence of low wages, given some minimum productivity levels. The training necessary for local labour in such activities is generally very small, limiting spill-over effects. Of critical importance is the absence of marketing know-how effects for the host country since the goods traded are within the captive markets of affiliates. Final product promotion is handled abroad by the foreign centres of decision-making.

The self-sufficiency school As Prebisch (1984) pointed out, the advocates of the second school which argued for the development of a self-sufficient economy based on the home market were concerned with a number of factors arising from the nature of the international economic system and the unique characteristics of developing countries. The question of major concern was the international dissemination of technology and the distribution of its fruits, given the inequality between the producers and exporters of manufactured goods, on the one hand, and producers and exporters of primary commodities, on the other. Developing countries were seen to be part of a system of international economic relations at the centre of which were the industrialised countries who manipulated the system to their own advantage. The countries were linked with the developed countries through their natural resources and were incorporated in this system in different ways and to different extents. It was further argued that for each developing country, the type and extent of its linkage with the centre depended mainly on its resources and its economic and political capacity for mobilizing them. This conditioned the economic structure and dynamism of each country, i.e. the rate at which technical progress could lead to an expansion in economic activities. Similarly, the system of international economic relations exaggerated the degree to which income in the developing world was siphoned off by the developed countries. Moreover, the penetration and propagation of technical progress in the developing countries was too slow to absorb the entire labour force in a productive manner. Thus, the concentration of technical progress and its fruits in economic activities oriented toward exports became characteristic of a heterogeneous social structure in which a large part of the population remained on the sidelines of development. The pattern of outward-oriented development was, therefore, incapable of permitting the full economic growth of developing countries.

To counteract this tendency, the proponents of the self-sufficiency school argued for a development policy that would be oriented toward the establishment of a new pattern of development which would overcome the limitations of the previous pattern. This new form of development had industrialisation as its main objective.

The aspects of particular importance underlining this development policy were clearly articulated by Prebisch (1950). The technology of the developed countries had penetrated mainly into activities connected with primary exports which responded to the needs of the industrial countries, but not into other activities of the developing countries where the productivity of a very large proportion of the labour force was very low. Raising the level of productivity of the entire labour force was, therefore, the basic problem of development. There was no prospect for achieving this through export activities as these suffered from serious limitations in that the possibilities of increasing commodity exports were restricted by the relatively slow growth of demand in the developed countries because of the generally low demand elasticity for primary products and protectionist policies in the developed countries. Therefore, industrialisation had a very crucial role to play in the employment of these large masses of manpower of very low productivity as well as the manpower released by further technological progress in export activities and in the production of agricultural goods for domestic consumption.

Recognising that the costs of production were higher in the developing countries than in the developed countries, the advocates of self-sufficiency development prescribed protection for solving the problem that would be encountered in the effort to develop industry. The rationale behind this was that further expansion of primary exports would only bring a fall in prices. Therefore, there was need to allocate productive resources to industrial production for domestic consumption since the income lost due to the higher cost of domestic industrial production in relation to imported industrial goods would not necessarily be greater than the export income lost through the fall in prices. Indeed, once beyond the point where such losses were the same, the option in favour of industrialisation was justified.

As Prebisch (1984) notes, it was argued that this point had already been passed and that additional primary exports that were already competitive would bring a loss of income through the deterioration of the terms of trade. From this, it was concluded that import substitution stimulated by a moderate and selective protection policy was an economically sound way to achieve certain desirable effects. This would help to correct the tendency toward a foreign exchange constraint on development resulting from the low income elasticity of demand for imports of primary products by the developed countries, compared with the high income elasticity of demand in the developing countries for manufactured goods from the developed countries. Import substitution by protection would also counteract the tendency toward the deterioration of the terms of trade by avoiding the allocation of additional productive resources to primary export activities and diverting them instead to industrial production. In addition to assisting the overall penetration of technology and creating employment, import-substitution industrialisation would further promote changes in the structure of production in response to the high demand elasticity for manufactures.

In relation to the unique characteristics of developing countries, one of the forceful arguments came from the work of the Economic Commission for Latin America (ECLA) which promulgated the problem of developing countries as being structural.[1] The ECLA argued that the causes of Latin American inflation lay not in excess demand but in particular structural bottlenecks that emerged during the process of development, especially in the supply shortfalls of the agricultural and export sectors, which limited the amount of output that could be produced (see Murinde, 1993). The main bottlenecks include the food bottleneck, export instability bottleneck and foreign exchange bottleneck. Orthodox monetarist measures could only suppress inflation by stopping the very process of economic development. This structural inflation could only be cured by well-devised economic development programmes. To overcome agricultural bottlenecks and foreign exchange shortages, developing countries were advised to change their structure of production and of imports and exports. Industrialisation via import substitution became the advocated strategy. To implement this strategy, ECLA's policies emphasized the need for programmed industrialisation via import substitution based on protectionist policies.

The argument in favour of import substitution due to the elasticity pessimism was influenced by the experience of the Great Depression and the growth of beggar-thy-neighbour exchange restrictions and other inward-looking policies that came in its aftermath. This was shared by many of the leading development economists of the time. For example, Nurkse (1952) argued that the developing countries were faced by the prospect that trade could no longer serve as an "engine of growth" and proposed an inward-looking, balanced growth which meant import-substitution industrialisation, since without the benefit of constant terms of trade, growth would have to reflect internal demands. Like Nurkse, Rosenstein-Rodan (1943) shared the elasticity pessimism and argued for balanced growth, but saw the need to have investments co-ordinated and interlocked in a balanced-growth pattern (see Chanthunya, 1991). He believed that the developing countries were trapped in a low level equilibrium with no effective inducement to invest: for example, the entrepreneur investing in shoes was not sure of selling shoes unless others invested simultaneously in textiles. This dilemma would disappear if the country faced constant terms of trade at which these entrepreneurs could sell whatever they wished. The balanced, co-ordinated growth required a planning framework. As Lewis (1984) pointed out, there were a number of other factors which the proponents of self-sufficiency cited in favour of import-substitution industrialisation. One of these was that the money cost was not the same as the real cost. It was argued that wages were always higher in manufacturing than in agriculture and, therefore, that the real cost of manufacturing was exaggerated. In this regard, it was pointed out that the development of primary commodity production for export, if successful, would give rise to unemployment. To illustrate this point, take, for example, an export industry such as the mining of bauxite that could afford to pay wages three or more times higher than the rest. Wages in that industry would pull up wages in all other industries beyond what they can pay. The success of this industry would, therefore, be paralleled by even greater unemployment elsewhere, but there would be no shortage of foreign exchange and no pressure to devalue the currency - a phenomenon that is now referred to as the Dutch disease.[2] This consideration made the use of shadow prices and benefit-cost analysis necessary in decisions involving international trade.[3]

Another factor that was cited in favour of import-substitution was the learning element. The development of managerial and technical skills was considered important in economic development. It was believed by many development economists that import-substitution encouraged learning-by-doing and since managerial and labour efficiencies were a function of time, there was need to set up domestic industries which had to be nurtured and nursed through protection over a period of time which was necessary for workers to acquire the necessary managerial and technical skills. Perhaps, this is the consideration behind the investment laws of many developing countries which require foreign investors to train local counterparts.

Another factor favouring import-substitution was the need to save foreign exchange, particularly in the wake of balance of payments difficulties. By producing at home what was being imported, the countries would save foreign exchange. Similar to this was the desire to generate savings from within which could be re-invested in the domestic economy so as to increase its productive capacity. The protection to import-substitution industry would turn the internal terms of trade against agriculture and in favour of industry, thereby increasing in industry profits which could be re-invested in the domestic economy, for stimulating further industrial growth.

Furthermore, it was argued that since import-substitution had a ready market for the new industries to be established, it would easily succeed as the new industries would merely produce what was previously being imported. By shutting off imports, import-substitution would avoid the uncertainties of estimating and hazards of creating new markets for the new industries to be established and secure an already established market of known dimensions.

The advocates of self-sufficiency also took into account external factors in arguing for import-substitution. For example, Schmitz (1984) argued that the international circumstances during the period 1914-45 were the most frequently cited explanation for the emergence of import substitution in developing countries, particularly in Latin America. The two world wars and the great depression made continued importation of industrial goods difficult, or even impossible, because earnings from exporting primary commodities fell and because the nations at war were unable to supply industrial goods. This sparked off a wave of industrialisation in developing countries in order to reduce their dependence on the industrialised countries for the supply of manufactured products.

In view of the arguments made in favour of import-substitution as a means for supporting modernisation industrialisation in developing countries, and given the arguments which were levied against the export of agricultural or mineral products, import-substitution greatly influenced development policies in the 1950s and 1960s and even subsequently. This coupled with political considerations and despite academic criticism against protectionism, industrialisation and planning, as well as the statistical evidence that the terms of trade had not shown a deteriorating trend, import-substitution dominated development policy in much of the developing world. As Fishlow (1984) pointed out, this happened not only because of the persuasiveness of the arguments in its favour but also because of the conditions that then prevailed. In the 1950s, the terms of trade were eroded for many countries from cyclical Korean War highs and discouraged investment in the primary sector. In addition, investment in many Latin American countries had already reached levels at which national producers represented a significant political voice. Furthermore, increased direct foreign investment made transmission of technology more effective than it had been earlier, and also compensated for increasing deficits on trade account and national autonomy and increasing state participation were popular political values. These views on the need for import-substitution spread to African countries, as well, some of which were influenced by Lewis' prescription of such a strategy for Ghana.

Critique of import-substitution   As argued by Schmitz (1984), there is evidence that in many countries that pursued import substitution policies, considerable advances were made in the degree of industrialisation. The share of manufacturing in GDP increased and the share of imports in total domestic supply was lowered significantly. Stewart (1985) also reported that the early import-substitution policies, with the special case of Hong Kong, were highly successful, and points out that savings, investment and growth rates rose to what were unprecedented levels for most countries, thus, indicating that import substitution played a significant positive role. However, many scholars and development planners have been disenchanted, even in the structuralist quarters of the ECLA, which had hitherto been among the main advocates of import substitution industrialisation. The disenchantment arose from many country and sector studies comparing the economic performance of countries that pursued import substitution with that of countries that adopted export-oriented industrialisation strategies. As a result of these studies, import substitution has since been severely attacked, the most severe attack having come from a comparative study by Little, Scitovsky and Scott (1970). The main criticism on import substitution is that protection was overdone and this led to an inefficient allocation of resources due to distortions in factor and product markets which were caused by the protection. It has often been pointed out that because of the resulting inefficient allocation of resources, import substitution brought more problems than it solved.

First, whereas it had been hoped that import-substitution would enable developing countries to be economically independent, it made them increasingly more dependent on the developed countries. The plant and machinery which had been acquired for the new industries required spare parts which could only be obtained from the developed countries. The same was true of the raw materials and other intermediate inputs. Disillusioned with the way import-substitution industrialisation had made developing countries more dependent on the developed'countries as a result of the need to import from them raw materials and spare parts, Sarkar and Singer (1991) wrote that he did not at first foresee the possibility that even national industrialisation, and even import-substituting industrialisation specifically geared to the home market, could take place in a context in which industrialisation, no less than the development of primary production for exports, could become the basis of continuing self-reinforcing relationship of dependency.

Secondly, since the domestic markets for the new industries were limited for the scale of plant and machinery which were installed, the industries produced below optimal capacity and, therefore, became high cost producers. In addition, the industries were unable to import necessary intermediate inputs, raw materials and spare parts due to lack of foreign exchange. This also led the industries to operate below installed capacity. The under-utilisation of capacity was also due to the fact that the industrialisation policies which were followed under import substitution shifted the distribution of income away from agriculture and led to too much diversification of investible funds which created more industrial capacity than could be used. Furthermore, the kind of products produced by the import substitution industries were mainly consumed by the elite in urban areas who were in the minority and their numbers not large enough for the scale of plants which were installed. Following from the argument that the products of import substitution industries were mainly consumed by the rich, is the criticism, as put forward by Krueger (1978), that these products were luxury products which were not essential and so their production led to inefficiency through a misallocation of resources.

The protection which was accorded to the import substitution industries is said to have taxed agriculture by raising the prices of manufactured goods in relation to agricultural goods in the home market; support of the exchange rate reduced the domestic currency receipts from agricultural exports on which

\opulation depended for livelihood. As a result, these industries
\itable ventures in the overall development strategy.

_, since the industries were not profitable they could not
_ enough revenue for importing spare parts and intermediate inputs
\which were necessary to keep them going. When this happened, there were
work-stoppages which led to loss of employment, an unfortunate event in the
wake of increasing labour force in the urban areas due to rising population and
rural-urban migration. The unemployment problem is said to have been
aggravated by the rural-urban migration which import substitution encouraged
and by the distortions in factor prices which made capital cheaper in relation to
labour and led to capital-intensive methods of production (see Todaro, 1996).
This neglect of comparative advantage led to the use of more capital for a
given value of industrial output which implied less investment in other more
productive sectors, thereby aggravating the unemployment problem.

Import substitution is further said to have led to more balance of payments
difficulties. The first reason for this is that the spare parts, raw materials, other
intermediate and capital goods had to be imported. The second reason is that
the import substitution policies discouraged exports by making the domestic
currency overvalued which reduced the domestic currency receipts for
agricultural products and made domestic exports expensive in export markets.
The overvalued currency also encouraged imports by making their prices
cheaper. The third reason is that the increase in the income of the urban elite
led to an increase in their propensity to import. The foreign exchange
problem was compounded by the fact that import substitution diverted
resources from the export sector and this reduced the availability of foreign
exchange, as the foreign exchange savings from import substitution were less
than the foreign-exchange losses due to the diversion of resources from
exports.

Import substitution is also accused of having inhibited the growth of other
industries because the protection it was accorded made the prices of raw
materials and intermediate inputs produced locally for use by other industries
more expensive than those quoted in the international market. The protection
also damaged the spirit of enterprise. Entrepreneurs who were secure from
competition were not cost conscious and were not ready to introduce modern
technology nor to take on the long-term planning and risk-taking involved in
setting up a large capital-intensive factory.

Import substitution is said to have been discouraging in other ways, too.
Since imports were kept out artificially, governments could pursue inflationary
policies and keep their rates of exchange overvalued, without feeling the
impact immediately on their countries' reserves of foreign exchange. The
inflation increased the risks (relative to other types of investments) of capital-

intensive projects that took a long time to mature and the difficulties of forward planning and reduced the likelihood of finding markets abroad for part of the output because of the overvalued exchange rates.

Another problem which is said to have beset import substitution is its reliance on controls. Policies to promote import substitution involved a proliferation of administrative controls and drastic intervention in the economy. This had a number of adverse repercussions on the economy. In the first instance, the intervention created uncertainty, particularly with frequent changes of government, and tended to dampen initiative. Delays caused by administrative regulations increased the capital-output ratio since manufacturers were either induced to hold excessively large stocks of imported inputs, as a precautionary measure, or were prevented from fully using industrial capacity by delays in obtaining foreign exchange for such inputs.

Investment decisions were also regulated but the delays involved in obtaining government's approval created havoc with business planning. A typical example of where such delays were probably great is India. Little, Scitovsky and Scott (1970) reported that procedures were complex and delays of more than a year were frequent. Investors applied in advance for investment licences and then failed to use them: since the allocation of licences was based on the number of licences granted, rather than on those used, actual investment was restricted to below the planned capacity targets. Other costs were the diversion of skilled manpower and the tendency of industry to be concentrated near administrative centres, to facilitate protracted negotiations with the government's administrative services. Corruption naturally resulted, and more productive private initiative was discouraged.

Little, Scitovsky and Scott (1970) argue that while prices may be an inadequate guide to social needs and scarcities and their defects can be remedied by controlling business decisions, investment decisions could only be efficiently made in the light of a detailed knowledge of the circumstances of each case. But central planners had no access to the information which was really required nor did they have large enough or sufficiently expert staff to process the available information. The same was true of decisions to import. It was impossible for central planners to obtain or digest the vast amount of information needed to control efficiently the thousands of decisions involved. It is no wonder that they fell back on rules of the thumb, based on such principles as "fair shares", which were far removed from social needs and scarcities. This often misfired: restrictions on imports of luxury consumer goods led to their manufacture locally. Similarly, discrimination in favour of imports of capital goods was accompanied by widespread under-utilisation of existing capacity, itself largely the effect of the import licensing system.

Another criticism that has been made against import substitution is that the scope for further progress was rather limited. Import substitution only went on for a limited number of years say, fifteen years, and then the countries run out of opportunities for further import substitution, a phenomenon that is said to have occurred particularly in a number of Latin American countries. Import substitution began with the final stages of production, and the first industries that were established were always those that assembled parts and components, and turned out finished consumer goods. Import substitution progressed in stages, beginning with the stage of "easy" import substitution which involved the production of such products as clothes, beer, soft drinks, confectionery. which could be produced for small markets; then proceeded to the increasingly "difficult" stages involving the production of intermediate goods and spare parts and finally to the production of capital goods; instead of beginning with the production of capital goods and ending up with consumer goods. As countries moved up the ladder, the opportunities for further import substitution declined more and more; contrary to the expectation that, since for a time at least it would allow a very rapid rate of industrial growth, it would produce a sufficiently dynamic change in the economic nature of a country and its consequences would include a higher rate of growth of income and, therefore, continued industrialisation based on a growing home market. Import substitution became exhausted, without having led to a dynamic and sustained industrial growth which would have made significant inroads on the problems of creating employment and fundamentally changing the economic structure. The sequential nature of import substitution also made technological advances difficult in that in the first stage, consumer goods were produced by means of the capital goods obtained from other developed and industrialised countries. The type of consumer-goods investment which took place determined the whole pattern of intermediate and capital goods industries, and there was little opportunity for changing the nature of techniques employed. This happened particularly in industries which began with the assembly of spare parts into finished products, and where industries producing the parts had then to conform exactly to the specification of similar industries in countries from which the parts originally came. As most investment was made by the subsidiaries of foreign companies, industrialisation by import substitution was very much less "learning intensive" than the industrialisation of the developed countries; it brought in complex technology, but without the sustained technological experimentation and concomitant training and innovation which are characteristic of the pioneer industrial countries. It is partly the lack of this experimentation and innovation which lies behind the failure of import substitution to lead to continued industrial growth, and so to real economic and social transformation (see Chanthunya, 1991).

In summary, it is argued that import substitution inherently suffers from the following weaknesses:

1. *Intrinsic problems of government interference* It is argued that excessive administrative regulations give rise to bureaucratization, corruption, uncertainty and delays, and thus discourage productive private initiative.

2. *Bias against exports* It is widely held that the existence of import restrictions leads to a higher exchange rate than would prevail under a free trade regime, reducing the relative gains from exporting.

3. *Bias against agriculture* It is also argued that the protection of local industry raises the prices of manufactured goods relative to agricultural products in the home market and the overvalued exchange rate reduces the domestic currency receipts for agricultural exports.

4. *Under-utilization of installed capacity* Some critics argue that since import controls do not apply equally to capital goods and since credit for installing machinery is relatively cheap, factories are over-equipped. Moreover, protection in product markets makes it possible to earn good profits even at low capacity utilization.

5. *Under-utilization of labour* It is useful to note that capital goods can be obtained relatively cheaply due to the combined effect of over-valued exchange rates, low import restrictions for such goods and subsidized financing conditions, resulting in a bias against employment of labour.

6. *Import intensity of import-substitution industries* It is argued that while the importation of consumer goods reduces substantially, this is achieved at the expense of increased imports of equipment and materials, resulting - contrary to expectations - in an even more rigid dependence on foreign supplies and renewed foreign exchange crises.

7. *The slowing down of import-substitution industrialization* It is argued that although initially industry can grow faster than domestic demand for manufactures, developing countries soon run out of import substitution possibilities. After that growth rates can only be maintained by a growth in domestic demand or in exports; but by then the structure and inefficiency of industry stand in the way of conquering export markets.

2.4 The theoretical basis of outward-orientation and inward-orientation

The proponents of outward-orientation emphasize the alleged virtues of competition and the benefits of resource allocation guided by the invisible hand of the market mechanism rather than the visible hand of bureaucracy. The price mechanism plays a very crucial role here in that it is believed that changes in prices bring about substitution in production and consumption, both at home and abroad. Through its effect on the price mechanism, trade permits a more efficient allocation of national resources. In order not to interfere with the operation of the price mechanism, outward orientation seeks to limit state action to the provision of public goods which are essential for the functioning of market processes, namely law and order, stable money and infrastructural activities that affect public goods (see, for example, Lal and Rajapatirana, 1987).

As to the reason for the superior performance of export promotion, it is generally argued that the policies which are adopted in pursuit of export-oriented strategies are closer to the optimum conditions for the achievement of economic efficiency and that the superiority of export-oriented strategies derives from this phenomenon. Writing in support of this claim, Krueger (1985) argued "the growth rates of the outward-oriented countries certainly suggest that something more than the direct impact of exports was at work in accounting for the superior growth performance of these countries. When one examines critically some of the bases upon which that superior performance may have rested, most of the factors earlier thought to have justified protectionist regimes in fact become arguments for intervention supporting exports instead of production for a protected domestic market". This "something more" is generally believed to be the operation of free market forces on the economy as a result of the absence of administrative controls which are not possible under an outward-oriented regime.

As argued by Krueger (1997), three sets of factors are believed to be at work in accounting for the difference in economic performance under the two trade regimes. Such factors are said to be technological, economic and politico-economic factors. The technological factors relate to market size, indivisibilities and economies of scale, factor intensities, infant industry, and interdependence and quality. With regard to market size, it is argued that the small size of domestic markets in developing countries limits their growth under import substitution only up to the size of the domestic market. It is pointed out that the expansion of an activity beyond the amount sold in the domestic market is seldom profitable under import substitution. In contrast, in an outward oriented economy, efficient activities can expand well beyond that point.

In relation to indivisibilities and economies of scale, it is pointed out that many processes or industries demand a minimum size for the plant to be efficient. As import substitution restricts local industries to reliance on sales in the domestic market, it leads to short production runs and high average variable costs. On the other hand, export orientation permits a developing country, regardless of the size of its domestic market, to establish economically efficient size plants and to maintain long production runs. Under such a regime, producers in a small country are also able to obtain specialised products which are not domestically produced at internationally competitive prices whereas under import substitution, either there are substantial delays in obtaining such items because of import licensing procedures and restrictions, or producers obtain them from high cost domestic producers.

In respect of factor intensities, it is argued that export promotion enables a faster growth of value added and employment of unskilled labour in industry for the same rate of human and physical capital formation, and the larger size of the international market encourages expansion of exporting industries that use relatively unskilled labour. The problem of import substitution is that it limits the expansion of these industries to the growth rate of domestic demand once production has expanded sufficiently to replace imports and thereafter, output growth is tied to increases in real income and demand.

In regards to the infant industry argument, it is asserted that the restriction of output levels to the domestic market reduces the dynamic gains to far smaller magnitudes than would be possible if the industry were induced to export (Meier, 1995). With regard to interdependence and quality, it is pointed out that efficient production of most manufactured goods involves the use of a wide variety of inputs. Owing to foreign exchange constraints and in order to enforce protection, inward orientation requires producers to obtain their intermediate inputs from protected local producers. As such products are of low quality, due to lack of competition, their use raises costs and lowers the quality of output in other firms. Under a liberal trade regime, exporters are free to purchase their inputs from abroad and from the cheapest and most reliable source and this reduces their own production costs.

Regarding economic factors, it is argued that the forces of competition to which outward orientation is subjected induces lower-cost activities in individual firms and greater economic and engineering efficiency. In addition, for any given distribution of costs within an industry, the possibility of exporting permits more rapidly changing market shares which in turn further accelerates the rate of increase of factor productivity and of the industrial sector.

Turning to the politico-economic factor, it is contended that outward orientation constrains government action because of several reasons. In the first instance, there are limits to the extent to which quantitative controls can be imposed in an export oriented regime. As exporters need ready access to the international market for their inputs, provision of that access substantially reduces the scope for quantitative restrictions upon any group of imports. If quantitative controls are highly restrictive, the reward for evading them is great and their enforcement is possible only with fairly detailed examination of all incoming goods, which is inconsistent with the ready access required by exporters. Thus, as some imports are intermediate goods used by exporters, this imposes a limit on the level of protection accorded to any productive activity through quantitative restrictions. In the second place, it is argued that outward orientation involves less variability in incentives as export policies inherently reward those who export and do not discriminate among exportables so that rewards depend on performance. Finally, it is argued that the negative effects of policies are more visible to policy makers under export promotion than under import substitution. For instance, an overvalued exchange rate is much more clearly reflected in lagging exports under an outward oriented policy than would be evident through rising premiums for import licences under import substitution. In contrast, under import substitution and direct controls over imports, firms have built-in incentives to misrepresent their activities in ways that induce the receipt of more import licenses and other permissions and privileges. These incentives are far smaller under export promotion.

The same is true with the procurement of intermediate inputs. It is not always true that such industries are required to purchase them locally from other import substitution industries. In any case, most of the intermediate inputs required by these industries are available abroad and these industries also try to source their intermediate inputs from the cheapest source. Thus, the procurement of intermediate inputs from the cheapest source is not unique to export oriented industries.

The advocates of outward-orientation seek to limit state intervention in the economy. One of the major reasons is to engender competition which is viewed as being very beneficial in that it forces exporters to improve their production processes, entrepreneurship and quality of their products; trade enables them to benefit from economies of scale which are associated with enlarged markets. But one can hypothesise a different possibility quite in the opposite direction, on a priori grounds. In Schumpterian fashion, for example, one can argue that the incentive to innovate is inversely related to competitiveness. The question of trade-related dynamic efficiencies can only, therefore, be settled empirically.

It is to be noted that the forces of competition which benefit exporters by forcing them to improve the quality of their products, production processes and entrepreneurship, exist abroad and not in the domestic market, presumably because of protection at home. This is why proponents of outward-orientation advocate active export-promotion policies so that producers of exports in the domestic economy can be subjected to the forces of competition abroad, in addition to benefiting from economies of scale. Interestingly enough, they also argue for free trade and dismantling of protection for the entire domestic market in order to foster efficiency through competition in all sectors of the economy. Thus, advocates of outward orientation, such as Bhagwati (1978) and Krueger (1978), are also against protecting industries producing for the domestic market. It is argued that this is harmful to growth in a number of ways in that it acts as an obstacle to the very development it seeks to achieve by reducing competition thereby worsening resource allocation and tying the country to an inefficient manufacturing system; that it restricts the extent to which economies of scale can be internalised by the country; and that, when combined with non-tariff barriers, as it is always the case, it reduces the efficiency of macropolicy.

In addition, it is argued that protection raises a country's production costs above the international standard and tends to overvalue the domestic currency, which further harms international competitiveness. Thus, protection places a country at a disadvantage with overseas competitors in material procurement when industrialisation begins its intermediate products stage. Moreover, protection makes profits on sales to the domestic market higher than to the export market, which places export sectors in a more difficult position in terms of resource allocation. Furthermore, protection is said to hinder the development of agriculture by turning the internal terms of trade in favour of industry and against agriculture and leads to a more unequal distribution of income.

Finally, it is argued that protection, particularly via quantitative restrictions, gives rise to rent-seeking or directly unproductive profit-seeking activities which exert a great cost on an economy. It is pointed out that under protection, entrepreneurs tend to evade the quantitative controls by diverting resources into unproductive ways of making income. Such resource-using unproductive activities are said to include tariff evasion and lobbying or corrupt practices, such as bribery, in order to get lucrative import and investment licences. It is argued that these wasteful activities cause additional distortions in production and consumption and that they are a major source of economic inefficiency since these activities use real resources to seek out rights to quotas and other rent-bestowing licences. It is pointed out that under perfectly competitive rent seeking, agents will invest resources to acquire licences until the value of rents equals the cost of rent seeking. But resources used in rent seeking produce no incremental output and are thus wasted.

As it has been stated, outward-orientation argues for active export promotion including the granting of export subsidies to encourage exports, contrary to the prescription of the neoclassical theory of trade which it embraces. The neoclassical trade theory argues against any form of intervention, whether through the use of import tariffs or export subsidies. This theory, as represented by the Heckscher-Ohlin model, shows how free trade increases the consumption possibilities of a country by equalising the marginal rate of transformation in production and the marginal rate of substitution in consumption and how any trade intervention - through an import tax or export subsidy - lowers welfare relative to the free trade situation. However, due to the existence of non-competitive conditions in the real world, particularly in the developing countries, neoclassical theory preaches the use of "optimal" intervention to correct situations which diverge from optimal marginal conditions. According to the optimal intervention theory, as advanced by Södersten (1980), a distortion should be corrected without recourse to trade intervention; the intervention should be as close as possible to the source of the distortion. A production subsidy or tax should be used to deal with a production distortion and a consumption subsidy or tax with a consumption distortion, and so on.

However, outward-orientation argues for export subsidies and against any subsidies for production or consumption in the domestic market. Presumably this is to compensate for what one perceives as existing distortions due to import-substitution measures so as to move relative prices nearer to "free trade" ones in order that exports can be promoted without any hindrance of distortion elements in the home market. Indeed, outward orientation argues that export subsidies are welfare-increasing rather than welfare-worsening if properly designed, in contradiction to the prediction of neoclassical trade theory.

In the economic literature, export subsidies such as export drawbacks have indeed been criticised on the grounds that they generate distortions in the input markets. As the exporter has access to foreign inputs which are exempted from tariffs, the domestic producer of inputs may be importing his own inputs, further back in the chain of production. As he is not an exporter, the duties paid on those inputs raise his costs, reducing his chances of competing with the inputs imported directly by the final exporter. Consequently, simple export drawbacks are biased against "indirect exporters", i.e., the domestic producers of inputs for final exporters. This bias persists even if the input is not internationally tradeable, as the tariff paid by indirect exporters raises the cost and price of the domestically produced input. The result is that simple export drawbacks can promote excessive reliance on foreign inputs and the development of an export sector detached from the domestic economy. Alternatively, simple export drawbacks can promote unnecessary vertical integration between final and indirect exporters. However, in a study of Chile, Korea and Colombia, Valdes-Prieto (1990) found that by extending export drawbacks in a carefully designed fashion, the granting of subsidies can be welfare-increasing. Thus outward orientation claims that its case for granting export subsidies is justified empirically.

With regard to the point that protection leads to rent-seeking and other directly unproductive activities which are a major source of economic inefficiency and loss of welfare, a study of the Philippines by Clarete and Whalley (1988) found no conclusive evidence of the welfare loss effect of such rent-seeking activities. According to the result of this study, trade policies and other distortions are indeed significant. However, in the presence of import quotas and rent-seeking, removing tariffs, even for a small open price-taking economy, is welfare worsening as in the presence of quotas, tariffs serve to reduce quota values and lower the social cost of rent-seeking. Thus, removing tariffs can be undesirable. The study also found that lifting tariffs could enhance welfare in situations where some goods are subject to quotas while other goods are not.

The gain from trade is expressed in the theory of comparative advantage which was formulated more than 150 years ago by David Ricardo who drew inspiration from Adam Smith. To Adam Smith, specialisation was a matter of absolute advantage: trade allowed countries to produce what they were best at, and to buy from abroad everything else. Ricardo demonstrated that even if a country had an absolute advantage in all lines of production, it could still gain from trading. The proponents of import-substitution, such as Nurkse (1959) and Lewis (1980), while accepting the importance of trade in growth, argue that there is little substitution in production or consumption at home or abroad so that changes in relative prices brought about by trade have negligible consequences for the allocation of resources and that what matters, instead, is the level of external demand. Therefore, the growth of developing countries depends indirectly on their ability to export and import and trade is an autonomous "engine of growth" or the single most important obstacle to it. The effect of trade on growth is both supply and demand based.

The supply effect of trade on growth derives from the incapability of developing countries to produce certain non-substitutable investment goods which they have to import in order to expand productive capacity. However, their ability to import such non-substitutable investment goods depends directly on their ability to export, if more foreign exchange cannot be obtained from foreign borrowing or redirected from the import of consumption goods.

Thus, limited substitutability of imported for domestic goods in consumption is what makes exports important for growth.

The demand-based effect of trade on growth derives from the dualistic nature of developing countries in that they typically have two independent sectors: a traditional, subsistence sector in which productive resources, mainly labour, are largely under-employed or unemployed; and a small enclave export sector with minimum links with the traditional sector which is caught up in the vicious circle of poverty. Thus, growth occurs only to the extent that the enclave sector expands to absorb the labour that is readily available in perfectly elastic supply from the traditional sector. Therefore, although exports matter for growth, their expansion depends on the prosperity and growth in the industrialised countries and other exogenous non-price determinants of the external demand for exports from the developing countries. Therefore, export performance of developing countries is determined by forces external to them. This is part of the foundation of import-substitution advocated by, *inter alia*, Prebisch, Myrdal and Nurkse who argued that while trade served as the engine of growth in the nineteenth century, it could no longer be relied upon to play that role in the twentieth century because of a slowdown in the growth of demand in the developed countries.

The experience of the South East Asian countries in the 1960-70 period, of course, proved Nurkse's prediction false. World trade expanded rapidly during the post-World War II period. As reported by Kaplinsky (1984), the estimates put the expansion of global trade in the two decades after 1953 at 8 percent per annum and at 11 percent per year for manufactured goods. However, as the 1970s wore on, the rate of economic growth fell and unemployment, inflation and balance of payments deficits became endemic in most of the major industrial countries. Consequently, the rate of growth of world trade declined. Thus, at least for this period, Nurkse's prediction was vindicated.

The problems which import substitution is said to have suffered from are not in dispute. What is in disagreement is the policy implication arising therefrom. Structuralists see the failure of import substitution to lie in the colonial heritage and in social class formation and economic control mechanisms which emerged during the neo-colonial period and gave way to several factors which worked against import substitution. These are:

1. that import substitution accepted the pattern of demand and the underlying distribution of income inherited from the past as given. For it to have succeeded, the distribution of income and consumption should have been radically altered;

2.   that import substitution encouraged foreign penetration of the economy, particularly the establishment of subsidiaries of foreign firms behind high tariff barriers which led to the elimination of many local producers and rendered the industrial structure monopolistic;

3.   that import substitution was based on foreign technologies from the advanced countries which were inappropriate to local conditions and led to heavy outflow of capital through transfer pricing and royalty payments;

4.   that import substitution resulted in the protected accumulation of the indigenous bourgeoisie in alliance with, or subordinated to, international capital; and

5.   that the overall effect of import substitution was transnational integration and national disintegration of the economy and society.

Therefore, according to the structuralists, as White (1984) has argued, the solution cannot lie in a greater reliance on market forces, but in more radical promotion of national or regional industrial policies which include greater control of foreign enterprises, greater scrutiny over imports of technology, reform of the tax and incentive system and redistribution of income. Put differently, these are policies which may require more fundamental political change, aimed at a different kind of inward-looking strategy.

Regarding the view by the advocates of outward orientation that countries should pursue free trade and produce and trade in accordance with the theory of comparative advantage, the advocates of import substitution point out that, in its neo-classical framework, as represented by the Heckscher-Ohlin model, the theory of comparative advantage is based on a number of simplifying assumptions, i.e. the prevalence of competitive conditions in commodity and factor markets; the absence of transport costs or other impediments to trade; all production functions are homogeneous of the first degree; the production functions are such that the commodities produced show different factor intensities; and the production functions differ between commodities, but are the same in all countries, and that there is no movement of factor inputs internationally - only trade flows. These assumptions do not correspond with the conditions that obtain in many developing countries, and a relaxation of these assumptions gives entirely different policy implications.

It is argued that there are a number of qualifications to these assumptions. One such qualification is the possibility of an "optimum tariff" which is based on the argument that if a country is large enough, it can depress the price of its imports on the world market by demanding less. In this way, it can use a tariff to improve its terms of trade and raise its export prices relative to its import

47

prices and this can improve its national welfare. The optimum tariff is that tariff which would maximise this gain. Orthodox economists regard the optimum tariff as immoral because the gains derived from it are at the expense of other countries and point out that trade policy ought to take into account the well being of the world as a whole. But for developing countries, the use of such a tariff could be morally justified. Orthodox economists argue that the use of the optimum tariff would trigger retaliation and that everybody would lose.

Another qualification is the infant-industry argument for protection. It is argued that new industries need to be sheltered when young as without such help, industries that might be profitable in due course would fail to establish themselves. This is predicated on the view that the market fails in some way; otherwise a new business would be willing to incur losses in the expectation of making big profits later. One such market failure is short-sighted financial markets which might make it impossible for a new business to finance its initial investment. Another type of market failure is "externalities". A new company may incur costs in starting up a venture that benefits others that follow it into the industry, e.g., the costs of adapting foreign technology for local use. The first company into the business is not fully rewarded as it cannot keep the benefits all to itself. Consequently, too few industries become established.

However, economic theory sees no case for infant industry protection. It argues that if a capital market exists and functions properly and if domestic producers have a correct view of the profitability of investment, they will invest in the industry even without a tariff. It is, therefore, concluded that the existence of internal economies is not a sufficient reason for protection. Using the theory of optimal intervention by Södersten (1980), it is argued that the best way of dealing with the infant industry case is either the use of a subsidy or a tax or both. But in developing countries capital markets are not well developed and governments rarely have enough financial resources to resort to the use of subsidies so that protection of infant industries may still be justified.

All these qualifications have long been recognised by economists but the case for free trade has remained almost universally accepted. Economists have regarded these exceptions to free trade as interesting but unimportant and the economic risks of trying to act on the exceptions have often been seen as out of all proportion to the likely costs, such as trade-policy retaliation by other countries and the danger that protection for infant industries would be captured by vested interests and extended through adolescence, adulthood and premature senility.

However, the virtues of free trade are now being challenged by a new body of economic theory and the case for free trade is now more in doubt than at any time since the 1817 publication of Ricardo's Principles of Political Economy. This new body of economic theory emphasizes the existence of increasing returns and imperfect competition in trade which call into doubt the extent to which actual trade can be explained by comparative advantage and open the possibility that government intervention in trade through import restrictions, export subsidies and so on may, under some circumstances, be in the national interest. As has been pointed out by Krugman (1987), the new body of theory argues that trade is not only caused by comparative advantage but also by other factors such as increasing returns, endogenous technological change, and economies of scale which can lead to imperfect competition. For instance, it has been recognised that economies of scale can lead to arbitrary specialisation by countries in products within monopolistically competitive industries and that countries specialise and trade, not only because of underlying differences, but also on account of increasing returns which are an independent force giving rise to geographical concentration of production of various goods, so that increasing returns are as fundamental a cause of international trade as comparative advantage.

It should be noted that the role of increasing returns is not a novel idea, but the new theory gives it more clarity and force than the formal models; it is emphasized that to the extent that trade driven by economies of scale is important in the world economy, imperfect competition is just as important as a causal factor. As Krugman (1987) has pointed out, international trade theory thus becomes inextricably intertwined with industrial organisation as most trade is in products of industries commonly classified as oligopolies.

The new theory of international trade argues that trade is, to an important degree, driven by economies of scale rather than comparative advantage and that international markets are typically imperfectly competitive. This new view has suggested two arguments against free trade: strategic trade policy argument which holds that government policy can tilt the terms of oligopolistic competition to shift excess returns from foreign to domestic firms; and externalities argument which calls for government policy to favour industries that yield externalities, especially generation of knowledge that firms cannot fully appropriate.

The contention of the strategic trade policy is that in a world of increasing returns and imperfect competition, lucky firms in some industries can earn higher than the opportunity costs of the resources they employ. For example, supposing that economies of scale are sufficiently large in some industry that there is only room for one profitable entrant in the world market as a whole, i.e., if two firms were to enter they would both incur losses. Then the firm which manages to establish itself in the industry will earn super-normal returns that will not be competed away.

49

Take the example of the aircraft industry where start-up costs are extraordinarily high. Let us suppose that two companies, Boeing and Airbus, are contemplating whether to build a new aircraft. If either goes ahead alone, it will make profits of £100 million. If both go ahead, they will each make a loss of £5 million. Now, assuming that Europe's governments agree to subsidize Airbus to the tune of £10 million, Airbus is certain to make a profit of £5 million, even if Boeing goes ahead, too. But for sure, Boeing will not go ahead as the subsidy makes it certain that Airbus will build its new aircraft, and certain, therefore, that Boeing will make a loss if it joins in. The result is that Airbus would make a profit of £110 million and repay its subsidy with ease. Assuming further that each company produces entirely for export, then Europe's subsidy of £10 million would secure a transfer of rents worth £100 million from America to Europe. We may take another example of an industry with just two firms, one being American and the other Japanese. In this industry, learning-by-doing reduces unit costs indefinitely as output expands. Japan closes its domestic market to the American firm while America keeps its own market open. As a result, the Japanese firm can increase its output, thereby lowering its unit costs. In due course, this competitive edge enables it to drive the American firm out of business. The rents that the American firm had extracted from American consumers now go to the Japanese.

These examples show that a country can raise its national income at other countries' expense if it can somehow ensure that the lucky firm that gets to earn excess returns is domestic rather than foreign. The strategic trade policy argument shows that at least under some circumstances a government, by giving support to its firms in international competition, can raise national welfare at another country's expense. The above examples show how this goal can be attained through a subsidy, but other policies can also achieve the same objective. In particular, when there is a significant domestic market for a good, protection of this market can raise the profits of the domestic firm and lower those of the foreign firm, in the case where both enter; like an export subsidy, this can deter foreign entry and allow the domestic firm to capture the excess returns. Thus, a protected domestic market can, under some circumstances, promote rather than discourage exports and possibly raise national income; contrary to the prognosis of classical trade theory.

The externalities argument is not a new idea of a strategic struggle over rents, as classical trade theory has shown. However, classical theory, being based on perfect competition, has not dealt satisfactorily with the most likely source of externality. This is the inability of firms to capture the fruits of expensive innovation. This is especially true in industries experiencing rapid technological progress, where firms routinely take each other's products apart to see how they work and how they are made. Investment in knowledge inevitably has a fixed cost aspect and once a firm has improved its product or technique, the unit cost of that improvement falls as more of the good is produced. The result of these dynamic economies of scale is a breakdown of perfect competition. Such external economies are found mostly in industries where R & D is an especially large part of a firm's costs. These external economies also offer a reason for government intervention in certain particular sectors of the economy and provides the rationale for deviating from free trade.

The objective conclusion of the new trade theory that much trade reflects increasing returns and that many international markets are imperfectly competitive has met with remarkably quick acceptance in the profession. However, the normative conclusion that this justifies a greater degree of government intervention in trade has met with sharp criticism and opposition. One of the leading critics of the application of the new trade theory is Bhagwati (1988) who insists that much of the economic reasoning that has long defended the classical view from infant-industry protection to the optimum tariff is directly relevant to the new ideas and that increasing returns and imperfect competition actually provide an even more justified case for free trade.

There are three criticisms which have been levied against the new theory of trade (see Chantunya, 1990). As in the case of the optimum tariff, the first of these criticisms is that trade policy should be looked at from the point of view of the well-being of the world as a whole and that this is unfair and would invite retaliation. It is, therefore, pointed out that if a cycle of retaliation and counter-retaliation sets in, every body would be worse off. The second argument is that governments lack the information needed to intervene intelligently. In this regard, it is often pointed out that to have any chance of making strategic trade policy work, governments would need copious amounts of information. In the Boeing-Airbus case, for example, the interventionist government would need to know how much profit would be earned by going ahead with a new aircraft, both with and without competition from abroad. Small mistakes in such calculations can mean that intervention makes the intervening country worse off, rather than better off. The third argument against the new trade policy theory, as advanced by Bhagwati (1988), for example, is that even if the government succeeds in intervening wisely, the gains from intervention will be dissipated by rent-seeking firms.

2.5   Some controversies on the choice of trade regime

The development of the NICs   The   reason that is always given by the advocates of outward-orientation for the success of the NICs is that these countries pursued the right policies by liberalising imports, adopting realistic exchange rates, providing incentives for exports and getting factor prices right so that their economies could expand in line with their comparative advantage; reliance on market forces and integration into the world economy yielded results superior to protection and dissociation from the world economy. The advocates of inward orientation argue that this is not completely correct. For example, Schmitz (1984) points out that the emergence of the NICs was a response to a set of international circumstances which produced relatively favourable access to markets of the advanced countries, dramatically increased access to international finance and increased relocation of production by multinational corporations to the periphery. It has been pointed out that these factors conditioned the emergence of the NICs rather than determined which countries were to seize the opportunities presented; thus the emergence of the NICs was determined partly by location and geographical significance, partly by the existence of a strong (repressive) internationally reliable regime; and partly by the existence of a technological infrastructure resulting from earlier import-substitution policies.   Furthermore, it has been pointed out that state control over industrial development was extensive and decisive in bringing about dynamic growth.

Role of multinational corporations   The background history to this is that from the mid-1960s onwards, various developments took place in the advanced countries: profitability declined, competition between themselves increased, especially more so with the advent of Japan as a major competitor in world markets; wages rose in Europe and North America and there were increasing difficulties in maintaining control over labour at the site of production. At the same time, advances were made in transport and communications technology. There also arose increased fragmentation of jobs which made it possible for complex tasks to be decomposed into simple tasks such that workers with only little training could achieve higher levels of productivity. Concomitant with these developments, a number of developing countries, especially the NICs, offered relatively cheap labour and generous incentives such as tax exemptions or subsidized infrastructure, culminating in a growing number of export processing zones. Under these conditions, producers in the advanced countries were attracted to set up production enterprises in developing countries, especially in countries which later came to be referred to as the NICs. This had far-reaching consequences on the host NICs. Multinational corporations invested heavily in these countries, the result of which was spectacular growth of both GDP and exports. Clearly, the setting up of production capacities by the multinationals in the NICs was not because these countries were pursuing "rational" economic policies which sought liberalisation of the economy around the price system. Therefore, the economic development that followed cannot be regarded as being the result of such rational economic policies.

Access to international finance   Apart from the factors that influenced multinational corporations to set up their production enterprises in the NICs, these countries were also favoured by their easy access to finance. A buoyant transnational banking market developed over the 1960s and 1970s, specialising in borrowing and lending of currencies outside the country of issue, known as the "Euro-dollar" market which developed mainly out of the US balance of payments deficits in the 1960s and out of the surpluses of the oil-exporting countries in the 1970s. The private transnational banks became the main channel for recycling these "petro dollars". Schmitz (1984) points out that credit from these banks expanded extremely rapidly between 1966 and 1978 (over 50 times) and by the end of the 1970s, over 50 percent of loans had gone to the developing countries; but the largest borrowers were the NICs with Mexico, Brazil, South Korea and the Philippines accounting for over 50 percent of the total accumulated debt to transnational banks in 1980.

Access to this private capital market allowed countries which obtained large volumes of credit to avoid the influence of the IMF conditionality on economic policy. Most importantly, these countries were able to sustain levels of imports well above those they could have afforded if such loans had not been available. The maintenance of this high level of imports enabled these countries to also maintain high growth rates of both investment and output. For example, Schmitz (1984) reports that Brazil was able to keep up its high growth rate through a "debt-led growth" strategy.

In the 1970s the poorest countries were unable to follow the example of the NICs and finance their balance of payments deficits by external private capital flows. Consequently, as Schmitz (1984) reports, their capacity to import declined which led during the 1970s to substantial decreases in per capita growth and declines in GNP per capita of 0.4 percent annually in the poorest countries of Sub-Saharan Africa. While there were many factors which contributed to this deterioration, constraints on their capacity to import played a major role, and larger external finance would have helped to achieve better performance, particularly in industry.

Role of the State   In addition to the favourable external environment, the State also played an important role in the development of the NICs. With the exception of Hong Kong and possibly Singapore, the NICs were not liberal, market-oriented economies as they have been portrayed by the proponents of export promotion. For example, in the case of South Korea, import restrictions were reduced selectively and gradually, suggesting an awareness on the part of the State that liberalisation must reflect the competitive strength of the evolving local producers. Restrictions on direct foreign investment were (and continue to be) extensive; and industrial policy was strongly reminiscent of Japan, with major decisions being taken on the basis of long-term objectives and in disregard of short-term efficiency. In general, the State played an active and central role in the allocation of resources. Datta-Chauduri (1981) suggested that the government directly or indirectly controlled the allocation of more than two-thirds of the investible resources, and a study by Luedde-Neurath (1983) on the trade front, emphasizes that Korea's export-oriented development success was neither preceded nor accompanied by significant across-the-board import liberalisation and that market forces were not given a free reign to allocate resources. Instead, there was a two-pronged import policy: liberal towards inputs for export manufacturing and highly restrictive towards the domestic market. Moreover, there was a tendency to "cross-tie" the domestic and the export market by making access to the (protected and hence profitable) domestic market conditional upon satisfactory export performance. Overall, it is concluded that the Korean import regime has been highly "managed" throughout the last two decades. Stewart (1985) also adds that while Korea abandoned across-the-board import protection, she maintained selective protection which enabled her infant industries to mature and that this is still true today as evidenced by a recent well publicised campaign against smoking foreign-made cigarettes in South Korea.

In Taiwan the State also pursued an active, selective interventionist role. Chou (1985) reports that a tariff structure that was designed for a completely different economy, that of the Chinese mainland, was adopted by Taiwan with the emergence of a bona fide need to impose foreign exchange controls. In this initial tariff structure, rates for raw materials were frequently set at the same levels as, or even above, those for processed goods. The tariff schedule underwent major revisions in 1955, 1959, 1965 and 1974, but the continuing relatively high levels of duties on primary and intermediate goods served to maintain the levels of effective protection characteristic of the early 1950s. In order to promote exports, the Taiwan Government adopted a discriminatory trade policy that was two-pronged: one that embodied strict import controls in respect of the domestic market; and another that provided incentives for exports. Under the export-incentive scheme, the government tried to reduce the bureaucratic red-tape to a minimum.[4] There were many bureaucratic

54

controls such as registrations, import and export licensing and supervision of foreign exchange transactions, the high administrative costs of which could not help but hurt price competition in the world market. To dismantle such impediments, the government in 1965 took certain measures which included the establishment of bonded factories and warehouses and the creation of export processing zones where exporting firms could enjoy all the tax benefits as well as a remarkable cutback in red-tape. Some organisations were also set up to promote exports. For example, the China External Trade Development Council was founded in July 1970 to promote exports and conduct market research. The China Export-Import Bank was also established in 1979 to provide loans to foreign buyers to facilitate the purchase of domestically manufactured capital goods. A system of low cost loans was initiated by the Bank of Taiwan in July 1957 to encourage exports. The export loan programme helped to meet the short-term fund needs of manufacturers in their export operations - from raw materials procurement to finished goods delivery. These loans were designed to offset the disadvantages of a weak private enterprise financial structure and one of the short-comings of the state-owned banking system - the almost complete lack of a programme for short-term operating funds. Thus, the benefit of such loans to exporting enterprises was quite considerable. In addition to these export incentives, there was a docile Chinese labour force. In the domestic market, the Government maintained its system of strict import controls. Domestic industries producing for the domestic market continued to be protected from foreign imports as before. The protection of domestic industry serving the domestic market kept the prices of domestically produced goods sold in the domestic market markedly high. This helped the government in providing subsidies in support of the export-incentives scheme through the tax system, i.e. domestic sales subsidized export sales. As Stewart (1985) reports, Taiwan still uses selective protection up to the present time which has been quite effective in keeping foreign goods out, as evidenced by the fact that she recently agreed to help reduce the current account surplus by liberalising import restrictions on such items as textiles. Clearly, it would be misleading to characterise Taiwan's development success story as being the result of "liberal trade policies" as the domestic market was highly protected.

In the case of South Korea, there was also significant industrialisation prior to the export expansion phase. As argued by Schmitz (1984), an impressive structure of manufacturing industries supported by an adequate infrastructure of transport and communications was inherited from Japan. Even though the Korean war led to considerable destruction, it did not destroy the accumulated industrial experience, technical skills and entrepreneurship which developed between the 1920s and 1940s. The same kind of argument can be extended to

Taiwan and Hong Kong. Although there was not the same degree of prior industrialisation as in South Korea, there was a considerable influx of people with technical and entrepreneurship abilities from mainland China. Singapore is an exception, but it relied so heavily on foreign capital that its case is consistent with the above argument.

State intervention was also extensive in the Latin American NICs. Schmitz (1984) points out that an analysis of the case of Brazil shows that internal cyclical features made an important contribution to the growth performance of the NICs. In the years immediately before the explosive growth of GNP and exports, industrial capacity in Brazil was heavily underutilised. Output growth did not take place because of the existence of idle capacity in the manufacturing sector but this was the single most important condition that permitted the boom. Until the early 1970s output was able to grow at a faster rate than the stock of capital, and only then did manufacturing investment accelerate significantly in response to continuing internal and external demand pressing upon productive capacity.

In the assessment of the other NICs, there has been little concern with internal economic cycles and it is difficult to judge how general the coincidence of liberalisation experience and upturn in the cycle was. However, as Chanthunya (1990) argues, if idle capacity was such a recurring feature under import-substitution, the availability of this capacity must have helped those economies which then tried to speed up their growth under the export banner.

Role of previous import substitution This raises a more general question, namely to what extent was import-substitution a precondition for successful export-led growth and how much sense does it, therefore, make to take the two as alternatives? There is an inherent difficulty in trying to produce evidence that protection under import-substitution generated externalities and learning which would have been lost without it. But it is probably not accidental that some of the successful exporters were countries in which import-substitution was relatively successful in building up an industrial structure which was not merely limited to local production of consumer goods. A case in point is Brazil which Schmitz (1984) also reports to have had its fair share of inefficient producers, but the degree of vertical integration achieved under import-substitution was such that from the simultaneous growth of industries which, to a large extent, were each other's customers, a remarkably balanced growth resulted and there simultaneously grew up many complementary industries which acted as self-reinforcing agents.

Use of fixed exchange rates The claim always made by the advocates of outward-orientation that the main reason for the success of the NICs is that these countries pursued the right policies by, inter alia, adopting realistic exchange rates is also not supported by empirical evidence. The evidence in the case of the Asian NICs suggests quite the contrary. As Hiemenz (1988) has revealed, the Asian NICs have always pegged their currencies to the US dollar, even before the launching of their export promotion industrialisation. The US dollar has been appreciating or depreciating at different time periods. This means that the currencies of the Asian NICs have also been appreciating or depreciating along with the US dollar. As a result, their currencies have been fluctuating in accordance with the movements in the economic fundamentals of the US economy and not of their own economies. Thus, although the locking of the NICs' exchange rates to the US dollar brought exchange rate stability, it also made their currencies overvalued during the time periods that the US dollar was appreciating. This made their products uncompetitive in export markets other than the US market during those periods.

The observations on the South-East Asian countries underline the importance of accumulating industrial experience for success in export manufacturing. The observations on the role of the state in the development of the NICs make it hard to agree with the argument of the advocates of free market policies that the countries applying outward-oriented development strategies provided for automaticity and stability in the incentive system and that they minimised price distortions and relied on the market mechanism for efficient allocation of resources and rapid economic growth. These show that the NICs relied far less on the "invisible hand" guided by enlightened market-oriented economic policies than is portrayed by the proponents of export promotion. These also show that the NICs pursued a combined strategy of export promotion in some sectors and import substitution in others. For example, Brazil and Korea built up their capital goods industry successfully during the 1970s through protective measures. Furthermore, these observations also indicate that the NICs owe their success to a favourable international environment which is no longer present. These beg the question of whether it makes sense to present outward orientation and inward orientation as alternatives and raise doubts on the proclamation that export promotion out-performs import substitution.

The current economic context for industrialisation Even if one accepted the dominant orthodox view about the virtues of free trade, the proponents of import substitution argue that there are serious obstacles to the adoption of outward orientation as the main trade strategy for development. There are several reasons for taking this position. One of the obstacles to the success of outward orientation for the developing countries is the problem which lies in the fallacy of composition, namely that what works for a limited number of countries does not work if it is adopted by the large majority. For example, Kaplinsky (1984) reports that in an analysis of the consequences of a generalisation of the East Asian model of export-led growth across all developing countries, it has been shown, on the basis of 1976 trade data, that if all the developing countries had the same export-intensity as South Korea, Taiwan, Singapore and Hong Kong, adjusting for differences in size and level of industrialisation, this would involve an increase of more than 700 percent in Third World manufactured exports which would increase Third World share of aggregate developed countries' manufactured imports from 16.7 percent to 60.4 percent. There can be little doubt, therefore, that the pursuit of export orientation throughout the Third World would provoke intensified protectionist response in the advanced countries. This implies that if export-orientation were to be pursued throughout the developing world, more modest targets would have to be set.

Growing protectionism Perhaps one of the main reasons for the scepticism over outward orientation is the growing protectionism in the advanced countries which discriminates most severely against manufactured exports from the developing countries. Bhagwati (1988) reports that since the mid-1970s, there has been a proliferation of non-tariff barriers in the industrial countries. Such proliferation of non-tariff barriers has involved the use of such diverse measures as orderly marketing arrangements, voluntary export restraints, import quotas, non-automatic licensing variable levies, countervailing duties and anti-dumping measures. Bhagwati (1988) also points out that between 1980 and 1985, seven industrial countries and the European Community initiated 155 anti-dumping cases and 425 anti-subsidy cases and adds that the effect of the use of these non-tariff barriers has been to nullify the substantial tariff reductions that have been accomplished under the GATT auspices. Interestingly enough, when it comes to advising the developing countries what they should do, he strongly advocates opening up their economies. His argument is that the increased use of the various non-tariff barriers by the developed countries is not effective, after all, in keeping out other countries' products.

This is an interesting self-contradiction. In one respect, the proliferated use of non-tariff barriers has nullified the effect of substantial tariff reductions achieved under GATT but in another respect, this has not had any effect in keeping out other countries' products! According to Bhagwati, this is because protection is often less than appearances suggest in that exporting countries use a variety of devices to circumvent a number of trade restrictions. For example, restrictions on imports of coats can be circumvented through the use of removable sleeves so that by importing sleeves unattached, the rest of the coat comes in as a vest, thereby qualifying for more favourable tariff treatment. Another example given is how exporters of running shoes to the United States avoided the high tariff on rubber footwear by using leather for most of the upper portion of the shoes, thereby qualifying for duty treatment as leather shoes. It is also interesting to note here that Bhagwati is using examples of avoiding high tariffs which, according to him, have been substantially reduced under GATT, instead of giving examples of how exporters can avoid the non-tariff barriers which, he acknowledges, have nullified the substantial tariff reductions accomplished under GATT, in terms of their protective effects. Non-tariff barriers, such as prohibitions on imports of certain products, cannot be circumvented as argued by Bhagwati. In my view, this is mixing up issues and does not provide a strong case why developing countries, in particular, should ignore the presence of these non-tariff barriers in the advanced countries and open their markets to the products of the developed countries, hoping that they will be able to penetrate their markets, too, with ease.

Bhagwati (1988) also recognizes that there are growing protectionist pressures in the developed countries such as the United Kingdom and the United States who are fearing that their own industries will collapse due to competition from Japan and the newly industrialising countries. However, he also strongly believes that the calls for protectionism in the developed world will soon be dissipated because of growing pro-trade views at the same time, beginning with the executive branch of governments of the developed world permeating through multinational corporations who are calling for free trade out of their own self interest. In addition, the work of GATT will ensure that markets of the developed countries will always remain open. GATT's track record has so far been disappointing for developing countries. Within the GATT rounds of trade negotiations, there has, of course, been an explicit recognition of the need to give special treatment to the developing countries. For example, in the 1973-79 Tokyo Round the developed countries agreed to introduce differential measures to the developing countries in ways that would provide special and more favourable treatment for them in the areas of the negotiation where this was feasible and appropriate. But the outcome has been different from the intention. Kaplinsky (1984) reports that by the end of the Tokyo Round in 1979, the average tariff on "developing-country type commodities" (7.9 percent in the nine major developed economies) exceeded that for "developed-country type goods" (i.e. 5.8 percent). Thus, industrialised countries also impose higher tariffs on the developing countries' manufactured exports than they do on exports from their fellow advanced

59

countries. In fact, the nominal tariffs on developing-country products increase with the degree of processing. Customs duties are usually low or zero on unprocessed materials, but increase with the degree of processing so that effective protection is usually much higher than the nominal protection for manufacturers. Processing of raw materials in developing countries is, therefore, discouraged by the escalating tariffs imposed by the industrialised countries. In addition to the tariffs, the industrialised countries impose non-tariff barriers, especially for textiles, clothing, and processed products. The non-tariff barriers are usually the most effective, a good example being the Long Term Arrangement in Cotton Textiles by which the main exporters among the developing countries agreed to limit their sales in order to avoid quotas being imposed. The industrialised countries also protect heavily their own production of agricultural goods, using among other techniques, guaranteed prices for their own producers, variable levies against imports (in the European Union). The United States of America uses a combination of high prices, government purchases and subsidised exports. Excise taxes on primary commodities are also often imposed by the developed countries. Restrictions are also imposed by foreign owners of firms, particularly where subsidiaries are engaged in the production of certain goods which could be exported where the foreign owner also has some interest. Thus, efforts by the developing countries to increase their exports to the industrialised countries, which offer lucrative markets, would be frustrated by the restrictions in markets of the industrialised countries or would merely result in lower prices and possibly lower receipts for their exports. It is, thus, difficult to agree with Bhagwati that the new World Trade Organisation (WTO) will ensure that the markets of the advanced countries are open to the manufactured exports of the developing countries.

Problem of shifting comparative advantage   Granting that export-oriented strategies are indeed superior to import-substitution, it is also not certain whether such strategies are still viable alternatives for the developing countries, in view of the changed conditions of the world economy in recent times. Major changes are taking place in manufacturing technology which are threatening to change the economics of location and are undermining the comparative advantage of the developing countries. Kaplinsky (1984) has shown how the use of these radical technologies is undermining the comparative advantage of the developing countries. The successful utilisation of electronics-based automation technologies benefits innovating firms in several ways. First, despite their software-intensity, fixed capital costs are often lowered as they have considerably fewer moving parts and require smaller support structures. Secondly, and more importantly, because of the greater control facilitated by computerised systems, working capital costs are generally also made considerably lower. Thirdly, there is increased labour productivity which arises from their effective use. Fourthly, due to optimising capabilities, material costs are cut significantly, both in high technology sectors and in traditional sectors such as garments. Fifthly, there is a reduction in product development lead-time, a factor which not only cuts costs but is also decisive in establishing market shares. Finally, there is the all-important question of product quality.

One relevant factor is the impact which a general reduction in the labour input is likely to have in reducing the advantage of low wage costs. Perhaps the most striking example in this regard is the case of the assembly of semi-conductors, one of the major sources of developing countries manufactured exports. Kaplinsky (1984) reports that with the manual technology of the 1970s, Hong Kong production costs were 33 percent of those in America; with the semi-automatic technology of the early 1980s, the advantage had fallen to 63 percent; but with automated assembly lines installed in 1983, production costs in Hong Kong were only marginally lower (8 percent) than those in the US.

The new electronics-based automation technologies are also having a profound impact upon the underlying engineering principles which affect scale economies in production, particularly in the discrete products industries. This is because their inherent flexibility is significantly reducing machine time-settings and their programmability is enabling machines to substitute for skilled labour. The result is the emergence of two opposite effects. At the mass production end of the spectrum, scale economies are being undermined, while at the batch production end, they are being injected. In either case, there are substantial implications for the location of industry and hence for the viability of production in peripheral production sites. The reduction of scale economies in the mass production industry is likely to take production closer to the final market and undermine the logic of building "world plants" and shipping parts around the world. By contrast, the injection of scale economies into batch production is likely to make it difficult for small-scale machinery suppliers, using conventional technology, to compete; a problem that is already confronting Southern European firms who are finding domestic and foreign markets being eroded by machinery produced with automated, flexible manufacturing systems.

There are also indications which suggest that the development in radical technical change will lead to trade reversals from developing to developed countries. The sector in which the technology has diffused most widely is the electronics sector itself and here, as Kaplinsky (1984) states, evidence has already been produced showing that the assembly of electronics circuits is being brought back from developing to developed countries and that the introduction of new technologies is likely to further reduce the need for cheap unskilled labour. Similar patterns are evident for the electronics consumer durable industry in which automatic-insertion devices and the utilisation of very large-scale integration components have enabled Japanese TV firms to withdraw from South Korea. There is also evidence that in some sub-processes of the garments industry trade reversal has already taken place and is likely to occur further and this is also likely to happen in some of those parts of the automobile components sector in which work is presently subcontracted to developing countries. This clearly shows that the utilisation of the new technologies will significantly reduce the rate at which production is subcontracted to Third World countries and that there will be a significant degree of trade reversal with subcontracted production being pulled back from low-wage Third World sites.

In short, the problems of market entry are forcing producers to locate closer to final markets. The costs of doing so are minimised by the introduction of radical electronics-based automation technologies. This bodes ill for outward-oriented strategies in the Third World, partly because the technology is diffusing unevenly across sectors and economic space, and partly because it has the effect of increasing economies of agglomeration.

To appreciate the significance of this development, one needs to recall that in the 1970s, US and Japanese companies established production capacities in Asian countries to take advantage of cheap qualified labour to produce light manufactures, such as clothing and textiles which are crucial in an initial export promotion industrialisation strategy for developing countries because of their labour intensity. In a study of trends in factor intensities in production, Yeats (1989) has shown how important labour intensity was in determining the products for export promotion in outward-oriented strategies. However, he has also shown that some of the products which used to be labour-intensive in the early period are now becoming capital-intensive and less suitable for export by developing countries. Such products include petroleum and coal products, food products and paper. The products which have become labour-intensive in production are metals; but textiles and clothing appear to have changed very little in labour intensity. Therefore, the current comparative advantage of the developing countries lies in metals, clothing and textiles and these are the products they would have to produce for export if they were to adopt an outward-oriented strategy. But, as Hiemenz (1988) has also shown, the advanced countries have also boosted the production of these very same products, particularly clothing and textiles under the umbrella of the "most favoured nation" clause.

This point is significant in that other developing countries, such as those in Africa, cannot hope to make any headway by adopting outward-orientation policies in that the products in which they still have a comparative advantage and which they would have to start with in such a strategy, like clothing and textiles, are already being produced by the advanced countries which would be the target markets for these products. The problem they would have to contend with is not only competition from the advanced countries' own goods but also those from the NICs who have been in the business for a much longer time.

Indeed, it is very unlikely that African countries will have such comparative advantage for a very long time to come. Their comparative advantage is also being threatened by the policy of the World Bank which has imposed family planning programmes on most African governments with a view to reducing population in already sparsely populated countries. It is argued that African governments do not have enough resources to provide adequate social services such as health and education to fast growing populations. What is often forgotten, however, is that the small population prevents the economic exploitation of natural resources in some of these countries. For example, Zambia which is a very large country with an area more than three times the size of the United Kingdom has a small population of only 8 million, 55 percent of which is urban. This means that there are too few people to till the land in the rural area and this is what is constraining that country's agricultural development. Limiting the population in such a country only ensures that it will remain in its present state of underdevelopment. This results in a kind of vicious circle in that the government gets its resources from the people who produce but since these are too few, inadequate resources are available to the government and for this reason cannot provide adequate social services to the population.

In addition to limiting the labour force which is necessary if the developing countries are to succeed with outward orientation, the IMF together with the World Bank are forcing African countries to also cut government expenditure on education, by removing education subsidies which are considered as a distortion. The effect of this is that most African countries will soon end up with small and uneducated labour forces and their comparative advantage in such labour-intensive products as clothing and textiles will be lost to other countries. The Asian NICs succeeded because they had an abundant and educated labour force!

2.6   The role of regional trading blocs

Developing countries, particularly African countries, must also come to grips with the new developments in the world economy towards the formation of trading blocs: the Americas, the European Union (EU) and the Asia-Pacific region. The United States has signed its free trade agreement with Canada as well as Mexico; there is a possibility of an American free trade zone spanning the whole continent of North and South America. There is also the Australia-New Zealand Free Trade Accord. As a result of these developments, it is being predicted that by the turn of the century there will be three main regions of broadly comparable economic strengths: North America, comprising the United States, Canada, and Mexico; Western and Eastern Europe, and the Western Pacific, comprising Japan, China, Australia, New Zealand and the nine rapidly growing developing countries.

The question that this poses is: what will happen to other developing countries, particularly African countries? Will African and other developing countries be left behind in the North's race for markets and spheres of influence or, for example, will the European Single Market be a free trade zone and act as a motor for the liberalisation of the world market or turn out to be a "fortress", more protectionist, inward-looking, and less sympathetic to the exporting needs of its developing African partners?

The main objective of these trading blocs is primarily for individual countries in Europe, America and Asia to avoid marginalisation in international trade and finance and collectively to effect changes which will ensure adequate balance of political and economic powers so as to sustain political independence and economic development through collective efforts. As such, these trading blocs will be able to defend their interests and to claim advantages of regional integration.

The implication of a single EU market is that different preferential treatment in national European markets of imports from various Third World countries will be done away with. On the surface this is advantageous; but as argued by Nomvete (1989), it means that African countries that have hitherto benefited from greater preferential treatment given by their traditional national European markets will now have to compete in an open market and they might lose out. For example, the single EU market may result in the elimination of special preference in some national EU markets for such agricultural products as bananas and sugar. The creation of a single market also means that trade barriers among the twelve EU markets would be eliminated. The beneficial effects of this is that African countries would no longer have to grapple with a mosaic of technical barriers to their exports in 12 different European national markets. Once inside the single EU market, African products would be entitled to free circulation in all EU countries. This would reduce marketing costs resulting from doing business in 12 separate national markets.

The advantages resulting from the elimination of intra-EU trade barriers would, however, be tempered by some snags. The elimination of intra-EU trade barriers would go hand in hand with harmonisation of national EU barriers to trade with the outside world. If the individual national restrictions to trade with Third World countries are replaced by a uniform harmonised system, which as a result of pressure from the hitherto most restrictive national markets, will reflect the level acceptable to those markets, the countries which enjoyed more liberal markets will now be disadvantaged counterbalancing, from the point of view of the subregional grouping as a whole, any advantage that might accrue to countries that were tied to the more restrictive markets.

It should also be noted that as a result of the elimination of internal barriers to trade among the EU countries and the establishment of a harmonised external barrier, the ACP-African countries will be exposed to greater competition from some countries of the Third World - Asia and Latin America; especially from the newly industrialising countries. African countries may no longer be entitled to special privileges over rivals in the third world and may also suffer from trade diversion effects as a result of their exports being replaced by cheaper exports from Europe. This will be hard on African countries in view of the narrow range of their export products to the EU markets.

Thus, the main loser in the unfolding world of trading blocs will be African countries where the process of economic integration is yet to be fully consolidated. By the beginning of the 21st century, the demand for Africa's traditional products is anticipated to fall (see Chanthunya, 1991). This is partly due to the fact that the advanced countries are moving away from manufacturing to services as the main form of economic activity. Indeed, with their fragile and uncompetitive economies, African countries are ill-placed to take advantage of any opportunities that the Europe of 1992 might offer.

On the basis of this reality it may, therefore, make economic sense for African countries to look to themselves and to Africa, to produce for themselves and for Africa, and to work and build together for their own survival. One could, of course, argue that perhaps what African countries need to do to solve their foreign exchange problem (which is one of the major obstacles to their development and which makes their continued access to the EU market essential) is to form a monetary union with one of the developed countries such as the US or Germany. However, this is not politically feasible as it would be regarded as a new form of colonialism.

Role of the Bretton Woods financial institutions Another issue that ought to be taken into account in proposing outward-orientation is the fact that industrialisation in the Third World is being further threatened by the policies which the IMF and the World Bank are enforcing on the developing countries. Ironically, while these institutions are among the main advocates of outward-orientation, their policies could in fact lead to a significant measure of de-industrialisation, thus undermining the long-run viability of any industrial strategy. Schmitz (1984) points out that evidence has shown that the success of export-oriented industrialisation was linked to the growth of Third World debt, although there are variations in the performance of individual economies. One of the major lending institutions throughout the last two or so decades has been the IMF. But the method of expanding access to IMF resources that has been chosen has the effect of forcing member countries into upper-credit-tranche conditionality much sooner than would occur if quotas had been adjusted appropriately. The extent to which developing countries have been forced into this conditionality has increased significantly in recent years - for example, by the end of 1988, 33 African countries had concluded Standby Agreements and twelve Extended Fund Facilities with the IMF.

Allied to the increasing participation of the IMF in policy-setting in developing countries is the participation of the World Bank with Structural Adjustment Loans. By 1995 there had been 22 agreements of this type between the Bank and African countries. As the IMF programmes often involve a re-examination of private and public investment policy and of the operations of public enterprises, the IMF has relied heavily and increasingly on collaboration with the World Bank in helping members in the formulation of these programmes. And linked with the co-ordination of the IMF and the World Bank, is the presence of the commercial banking system which after the mid-1970s became an important source of finance for developing countries. However, the commercial banks have increasingly tended to extend financial resources to developing countries only if the developing countries concerned have a programme with the IMF or the World Bank. This interlinkage of IMF, World Bank and private banking conditionality is important, so that without the IMF "seal of approval" it is unlikely for developing countries to obtain significant financial resources from the international capital markets including bilateral donor countries. It is, therefore, instructive to focus on the general orientation of the policies enforced by the IMF and the World Bank conditionality. Leaving aside the fallacy of the "composition" problem - that is, if all competing countries devalue simultaneously, the effect is nullified - two elements of conditionality are relevant to the industrialisation of developing countries, namely the "appropriate" role of the state, and trade and tariff policies.

The IMF has always taken a strong line on the appropriate role of the state in developing countries, basing its presumptions on an idealised market - economy model. On many occasions, a reduction in the role of the State has been an explicit component of IMF conditionality. But in recent years the World Bank has also made a reduction of the role of the State a primary condition for assistance and it is one of the Bank's key policy prescriptions for Sub-Saharan Africa. Thus, in its early policy document for the region the "Berg Report", the World Bank (1982) states "it is now widely evident that the public sector is over extended, given the present scarcities of financial resources, skilled manpower, and organisational capacity. This has resulted in a slower growth than might have been achieved with available resources, and accounts in part for the current crisis". Implicit in this is the view that the state is an inefficient allocator of resources, since if this were not the case there would be no point in reducing the role of the state in production. But the history of industrialisation is replete with examples of countries which have industrialised with the state playing an active, interventionist role, not just in policy-setting but also directly in production. The role played by the state in the industrialisation of the South-East Asian countries, as has been seen above, is pertinent here. Not only is this a historical fact but there are also powerful analytical factors which justify this participation. Notably when external economies exist (as it is almost always the rule) or when there are dynamic learning effects, there is likely to be an under-investment by private capital in industry. Moreover, the practical effect of reducing the role of the state may be to increase the role of foreign capital. But, as we have argued above, in the changing economic climate of the recent times, foreign investors will most likely become increasingly reluctant to use developing countries as production platforms for the world market.

The position of the IMF and World Bank on trade tariff policies is heavily influenced by the apparent link between protection and "inefficiency", that is, the extent of value-added in world prices on the one hand, and between "free trade" policies and export success, on the other. The normal prescription is that tariffs should be substantially reduced so that rates of effective protection do not exceed 10 percent, and that specific infant industry protection should not exceed 5 to 8 years.

However, such prescriptions reveal a general lack of historical analysis. For both at the macro- and sector - specific levels, export oriented industrialisation was generally preceded by industrial experience accumulated over many decades. Thus, while much of the import-substitution industrialisation in the developing countries may appear to be "inefficient" and ephemeral, it may well be an important investment in the long run. Consider, for example, the case of sugar technology. Kaplinsky (1984) reports that the development of the dominant vacuum-pan technology took around 100 years (1820-1920); beet sugar technology matured over a period of 50 heavily protected years (1800-50) and the Indian development of open-pan technology (which has recently "matured" and become competitive) took around 50 years (1925-80). A review of infant industries in the case of developed countries identifies similar long-time horizons. But the sort of time-frame implicit in the IMF/World Bank conditionality is considerably shorter and this has a very important implication for technical "mastery", technical change and technological capability. While the shorter time-periods may be ideal for importing technology from abroad and rooting out X-inefficiency, they have little relevance to developing some form of indigenous capability or technological "mastery", which takes a much longer period of time and is a pre-condition for sustained, long-run industrialisation.

This argument is not intended to provide a blanket justification for protection, as some industrialisation in developing countries cannot be justified whatever the conception of "efficiency", besides protection is not a sufficient condition for indigenous technological change. However, as pointed out by Kaplinsky (1984), the form in which conditionality is actually being implemented is, despite some protestations to the contrary, blunt and the general effect is to enforce de-industrialisation on the developing countries.

2.7   Impediments to export promotion

Even if the economic context were favourable, there are other problems which export promotion has to contend with. Such problems relate to some of the measures which are recommended to accompany a development strategy that is based on export promotion.

Problem of devaluation   One of these problems concerns the use of the appropriate exchange rate. It is pointed out that where a developing country may indeed have a comparative advantage in the costs of production of a certain product, it may not have a price advantage vis-à-vis foreign producers - including transport, insurance and other expenses of shipping the product. An absolute price advantage is said to depend on the exchange rate. This is perhaps viable for the economic structures of developed countries which are fairly similar and as such changes in the exchange rate of one would, apart from making existing exports more (or less) competitive, open (or close) overseas markets for many other products. In developing countries, where only one or two manufactures would possibly qualify for export in the foreseeable future, the situation is different. In order to develop these exports, a very low exchange rate might be needed. This may not be appreciated by the authorities or it may not be politically expedient because of its inflationary effects and other implications for other sectors of the economy and for the distribution of income. If a low exchange rate necessitates devaluation, it could also affect the prices of traditional exports, at a cost in foreign exchange. Moreover, this could set in motion price rises and wage increases which could eliminate the price advantage required to export manufactures, thus creating further pressures for more and more devaluations, with developing countries literally no floor to which the exchange rate can fall.

The advocates of free trade argue that devaluation need not be inflationary, especially where there are quantitative controls and a high incidence of parallel markets, as is often the case in developing countries. Parallel markets are unofficial markets which arise from difficulties of obtaining goods in the official market such as foreign exchange. As people in need of such goods know that they cannot obtain them from the official market, they offer a higher rate to those who can sell to them outside of the official market. In such situations, it is pointed out that devaluation can actually result in a fall of the general price level. Chanthunya (1990) has given several reasons why devaluation can produce this result. In this regard, the first point made is that the domestic costs of imports is based on the parallel foreign exchange rate, although the greater proportion of them is purchased on the official market. Therefore, as the official rate is devalued, most producers and consumers switch their supply from the parallel to the official market and this results in the appreciation of the exchange rate in the parallel market. This means that the cost of goods in the parallel market falls and this leads to a fall in the general price level. Secondly, as devaluation leads to a diversion of resources from the production of non-traded to export goods, the supply of export goods increases, with sales to the parallel market contracting. And since the parallel rate equilibrates the total demand for and supply of foreign exchange in the economy, the parallel rate appreciates not only relative to the official rate but also in absolute terms. The parallel rate appreciates even more if the central bank increases sales of official reserves. It is pointed out that this is usually the case as devaluation is often supported by official sector borrowing.

Thirdly, it is pointed out that if devaluation is anticipated, it brings about a temporary decline of the price level. This is because it leads to a contraction in the demand for foreign currency holding and to a rise in the demand for domestic currency holding in the parallel market. To maintain equilibrium, the exchange rate in the parallel rate appreciates and the price level falls, in consequence, until the devaluation takes place. At this point, a return to foreign currency holding takes place in the parallel market which causes the price level to jump back to its original level. An observer at this point would erroneously conclude that the devaluation in the official market led to an increase in the price level, when what actually happened is that it led to a temporary price fall which later returned to its original level.

On the other hand, it is pointed out that an unanticipated devaluation leads to an increase in total output as it raises the demand for domestic money, thereby exerting downward pressure on the domestic price level. This is reinforced by a fall in the price of imported goods in the parallel market as a result of the appreciation of the exchange rate in that market.

It is also argued that policy makers tend to focus on the consumer price index instead of on the aggregate price level when examining the effects of devaluation. As the consumer price index is much narrower in scope than the aggregate price index, in that it excludes certain imports purchased in the parallel market, policy makers often mistake an increase in the consumer price index for an increase in the general price level and erroneously conclude that devaluation of the official rate has an inflationary effect, as measured by the official consumer price index, even though the aggregate price level, as measured by the domestic expenditure deflator, remains the same or actually falls.

Finally, it is argued that in any case, the imposition of quantitative controls as a substitute for a formal devaluation does not avoid the adverse repercussions that a devaluation has on the rate of inflation or real wages. It is pointed out that the emergence of a parallel market in response to such controls and the depreciation of the exchange rate in this market have inflationary consequences similar to those of an official devaluation. Moreover, the illegality of transacting in the parallel market gives rise to real resource costs that are absent in a unified exchange system and result in loss of welfare. Such a dual market also provides an environment conducive to corrupt practices and permits economic rent to accrue to certain groups that are in a position to exploit the exchange rate differential between the two markets.

However, the conclusion that quantitative restrictions lead to loss of welfare is not conclusive. Falvey (1978) has shown that the smuggling which the quantitative restrictions give rise to actually lead to an unambiguous welfare gain. This is because illegal imports compete with higher cost domestic production and leave lower cost legal imports unchanged, thereby eliminating the source of a potential welfare loss under tariff protection.

The assumption that the domestic cost of imports reflects the parallel exchange rate is also too strong to have general applicability in developing countries. Where quantitative restrictions are used, there are also strict controls on prices so that the prices of domestic inputs and final products are, to a large extent, based on those obtaining on the official market. In addition, the amount of foreign exchange that circulates on the parallel market is very small and sometimes insignificant in relation to that on the official market. This means that the proportion of output purchased on the parallel market is very small or insignificant relative to the total domestic output. As most African countries are highly dependent on imports to sustain production, investment and basic needs, devaluation immediately results in an increase in their price level through the direct increase in the cost of imports.

The inflationary effect of devaluation also depends on the stance of domestic monetary and fiscal policies. In many developing countries this tends to be accommodating in that the government usually has little room for manoeuvre. To suppress the inflationary effect of devaluation, a tight monetary and fiscal policy is required. In developing countries, this means reducing domestic credit and government expenditure. The reduction in domestic credit runs counter to the objective of devaluation itself which is to bring about a supply response that will increase exports. To increase exports requires additional investment but if domestic credit is reduced then there are no loanable funds which can be used to make the additional investment required to increase the supply of exportable products. The rise in interest rates also means that the cost of such investment rises and results in more inflationary pressures as this increases the cost of production. In some instances, commercial banks do not abide by the instructions of the central bank on credit limits. This is especially true of international commercial banks with headquarters abroad which supply them with additional funds for on-lending to their customers. This means that such banks are able to extend additional credit in excess of the central bank limits because they have other sources of liquid financial resources. The result is that the overall level of domestic credit is not reduced and may well exceed the limit leading to an expansion of the money supply which further increases the inflation. In any case, the devaluation increases the money supply in the first place as exporters get the local currency receipts for their exports at the new devalued exchange rate. With regard to government expenditure, the high import content of government spending leads to increased expenditure if the currency is devalued. In addition to this, the inflationary effect of the devaluation forces the government to award pay increases to its workers. Indeed, wages throughout the entire economy go up as workers demand compensation for the rise in the cost of living due to the devaluation, thus adding to more inflationary pressures.

There is also the all-important question of whether devaluation always succeeds in bringing about its desirable consequences. A devaluation is expected to result in a reduction in imports by making them more expensive and in an increase in exports by making their prices more competitive in world markets, thereby improving the trade balance. By making the cost of imported goods higher, devaluation is expected to result in expenditure switching from imports to locally produced non-tradeable goods. However, the effect of devaluation in promoting exports of African countries is rather doubtful. This is because the exports of most African countries are mainly agricultural and mineral products whose demand on the world market is falling due to various factors such as advancements in technology which are resulting in the production of synthetic substitutes and in the use of less and less materials in the production of final goods, in addition to campaigns against the consumption of certain products like tobacco due to their health hazards. Furthermore, the advanced countries are moving away from manufacturing to services as their main economic activity. This means that the demand for primary products on which African countries depend for export earnings is likely to continue to fall. On the other hand, the imports of African countries are mostly essentials, mainly food, raw materials and goods as inputs for their industries. A devaluation does not, therefore, lead to a reduction in these imports but merely to an increase in the import bill in local currency, which largely explains the inflationary effects of devaluation in less developed countries.

There is a further problem with devaluation in that it requires adaptability of the economic system in order to reap its advantages. This is to say that it requires the ability of the economic system to move resources (capital, land, labour, etc.) from one line of production to another in response to changes in the relative prices of final products or factors, and the organisational capacity to combine these factors efficiently in order to produce those goods where the country concerned enjoys a comparative advantage. And the process of adaptation should be quick; otherwise, if it takes five years to adapt the economy to changing patterns of world demand and supply, a new set of circumstances will be confronting the country by the time this process is completed and a new process of adaptation will have to be set in motion.

Typically, developing countries are not adaptable. What is more, those commodities which they can produce relatively easily have poor prospects in world markets. As it has been pointed out above, their exports consist mainly of primary commodities whose world demand is usually price-inelastic, that is to say, an increase in the volume supplied by say 5 percent would reduce prices by more than 5 percent. Clearly in such a case it would not pay to increase the volume of exports as the total amount of foreign exchange received by exporting a larger volume of exports would be less than would be received by exporting a smaller volume. It might, of course, be asked: "if demand is inelastic why not reduce the volume of exports? Prices would rise by a higher percentage than the fall in volume and the total inflow of foreign exchange would be increased." This is indeed what some countries do. Brazil sometimes burns her surplus coffee and Canada often prefers to stock great quantities of wheat rather than spoil the market. However, such action is not plausible for developing countries. When there are many countries exporting the same commodity, co-ordination among them to raise the price is difficult. Moreover, to exploit the advantage an inelastic demand curve offers to exporters can be very risky as higher prices can and do stimulate the development of synthetic or other substitutes.

The ground for doubting the effectiveness of devaluation is further provided by the experience of the Asian NICs themselves. The US import surge arising from the huge budget deficit, the depreciating US dollar since 1985 to which the exchange rates of the Asian NICs are pegged, and the signing of a cooperation agreement between the Association of South East Asian Nations (ASEAN) countries and the EU in 1980, should have provided a favourable climate for continued export expansion. The depreciation of their currencies due to the depreciating US dollar should have made their exports more competitive in non-US markets, especially in the EU, given the appreciation of the Deutsche mark, and in the Japanese market with the appreciation of the yen. But, as pointed out by Hiemenz (1988), this did not improve the ASEAN competitiveness in the respective import markets.

The case of Ghana which has been dubbed as a success story in Africa of the IMF/World Bank structural adjustment programmes is also instructive here. Under the IMF/World Bank structural adjustment programme, Ghana has devalued its currency quite substantially by any standards. The value of the Cedi has been reduced from 1.15 Cedis per US dollar in 1977 to 337.84 Cedis per US dollar in the third quarter of 1990 (see IFS 1990 Yearbook and March 1991 IFS). But, despite this massive devaluation, cocoa exports, on which the country depends for foreign exchange earnings and which have been the target of this devaluation, have not picked up. The production response simply has not been forthcoming and as noted by Frimpong-Ansah (1990), in his examination of the effect of the economic liberalisation measures in an attempt to resuscitate Ghana's economy, that country's stock of cocoa trees which had declined to its 1917 level, before the start of the economic liberalisation programme, is still at that level, despite the massive devaluation the Cedi has undergone.

The above arguments are not intended to show that devaluation is completely useless but rather that its desirable effects are not always guaranteed. The use of an appropriate exchange rate is indeed necessary if a country wishes to maintain her export competitiveness in world markets. An overvalued exchange rate, for example, would make its exports expensive and its imports cheaper in addition to shifting its consumption towards exportable goods which tends to reduce the availability of export commodities. The result is a payments imbalance which cannot be sustained. Therefore, an appropriate exchange rate should be maintained all the time. Such a rate is the market rate which equates the demand for and supply of foreign exchange and should be maintained all the time to ensure that it does not deviate from this equilibrium level, otherwise a large devaluation would be necessary with all the adverse consequences discussed above and as such ought to be avoided.

Lack of exporting infrastructure   Lack of exporting infrastructure is yet another problem involved in export promotion. Even if a country succeeds, by devaluation or other means, in making potentially profitable a new line of exports, it has other problems to solve. Firms in developing countries rarely have institutional links with wholesalers or retailers in the industrialised countries. Therefore, much time and money have to be spent prospecting potential markets, designing products according to the requirements of these markets which are usually different from the domestic markets, establishing sales organisations, investing in new plant to produce the required goods, achieving adequate quality control, and so on. None of these steps would be taken unless there is a reasonable expectation that domestic policies encouraging such exports will continue in the future. However, the risks are often considerable because production for export cannot be supported by production for the home market since goods sold at home are usually of a type and quality not accepted in international markets.

Limited role of countertrade   An argument that is now often heard is that if traditional methods, such as devaluation, fail to produce results by way of increasing a country's exports, the use of countertrade can succeed in achieving this objective. Its apologists argue that countertrade is a necessary expedient to facilitate the development process and that it can allow world trade to grow. This is, of course, an admission that the pursuit of free trade alone cannot always bring about desired results.

Growing protectionism, depressed commodity markets and prices, debt burdens and lack of marketing channels are the factors behind the growth of countertrade in recent times. Following the lead given by the East European countries in the early sixties, developed and developing countries alike have entered into countertrade activities as a supplementary trade financing mechanism. The term countertrade subsumes specific mechanisms of reciprocal or interlinked trade. Countertrade is, thus, a "tied" or "conditional" transaction in which a firm or a country is compensated partially or fully by non-monetary means (see Murinde, 1996).

The experience of African countries with countertrade is rather limited. Most African countries avoided to countertrade their products for fear that they would barter them in exchange for obsolete machinery or equipment. They, therefore, chose to keep their products until they could sell them in the open markets for foreign currency which they could then use to buy high quality or the latest machinery or equipment. As Banks (1983) has pointed out, one other reason for the limited use of countertrade by African countries is that most of them lack the required expertise to successfully conclude countertrade deals. Countertrade is slow, complex and risky particularly in the area of negotiations and financing and is a costly way of doing business, in addition to restricting trading opportunities as it tends to be bilateral. Therefore, a country lacking such expertise may not derive significant benefits from countertrade.

Thus, countertrade is not a cornucopia which opens up unlimited opportunities which would enable developing countries to increase their exports in the face of protectionism in the advanced countries, depressed commodity markets and prices, debt burdens and lack of marketing channels. The proponents of free trade must also accept that countertrade is not a first-best option in that it undermines open multilateral trade and encourages uncompetitive trade practices, the very things that they are against.

The problems cited with regard to export promotion demonstrate that for a developing country dependent on one or two primary products, the problem of increasing exports is as severe as one of securing an efficient increase in output; the mere institution of trade liberalisation and free market forces alone may not necessarily bring about positive results in restoring economic growth and development.

Need for industrialisation in developing countries There are valid theoretical arguments why the rehabilitation and growth of industry is essential for the economic development of less developed countries. Industrialisation and more specifically the development of the manufacturing sector, provides the "dynamism" for increasing productivity and growth. It is this sector that has an "indefinite scope for technological progress through a continual increase in specialisation and the subdivision of productive processes", and generates both static and dynamic economies. In this way, manufacturing industry also imparts a technological dynamism to other sectors of the economy.

Singh (1982) outlined the following reasons for the need for rapid industrialisation in Africa (see Chanthunya, 1991):

1. manufacturing industry plays a leading role in economic development in the specific sense that a 1 percent increase in gross domestic product is normally associated with a more than 1 percent increase in value added in manufacturing;

2. the lower the level of a country's per capita income, the greater the growth elasticity of manufacturing. For African countries the value of this elasticity has been estimated to be about 1.6;

3. since income elasticity of demand for manufacturing is considerably greater than for food and agricultural products, manufacturing can be expected to grow at a relatively faster rate;

4. because of favourable demand elasticities and dynamic economies of scale, manufacturing industry not only grows more quickly than other sectors, but its growth is normally associated with increased employment;

5. expansion of manufacturing industry helps to raise the growth of productivity in agriculture in two ways: (i) by absorbing redundant labour, and (ii) by providing modern industrial inputs which incidentally raise both land and labour productivity; and

6. expansion of manufacturing industry also increases the pace of technical change and helps to raise productivity growth in sectors other than agriculture.

Of particular importance is the development of a capital and intermediate goods sector as it is this sector which has the greatest potential for dynamic economies and technological change. In addition, the expansion of capacity in this sector feeds upon itself by increasing the growth rate of demand for its own output and so provides both the incentives and the means for its own expansion. The establishment of a capital goods sector thus provides for a built-in element of accelerating the growth of demand for manufactured goods.

One major objection against industrialisation that has been voiced in recent times by the International Labour Organisation and other agencies is that industrialisation in Third World countries helps very little to expedite the provision of basic needs to the poorest sections of the population and that industrialisation may often be pursued at the expense of basic needs. But in many poor countries it is impossible to achieve the twin objectives of economic growth and elimination of poverty without rapid industrialisation.

The popular approach to tackling poverty in developing countries nowadays is to provide as quickly as possible the essentials needed by the poorest sections of the population. The significance of industrialisation to the elimination of poverty is explained by Singh (1979) in the context that accelerated industrialisation and a substantially redistributive fiscal policy (i.e., a more equitable distribution of gains from economic growth by fiscal means) must be the two pillars of any well conceived basic needs programme. Rapid industrial growth is necessary to provide essentials for the poor. A poor country that wants the basic needs of its people fulfilled must greatly increase its national income. In African countries, this requires a very great expansion of manufacturing. African countries suffer from a very low level of industrial development. As Singh (1982) has pointed out, in most of them, manufacturing accounts for less than 10 percent of GDP and industry produces a limited range of relatively simple products. The capital and intermediate goods sector is virtually non-existent. In order to achieve fast economic growth, African countries need to change the structure of their economies by substantially raising the share of manufacturing in national output and corresponding changes within the structure of manufacturing industry itself to ensure that it contains a sizeable capital and intermediate goods sector.

The task of developing manufacturing industry cannot be accomplished by simply adopting open market policies as it is suggested by the advocates of outward orientation. It calls for active state intervention to create the necessary conditions that will be conducive to the development of manufacturing industry. One such condition is the protection of "learning processes" which form an inherent part of the development of a country's potential to produce technological changes. The industrial development of African countries will require a significant degree of government intervention to bring about such necessary economic changes, particularly for facilitating the planned build-up of a capital in the intermediate goods sector.

2.8   Conclusion

The neoclassical view of development policy is that governments should not intervene in their national economies and that their role should simply be to establish an economic environment in which market forces will realise the efficient allocation of resources. The appropriate instruments for creating such an environment are said to be prices and price-denominated policies. Thus, governments of the developing countries are called upon to rationalise and liberalise economic policy around the price system so that they can allow the free play of market forces. In addition, they are advised to eliminate tariffs and quotas, or to reduce them substantially, and to devalue their currencies. It is pointed out that such policies would bring their countries' productive structures in line with comparative advantage which will enable them to achieve fast economic growth.

To be able to do this, developing countries are advised to emulate the example of the newly industrialising countries by adopting outward-oriented industrialisation strategies which are said to have been behind the marvellous economic success of these countries. It is pointed out that outward-orientation made these countries pursue rational economic policies by liberalising imports, adopting realistic exchange rates, providing incentives for exports and, above all, getting factor prices right so that their economies could expand in line with their comparative advantage; and reliance on market forces and integration into the world economy yielded results far superior to protection and dissociation from the world economy.

What has been seen in this chapter is that this is far from the truth. Most of the NICs adopted a system which involved government intervention with some controls and selective protection of some industries; and this system of planning was not abandoned by these countries, even when they turned to export-orientation. In particular, the prior success of import substitution played a crucial role in the success of the outward-orientation strategy of these countries. Furthermore, a favourable international environment, such as easy access to international finance and growing world trade, and re-locational activities of multinational corporations contributed greatly to the success of this strategy.

With regard to the theoretical basis, it has been seen that there are also valid reasons for government intervention and a policy of import substitution. These include the strategic trade theory and the problems of promoting exports due to such factors as the growing protectionism in the developed countries, the problem of shifting comparative advantage, the formation of regional economic blocs in the world economy, the recent market reforms in Eastern Europe, the role of the Bretton Woods institutions in de-industrialising the developing countries and the limited effect of facilitating instruments such as devaluation and countertrade.

There is, thus, no theoretical basis for the view that an "undistorted" price system, which outward-orientation is said to foster, leads to faster economic growth than government intervention or a policy of import substitution. Indeed, the development of the NICs was facilitated by active state intervention. Thus, it may be argued that the question of development policy is not simply one of choosing between outward-orientation and import-substitution. The essential aspect of development is structural change. This is what Africa needs most if it is to get out of its abnormally low level of development. African countries need to increase their manufacturing industries and to establish a capital and intermediate goods sector which will act as a propelling force in inducing further industrial growth. The growing importance of manufacturing industry was an important feature in the development of the now advanced countries and remains so even for the newly developing countries. It matters less whether the process of industrialisation is achieved by import substitution or export promotion.

This is a point which African countries should bear in mind. There is not just one way of achieving industrialisation and African countries should not be misled into the view that this can only be done by adopting a strategy of outward-orientation simply because the Bretton Woods institutions which lend them money say so. Indeed, African countries should exercise care in obtaining financial assistance from the Bretton Woods institutions in support of the so-called structural adjustment programmes. The foreign exchange resources obtained under these programmes are mainly, if not totally, used for import liberalisation which is no more than the financing of consumption with borrowed funds instead of using such resources for upgrading their productive capacities. If this is not watched very carefully, it might lead, in future, to a new economic crisis of far greater proportions with increased debt service difficulties.

Import substitution is still a viable option that is available to African countries, which they can also pursue as part of a wider strategy to lay a firm basis for developing exports later on. This is not to say that export promotion is not a viable strategy which can be pursued from the very beginning. The two can go hand-in-hand. However, one would like to exercise caution here. As it has been seen, the prospects for outward-orientation are not very promising due to various unfavourable factors in the international environment. Given this situation, African countries would probably do better if they paid more attention to import substitution. However, the narrow and fragmented national market in Africa is a major constraint and they should, therefore, base such import substitution on regional markets within Africa. The African regional economic integration groupings, such as the Economic Community of West African States (ECOWAS) and the Common Market for Eastern and Southern Africa (COMESA) the Preferential Trade Area for Eastern and Southern African States (PTA) have provided a framework for making this possible. Here is where their opportunity lies to make their import substitution industries succeed based on regional markets where they would not contend with stiff competition from the advanced and the newly industrialising countries, as their products are discriminated against as third country products in these markets. The competition in these markets is among equals with more or less the same level of development and producing products of more or less the same quality. It would be after gaining experience in these markets that they will be able to compete far afield. But by then their countries will have achieved a significant measure of industrialisation and development for the well-being of their people. Manufacturing industry holds the key to economic development and African countries should take advantage of the African regional integration groupings to develop their manufacturing industries on the basis of import substitution for national and subregional markets.[5]

To develop manufacturing industry based on national and subregional markets will require African countries to also pay attention to other sectors of the economy. Of particular importance is an increase in agricultural productivity and growth without which industrial development will be difficult to sustain. The expansion of general education is also of critical importance as it is vitally essential to inculcate a scientific and experimental outlook in the population at large to internalise the factors necessary for sustained industrial development.

Notes

1. Structuralist explanation of inflation in Latin America rejected the view that high inflation was caused by monetary indiscipline by the government; see Meier (1995, p.12) and Murinde (1993).

2. According to Corden (1984), the term "Dutch disease" first appeared in an article in *The Economist* of 26 November, 1977. This article reported that the Netherlands enjoyed a large surplus in its balance of payments with a strong guilder because of her rich deposits of natural gas, but that its domestic manufacturing industries were extremely inactive and the unemployment rate was renewing its record. This was called the "Dutch disease", and its symptoms were reckoned to be "external health but domestic illness".

3. This view is expressed in Lewis (1953), recent expositions include Meier (1995).

4. The Taiwanese trade control system in Taipai relies on a system of export processing zones.

5. See, for example, the United Nations Economic Commission for Africa (1989).

3 Critique of empirical literature

3.1 Introduction

This chapter surveys some of the empirical work that has been undertaken on the relationship between trade regime and economic growth. An attempt is made to examine the approaches, models and results of these studies and assess their commonalities and differences and draw some conclusions. An overall assessment will then be made with a view to drawing lessons for developing countries, particularly for African countries, regarding the appropriate trade regime they should follow in order to achieve economic transformation and self-sustaining growth.

Following the pioneering work of Little, Scitovsky and Scott (1970), many other studies have been undertaken with a view of testing the hypothesis that export-promotion is superior to import-substitution. These studies have mainly followed two approaches: (i) those that have compared the economic performance of countries pursuing the two different trade strategies or the economic performance of the same country in different periods when the country was pursuing the different strategies; and (ii) those that have simply examined the statistical relationship between exports and economic growth. Notable among the first group are the studies by Bhagwati (1978) and Krueger (1978) and the World Bank (1987).

The Bhagwati-Krueger study was undertaken under the auspices of the NBER and covered Brazil, Chile, Colombia, Egypt, Ghana, India, Israel, South Korea, Pakistan, the Philippines and Turkey. The project focused on the quantification and analysis of individual developing countries' experiences with exchange control regimes and attempts at liberalising those regimes, and on the interaction between the countries' trade and payments regime and their economic development. Each country study was undertaken within an analytical framework devised and agreed upon in advance by all the research participants.

For each country covered by the project, individual researchers were asked to study their country's experience with a view to identifying:

1. when and why exchange control was adopted and how the control regime was intended to relate to the country's domestic economic goals;

2. the evolution of quantitative restrictions after their initial imposition;

3. efforts, if any, to ameliorate the undesired results of the payments regime;

4. experiences with attempts at liberalization and the timing of the economy's response to those attempts; and

5. the resource-allocational, income-distributional, and growth effects of the country's experience. Within that framework, each country's author singled out for in-depth analysis a particular point in time during which the detailed working of the exchange-control regime was analyzed, and selected one liberalization effort for intensive analysis.

The research output was disseminated in two volumes edited by Bhagwati (1978) and Krueger (1978), respectively; the former examined the anatomy and consequences of exchange control regimes while the latter focused on liberalization attempts and consequences. Specifically, the Bhagwati synthesis volume addresses the static efficiency and dynamic aspects of exchange controls. It is a taxonomy, based on detailed cross-country observations of the ways in which governments in developing countries intervened in foreign trade at the flood tide of protectionism based on quota restrictions. The Krueger volume traces out the fluctuating character of exchange controls over five distinct phases through which any one country might pass. From the experiences of the group of ten countries, the Krueger volume considers the implications of major changes in trade policies for domestic income, employment, and inflation as well as for the balance of payments. Both volumes conclude by comparing a development strategy based on import substitution to one based on export promotion. Table 3.1 below shows some of the findings of their study on the comparative economic performance of the countries pursuing the different strategies. For Brazil, the table shows that during the period 1960-67 when the country was pursuing an inward oriented strategy, she only achieved an annual average growth rate of exports of 3.7 percent and total exports amounted to only 7 percent of GDP, and her annual average growth of real GDP was only 4.1 percent during that period. Following a change-over to outward orientation, her economic performance improved considerably so that for the period 1968-73, the growth rate of her exports shot up to an annual average of 16.5 percent which raised the share of exports in GDP to an annual average of 8 percent; and this caused real GDP growth to jump to an average of 11.5 percent per year.

Table 3.1
Experience of some successful exporters

Country	Period	Annual rates of growth of:			
		Real dollar exports	GDP	Value of exports (as % of GDP)	Investment (% of GDP)
Brazil	1960-67	4.1	3.7	7	14
	1968-73	11.5	16.5	8	23
Hong Kong	1963-78	8.2	9.2	99	28
Korea	1953-60	5.2	5.7	3	11
	1960-78	9.6	28.4	29	35
Singapore	1965-78	8.6	8.7	187	39
Taiwan	1960-76	8.7	20.9	47	28

Source: Krueger (1985, p.21).

Similarly for Korea, the table shows that for the period 1953-60 when she was following inward oriented policies, her exports grew at 5.7 percent per year on average and that these constituted only 3 percent of of GDP. Consequently, her real GDP grew at a low annual average rate of 5.2 percent. Following the policy change to outward orientation, economic performance in the 1960-78 period was far superior. During this period, the growth of exports averaged as high as 28.4 percent per year and the share of exports in GDP as high as 29 percent. Consequently, annual real GDP growth averaged as high as 9.6 percent.

The table also compares the economic performance of Hong Kong, Singapore and Taiwan, presumed to be outward oriented during the respective periods given, to that of Brazil and Korea before they changed to outward orientation. For example, it shows that Hong Kong's exports amounted to an average of 99 percent of GDP year during the period 1963-78 and grew at an average rate of 9.2 percent per year and this enabled Hong Kong to achieve an average growth of real GDP of 8.2 percent per year which is higher than that of 4.1 percent for Brazil during the period 1960-67 and that of 5.2 percent for Korea in the period 1953-60. The same comparison is made for Singapore and Taiwan.

However, the evidence appears to be flimsy. There are only two countries where economic performance has been contrasted before and after the policy change. This has not been done for the other three countries and as a result we are not able to tell what difference outward orientation made to the economic performance of these majority countries. But even if this had been attempted, we would still have been left with the problem that we would not know what contribution past policies of inward orientation made to the success of outward orientation in promoting exports in the latter periods. This also applies to the other two countries. It was seen in Chapter 2 that earlier import substitution contributed a great deal to the export success of Korea and Brazil.

However, according to the results of the NBER research project, export-oriented strategies have, by and large, intervened virtually as much and as "chaotically" on the side of promoting new exports as other countries have on the side of import substitution. Yet, the economic cost of incentives distorted toward export promotion appears to be less than the cost of those distorted towards import substitution, and the growth performance of the countries oriented towards export promotion appears to have been more satisfactory than that of the import-substitution oriented countries. An important conclusion drawn from the outcome of the research project is that policy should err on the side of allowing a higher marginal cost for earning than for saving foreign exchange. This would be achieved by liberalization of the trade and payments regime.

The World Bank (1987) study, covered 41 developing countries, for the period 1963-85. The data collected were then used to divide the countries into "strongly outward-oriented", "moderately outward-oriented", "strongly inward-oriented", and "moderately inward-oriented" economies. Due to the fact that policies change, and world trade has been unsettled since 1973, each group was examined for two periods: 1963-73 and 1973-85. The criteria for the four categories are as follows:

Strongly outward oriented Trade controls are either nonexistent or very low in the sense that any disincentives to export resulting from import barriers are more or less counterbalanced by export incentives. There is little or no use of direct controls and licensing arrangements, and the exchange rate is maintained so that the effective exchange rates for importables and exportables are roughly equal.

Moderately outward oriented The overall incentive structure is biased toward production for domestic rather than export markets. But the average rate of effective protection for the home market is relatively low and the range of effective protection rates relatively narrow. The use of direct controls and licensing arrangements is limited, and although some direct incentives to export may be provided, these do not offset protection against imports. The effective exchange rate is higher for imports than for exports, but only slightly.

Moderately inward oriented The overall incentive structure distinctly favours production for the domestic market. The average rate of effective protection for home markets is relatively high and the range of effective protection rates relatively wide. The use of direct import controls and licensing is extensive, and although some direct incentives to export may be provided, there is a distinct bias against exports, and the exchange rate is clearly overvalued.

Strongly inward oriented The overall incentive structure strongly favours production for the domestic market. The average rate of effective protection for home markets is high and the range of effective protection rates relatively wide. Direct controls and licensing disincentives to the traditional export sector are pervasive, positive incentives to non-traditional exportables are few or non-existent, and the exchange rate is significantly overvalued.

Based on these definitions, the World Bank classified the 41 developing countries as shown in Table 3.2 below. From the indicators of the macroeconomic performance of these countries, grouped by the strategies defined above, the study concluded that the economic performance of the outward-oriented economies is broadly superior to that of the inward-oriented economies in all respects, including the average annual growth rates of real GDP and per capita income, the gross domestic savings ratio, the average incremental capital-output ratio, the average annual growth rate of real manufactured exports and the average annual rate of inflation.

Table 3.2
World Bank classification of developing countries by trade orientation

Period	Outward oriented		Inward oriented	
	Strongly	**Moderately**	**Moderately**	**Strongly**
1963-73	Hong Kong	Brazil	Bolivia	Argentina
	Korea	Cameroon	El Salvador	Bangladesh
	Singapore	Colombia	Honduras	Burundi
		Costa Rica	Kenya	Chile
		Cote d'Ivoire	Madagascar	Dominican Republic
		Guatemala	Mexico	Ethiopia
		Indonesia	Nicaragua	Ghana
		Israel	Nigeria	India
		Malaysia	Philippines	Pakistan
		Thailand	Senegal	Peru
			Tunisia	Sri Lanka
			Yugoslavia	Sudan
				Tanzania
				Turkey
				Uruguay
				Zambia
1973-85	Hong Kong	Brazil	Cameroon	Argentina
	Korea	Chile	Colombia	Bangladesh
	Singapore	Israel	Costa Rica	Bolivia
		Malaysia	Cote d'Ivoire	Burundi
		Thailand	El Salvador	Dominican Republic
		Tunisia	Guatemala	Ethiopia
		Turkey	Honduras	Ghana
		Uruguay	Indonesia	India
			Kenya	Madagascar
			Mexico	Nigeria
			Nicaragua	Peru
			Pakistan	Sudan
			Philippines	Tanzania
			Senegal	Zambia
			Sri Lanka	
			Yugoslavia	

Source: World Bank (1987, p.83).

In the first instance, growth rates of GDP showed a clear descending pattern from the strongly outward-oriented to the strongly inward-oriented economies. For the 1963-73 period, the annual average was 9.5 percent for the strongly outward-oriented group, more than double the 4.1 percent attained by the strongly inward-oriented group. The respective rates for 1973-85 (7.7 percent

86

and 2.5 percent) showed that the gap had widened. As a result of these trends in GDP, the average annual growth rate in real per capita income for 1963-73 was highest in the strongly outward-oriented economies (6.9 percent) and lowest in the strongly inward-oriented economies (1.6 percent).

Table 3.3
Comparative economic performance

	Outward-oriented countries		Inward-oriented countries	
	Strongly	Moderately	Moderately	Strongly
Initial per capita GNP level (1965) for period 1963-73				
Unweighted average	406	426	248	263
Weighted average	179	497	258	148
Initial per capita GNP level (1973) for period 1973-85				
Unweighted average	1281	974	397	351
Weighted average	593	692	336	189

Notes: (a) Current US$.
　　　 (b) Weighted by population share within each group of countries.
Source: Singer (1988, p.234).

During the 1973-85 period, per capita income in the strongly outward-oriented countries grew by an annual average rate of 5.9 percent, whereas in the strongly inward-oriented countries it fell on average by 0.1 percent a year. Performance differences were less marked between the moderately outward-oriented and the moderately inward-oriented economies.

This chapter presents a critique of selected empirical literature on the relationship between trade regime and economic growth. In what follows the chapter is structured into four sections. Section 3.2 discusses some basic flaws in the seminal empirical work in this area, namely the two volumes edited by Bhagwati (1978) and Krueger (1978) for the NBER as well as the World Bank (1987) study which was published in the World Development Report for 1987. A summary of selected statistical studies on the link between export growth and economic growth is presented in Section 3.3. The question of trade regime bias is further explored in the context of the literature on economic integration, in Section 3.4. Finally, concluding remarks are offered in Section 3.5.

3.2 Flaws in the Bhagwati-Krueger and World Bank empirical studies on trade regime and economic growth

There are conceptual and practical problems with both the Bhagwati-Krueger and World Bank studies on the relationship between trade regime and economic growth. We argue that in order to conclude that export promotion is superior to import substitution, three conditions should be fulfilled. First of all, the outward orientation strategy should be clearly distinguished from non-outward orientation. Secondly, a causal link between outward-orientation and export performance should be established. Finally, a causal link between export performance and economic growth should be established.

None of the studies has fulfilled all of these three conditions. Indeed, all the statistical studies have failed on all these accounts while the Bhagwati-Krueger and World Bank studies failed on the first and third accounts. Therefore, none of these studies has conclusively shown that export promotion is superior to import-substitution.

Take the Bhagwati-Krueger study for example. To meet the first and second conditions, i.e. to distinguish outward-orientation from non-outward-orientation policies and to establish a causal link between outward orientation and economic performance, the study tried to identify separate phases of trade policy and compared the growth rates of exports and GDP in the periods of different phases of trade policy. But this was a futile exercise because of difficulties involved in trying to identify different policy stances of countries at any given point of time. Countries pursue mixed policies all the time. Therefore, characterization of different phases of trade policies would be very arbitrary and pinpointing the precise date at which a country shifted from one phase to another is a difficult exercise in its own right.

To characterise the different phases of trade policies and to determine the dates separating the different phases, the Bhagwati-Krueger study used a working definition of trade liberalisation as a process of moving away from quota restrictions at, possibly disequilibrium exchange rates, to one where only tariffs are used at equilibrium exchange rates. Thus, according to the Bhagwati-Krueger study, India which was rife with exchange controls, licensing, and import quotas was, by this definition, very restrictive and very inward-looking; whereas Brazil which relied mainly on tariffs, some of which were very high to protect domestic industry, was distinctly very liberal and very outward-oriented. But tariffs can be equally protective as quotas. It is not difficult to imagine a tariff that is sufficiently high to keep imports of a certain good completely out. This would have more protective effects than a quota that at least allows importation of a certain amount of the good.

Therefore, interpreting the use of quantitative controls as representing inward-looking and the use of tariffs as outward-orientation can be very misleading.

Comparing export performance in different phases of trade policies in an attempt to establish a causal link between outward-orientation and economic performance is an equally futile exercise, even if one succeeded in correctly characterizing the different phases of trade policy. This is because one cannot tell whether the export performance is due to some other factors than any conscious government policy to promote exports. In addition, the export performance observed in an outward-orientation phase could be the result of previous inward-orientation policies. We have seen from the previous Chapter that Korean and Brazilian export booms were preceded by significant prior import-substitution industrialisation, which provided a foundation for the subsequent export stage. Export performance does not measure an index of a government's commitment to export promotion. Countries pursue mixed policies and even when a country may be pursuing inward-looking policies, industries may still export because their outputs are too large to sell everything in the domestic market.

The World Bank study also suffers from the same defects. The definition used by the World Bank to classify the 41 developing countries into four groups of "strongly outward-oriented", "moderately outward-oriented", "moderately inward-oriented", and "strongly inward-oriented" is one of neutrality of incentives between tradeables and non-tradeables. This curious definition is very difficult to apply to classify the countries in the four groups in a precise way. As we have pointed out, outward-orientation argues for export subsidies, presumably to offset the distorting effects of import-substitution measures that may be in place such as tariff and non-tariff barriers. But measuring the extent of the protection accorded by such measures and the extent of the export incentives which must be given to export industries so as to neutralise the protective effects of the import-substitution measures is a very difficult, if not totally impossible, task to perform in practice, and no one should be deluded that it can be done precisely. The World Bank was well aware of this problem and used a combination of the following qualitative indicators: (i) effective rate of protection - the higher it was, the more inward-oriented and vice versa; (ii) use of direct controls such as quotas and import licensing - the greater the reliance on this, the more inward-oriented and vice versa; (iii) use of export incentives - the greater the use of export incentives, the more outward-oriented and vice versa; and (iv) degree of exchange rate overvaluation - the greater the overvaluation, the more inward-oriented and vice versa. But all these steps must have involved measurement difficulties which magnified the error in the final result.

The second problem with the World Bank study is that the choice of its countries for classification into the four groups is very biased; thus, making the conclusion of its study meaningless. The main evidence of the study in claiming that outward-orientation is superior to import-substitution is that when countries are grouped according to the four categories, their economic performance, including GNP growth, tends to decline as we move along the scale from the strongly outward-oriented towards the strongly inward-oriented. But the strongly outward-oriented comprises only South Korea and the two city states of Hong Kong and Singapore, in effect comparing the economic performance of the rest of the countries with that of these cities. What sense is there in comparing the economic performance of a poor large country like Zambia with the city of Hong Kong? It would, perhaps have made more sense to compare the City of Lusaka with the City of Hong Kong. But even here we would encounter a problem in that the growth of the City of Lusaka is influenced by the growth of the whole of Zambia while that of Hong Kong is only influenced by its own growth. Thus, if we disregard the two city states of Hong Kong and Singapore, we are only left with South Korea in the strongly outward-oriented group. Therefore, the strongly outward-oriented group only represents the successful performance of Korea.

The other problem is that the inward-oriented, especially the strongly inward-oriented countries, consists of poorer countries than the outward-oriented countries; and as we move along the scale there is a regression in per capita income level (see Table 3.3). The inward-oriented countries started off the two periods analyzed, i.e., 1963-73 and 1973-85, with much lower initial income levels. As Singer (1988) has rightly observed, the exception to the rule of lower income levels as we move from outward-orientation to inward-orientation is the weighted average figure for the strongly outward-oriented which is conspicuously low for 1963-73. This is due to Korea's domination which had a very low income level in 1963 and was still among the poorest countries in the world. We have seen that Korea's export boom was preceded by significant earlier import-substitution industrialisation and that the Korean government played an active interventionist role in its development. Therefore, to represent Korea's case as outward-orientation is an oversimplification and it is misleading to argue and give policy advice from one single case; and if each country's experience were to be counted as equally important, then the unweighted average per capita GNP level would be more significant than the weighted average. Disregarding the first category of strongly outward-oriented which consist of one country and two cities altogether, the lower per capita incomes among the more inward-oriented countries emerge very clearly. Thus, all that the World Bank analysis really shows is that poorer countries have lower per capita income than countries further up the development ladder such as the NICs and the middle-income countries. Yet this essential piece of information about the different initial GNP levels of the four categories is not taken into account in the demonstration that "outward-orientation works".

3.3 Summary of some previous statistical studies on exports and economic growth

Rather than focussing on studies of comparative economic performance between countries pursuing different types of trade regime, or between two time periods when a country was pursuing different types of trade regime, most scholars seem to have focussed their attention on statistical studies. Presented below is a summary of some of the statistical studies undertaken between 1973 and 1989 by various scholars, summarising the models used in estimation of parameters of the assumed explanatory variables, the econometric method used in estimation of the model equations and the main results of the estimated model, and characterisation of their results.

Voivodas (1973):

Data Set: Cross-country (1956-67).
Estimated equation:
$dY_t/Y_t = a + b\,X_t/Y_t$ i.e. GDP growth on export share where
$Y = GDP$; t = time; X_i = an index of dollar value of exports; $\qquad$ (3.1)
Econometric technique: ordinary least squares.
Results:
$dY_t/Y_t = 3.261 + \quad 0.200\,X_t/Y_t$
$\qquad\qquad\qquad (2.303)$
$R^2 = 0.206$
Characterisation of results: export promotion supported.

Krueger (1973):

Data set: cross-country (1954-71).
Estimated equation:
$\log GNP_i = a_{oi} + b_{it} + c\,(\log X_i) + e\,D_{i2t}$ $\qquad$ (3.2)
(t = time; X_i = an index of dollar value of exports of country i; $D_{i1} = 1$ during periods of trade controls and zero otherwise).
Econometric technique: ordinary least squares.

Results:

> General coefficient for:
>> Exports = 0.11
>>> (4.29)
>>
>> R^2 = 0.99
>> F   = 395485
>> D.W.   = 0.92

Characterisation of results: export promotion supported.

Fajana (1979):

Data set: time-series (1954-74), Nigeria.
Estimated equation:
$dY_t/Y_t = a + dX_t/Y_t$
(i.e. GDP growth on proportion of export change to GDP).   (3.3)
Econometric technique: ordinary least squares.
Results:
$dY_t/Y_t = 5.9854 + 1.4636\ dX_t/Y_t$
                    (3.2461)
$R^2 = 0.4721$
Characterisation of results: export promotion supported.

Tyler (1981):

Data set: cross-country for the period 1960-77, middle income countries.
Estimated equation:
$dY_t/Y_t = a + b_1\ dK_t/K_t + b_2\ dL_t/L_t + b_3\ dX_t/X_t$ (3.4)
i.e. GDP growth on growth of capital, labour and exports, where K = capital, and L = labour.
Econometric technique: ordinary least squares.
Results:
$dY_t/Y_t = 1.997 + 0.254\ dK_t/K_t + 0.981\ dL_t/L_t + 0.57\ dX_t/X_t$
               (5.921)   (2.576)   (1.694)
$R^2 = 0.685$
Characterisation of results: export promotion supported.

Feder (1982):

Data set: cross-country (1964-73), 1 time period.
Estimated equation:
$dY_t/Y_t = a + b_1\ I_t/Y_t + b_2\ dL_t/L_t + b_3\ [(dX_t/X_t)(X_t/Y_t)]$ (3.5)

i.e. GDP growth on ratio of investment to GDP, population growth and exports growth multiplied by ratio of exports to GDP where I = investment. Econometric technique: ordinary least squares. Results:

$$dY_t/Y_t = 0.002 + 0.178 \ I_t/Y_t + 0.747 \ dL_t/L_t + 0.422[(dX_t/X_t)(X_t/Y_t)].$$
$$ (0.180) \ (3.542) (2.862) (5.454) (3.6)$$
$$R^2 = 0.689$$

Characterisation of results: export promotion supported.

Kavoussi (1984):

Data set: cross-country (1960-78), 1 time period divided into low and middle income countries - benchmark being per capita income of US \$360.
Estimated equation:
$$RY = a + b \ RK + c \ RL + (d_1 + d_2 \ MX)RX$$
$$ = a + b \ RK + c \ RL + d_1 \ RX + d_2 \ MRX (3.7)$$
where $MRX = (MX)(RX)$.

(i.e. GNP growth (RY) on growth of capital stock (RC), labour force (RL) growth, growth of exports (RX) and on share of manufactured goods in exports (MX)multiplied by growth of exports.

Econometric technique: ordinary least squares.
Results:

For total sample:
$$RY = 2.03 + 0.227 \ RK + 0.441 \ RL + 0.083 \ RX + 0.00061 \ MRX$$
$$ (4.02) \ (5.23) (1.84) (2.33) (0.97)$$
$$R^2 = 0.58$$

For low income countries:
$$RY = 0.58 + 0.236 \ RK + 0.930 \ RL + 0.093 \ RX - 0.00054 \ MRX$$
$$ (0.59) \ (3.70) (1.96) (2.48) (0.75)$$
$$R^2 = 0.58$$

For middle income countries:
$$RY = 2.43 + 0.243 \ RK + 0.463 \ RL - 0.072 \ RX + 0.00496 \ MRX$$
$$ (4.95) \ (5.59) (2.12) (1.01) (4.19)$$
$$R^2 = 0.78$$

Characterisation of results: export promotion supported.

Jung and Marshall (1985):

Data set: time series (1950-81).
Estimated equation:

$$X_t = \sum_{i=1}^{m} a_i X_{t-i} + \sum_{j=1}^{n} b_j Y_{t-j} + \mu_t \tag{3.8}$$

$$Y_t = \sum_{i=1}^{r} c_i Y_{t-i} + \sum_{j=1}^{s} d_j Y_{t-j} + v_t \tag{3.9}$$

Econometric technique: ordinary least squares for a Granger causality test. Results: Many estimates of F-statistic and modified Box-Pierce statistic. Characterisation of results: export promotion, internally generated exports, export reducing growth, growth reducing exports and indeterminate results.

Chow (1987):

Data set: cross-country sample of 8 NICs (1960s-80s).
Estimated equation:

$$X_t = a + \sum_{j=-k}^{m} b_j MFG_{t-j} + \mu_t \tag{3.10}$$

$$X_t = c + \sum_{i=-k}^{m} a_i X_{t-i} + r_t \tag{3.11}$$

where MFG = growth in industrial output, and $-k$ denotes the lead length of future values of a variable.
Econometric technique: ordinary least squares in Sim's causality test.
Results: various F-statistics for the different countries studied. Characterisation of results: no causality for one country but rest supported bi-directional causality between exports and industrial development (export promotion supported).

Ram (1987):

Data set: cross-country (88), time-series - 2 time periods.
Estimated equation:

$$Y = a + b L + c I/Y + d X \qquad (3.12)$$
$$Y = a + b L + c I/Y + d[X(/Y)] \qquad (3.13)$$

Econometric technique: ordinary least squares.
Results:

Equation (3.13):
1960-72:

$$Y = a + \underset{(2.20)}{0.515 \, L} + \underset{(3.25)}{0.090 \, I/Y} + \underset{(4.59)}{0.180 \, X}$$

$R^2 = 0.38$
$F = 17.45$

1973-82:

$$Y = a + \underset{(1.51)}{0.457 \, L} + \underset{(3.95)}{0.134 \, I/Y} + \underset{(6.17)}{0.302 \, X}$$

$R^2 = 0.44$
$F = 21.87$

Equation (3.12):
1960-72:

$$Y = a + \underset{(2.41)}{0.548 \, L} + \underset{(2.52)}{0.071 \, I/Y} + \underset{(5.12)}{0.476 \, X(X/Y)}$$

$R^2 = 0.41$
$F = 19.65$

1973-82:

$$Y = a + \underset{(1.22)}{0.395 \, L} + \underset{(3.33)}{0.123 \, I/Y} + \underset{(4.79)}{0.596 \, X(X/Y)}$$

$R^2 = 0.36$
$F = 15.67$

Characterisation of results: export promotion supported.

Hsiao (1987):

Data set: cross-country (1960s-early 1980s). Estimated equation: As in Jung & Marshall and in Chow above. Econometric technique: ordinary least squares in Granger causality test and AR(1) in Sim's causality test.

Results: Various F- ratios and R^2 and autocorrelation coefficients for the various countries.

Characterisation of results: Indeterminate (uni-directional causality from GDP to exports for one country in both tests, for three countries Granger Causality test found no causality relationship whereas Sim's Test found bi-directional causality relationship.

Moschos (1989):

Data set: cross-country for (1970-80).
Estimated equation:

$$YG_i = a_o + a_1 XG_i + a_2 DXG_{i*i} + b LG_i + c KG_i + u_i \qquad (3.14)$$

i.e. GDP growth on growth of exports, growth of labour force and capital; DXG_{i*i} incorporates a multiplicative dummy variable which takes value of zero for all observations in which the level of development is at or below its hypothesized threshold and the value XG_i for remaining observations.
Econometric technique: ordinary least squares.
Results:

$$YG_i = \ 0.005 + \ 0.129 \, XG_i \quad 0.093 \, DXG_{i*i} + \ 0.761 \, LG_i + \ 0.229 \, Kg_i$$
$$ (0.80) \quad (1.91) \qquad (1.35) \qquad\quad (3.22) \qquad\quad (6.90)$$

R^2 $\quad = 0.656$
SSR $\quad = 0.01569$
SE $\quad = 0.01542$
H $\quad = 5.17$

Characterisation of results: export promotion supported.

From the above, two main types of models that have been used in the statistical tests that have tended to support the superiority of export promotion can be distinguished. The first type employs a Cobb-Douglas type production function in which exports are included as one of the inputs or factors in the production function explaining output growth. The model used takes the following general form:

$$Y = a + bK + c L + d X \qquad (3.15)$$

where Y = real GDP; K = real capital stock approximated by the ratio of gross investment to GDP; and L = labour force approximated by total population.

The analysis of the model focuses on the coefficient of the export variable. The hypothesis made is that due to scale effects and externalities associated with export production, marginal productivities are higher in export production. Thus, given the labour force and capital stock, a strategy of export promotion will raise the growth of GDP; (this is the approach used by Tyler (1981), Kavoussi (1984), Ram (1987) and Moschos (1989).

A variant of this approach is one by which the economy is divided into export and non-export sectors in order to provide a formal rationalisation for the inclusion of exports as an added factor of production. The rationale of this method is that export production provides positive externalities to non-export production. The Cobb-Douglas type production function model in this approach is of the following form:

$$Y = a + b \, I/Y + c \, L + [d/(1+d)+F_x][XG.X/Y] \qquad (3.16)$$

where the export growth variable $X.X/Y$ has export growth weighted by the share of exports in GDP, and the coefficient of this variable, $[d/(1+d)+F_x]$, combines the sectoral productivity differential, d, with the externality effects of exports on the non-export sector, F_x. This is interpreted by Feder (1982) as a measure of the gains from shifting factors of production to exporting which is a high productivity sector. This is also the approach used by Feder (1982), Kavoussi (1984) and Ram (1987).

The other difference we can notice among some of the scholars employing the Cobb-Douglas type production function is in their use of an additional factor. Kavoussi (1984) took account of the level of development to see whether this had any effect on the role of exports in growth by dividing his sample countries into middle and low income in testing his model. His conclusion from his results was that higher rates of economic growth were associated with higher rates of export growth in all cases.

Moschos (1989) also took account of the level of development but incorporated in his equation model a switching variable to determine a threshold level of development below and above which each of the main factors of growth have dissimilar effects on output growth. From his results he also concluded that the positive effects of export expansion on economic growth was applicable in all countries.

Ram (1987) took account of the level of development as well as the international economic environment to capture structural shifts that occur with major changes in the international economic environment. His study was, therefore, conducted for the period 1960-72 before the oil-shock and 1973-82 after the oil-shock for middle and low income countries. His overall result was that exports played an important role in growth in all countries and, when analyzed for countries at different levels of development before and after the oil-shock, that its impact was greater after the oil shock particularly for the low income countries.

However, the use of the Cobb-Douglas type production function models begs the question whether there are not other production categories besides exports whose growth has a similar relationship to GDP. For example, agriculture and infrastructure are often cited as bottleneck sectors in developing countries and it could well be that an increased allocation of resources to these sectors would raise GDP growth. Sheehey (1990) has demonstrated that the strong empirical link between exports and GDP growth in the application of the Cobb-Douglas type production function model or similar models is not unique to exports but, in fact, is common to all the major production categories such as agriculture and infrastructure. Therefore, if the link between sectoral growth and GDP growth is common to all sectors, it clearly cannot be due to relative productivity differences and externality effects assumed in these studies. Since there is considerable underemployment of labour and much less utilization of production capacities in less developed countries, this suggests that exports can be increased without a reduction in the output of import competing industries.

This, however, does not throw overboard the case for export promotion. But it makes the important point that the large body of evidence that is supposed to demonstrate the superiority of export promotion has no bearing on this controversy. The same tests support the promotion of all the sectors of production. Therefore, an export promotion strategy, if it really provides the benefits widely attributed to it, must rely on evidence other than these cross-country tests.

The other main type of statistical tests simply relate exports to GDP, with exports as the explanatory variable in the following general equation model:

$$GDP = a + b X + u_t \tag{3.17}$$

where X is exports, and u_t is a stochastic error term. This is the approach used by Viovodas (1973), Krueger (1978) and Fajana (1979).

There is also some variation in approach among this group of researchers. The study by Viovodas (1973) is a simple cross-country study, using 1956-67 data of 22 countries. Krueger (1978) also undertook a cross-country study, but in two different time periods to capture the linkage between trade policies and exports and growth. The study by Fajana (1979) is a time series analysis undertaken for one country only.

A common feature of both these studies (i.e. both those employing a Cobb-Douglas type production function and those that simply relate exports to

98

growth) is the use of ordinary least squares in the estimation of their equations. It is not surprising, therefore, why the majority of the statistical results are of low power, a result that makes these studies of less value than has been claimed elsewhere.

The major weakness of most of the above studies is that they are prone to a simultaneity bias. The approach used in testing the hypothesis of export promotion involves regressing real GDP growth on contemporaneous real export growth and to infer support for the proposition that export growth causes output growth from the significance of the export growth coefficient, although additional supply variables of foreign exchange and/or demand side variables have been included in some of these studies. Such an approach has a serious methodological weakness in that it presupposes, *a priori*, that exports growth causes economic growth and not that economic growth causes exports growth, which would lead to quite different policy implications.

To understand this counter-hypothesis, consider a growing economy where learning and technical change are proceeding rapidly in a few industries. The learning and technical changes that are taking place may have very little to do with any conscious government policy to promote exports or even to promote production in those industries. These changes may be more related to the accumulation of human capital, cumulative production experience, technology transfer from abroad through licensing or direct investment, or physical capital accumulation. In other words, important primary causal factors behind this unbalanced growth may be unrelated to any special export promoting incentives and may foster growth even in the absence of such incentives.

Given this unbalanced growth, it is unlikely that demand for goods from these boom industries will grow as rapidly as their production and producers are likely to turn to foreign markets to sell their goods. The causal relationship in this instance is then one that proceeds from output growth to export growth. In this circumstance, although output growth and export growth are likely to be correlated, it would be a serious mistake to characterise such a situation as one in which export promotion has induced growth. Ordinary correlations between export growth and output growth are unable to discriminate between the export promotion hypothesis and the internally generated exports hypothesis.

Negative correlations are also not devoid of plausibility. Increased output growth might lead to a decrease in export growth. For example, real growth that is induced by an exogenous increase in consumer demand that is heavily concentrated in exportable and non-traded goods could lead to a decline in exports. Thus, output growth could cause decreased export growth because most tradeable products are consumed at home due to the increase in domestic income. Increased exports arising from some types of inward foreign direct investment might also lower domestic output due to various distortions. Export growth might, therefore, cause reduced output growth. Thus, a discriminating test of the export promotion hypothesis should attempt to focus on the direction of the causal relationship between exports and growth as well as on the sign of this relationship.

Jung and Marshall (1985) addressed this empirical issue using the Granger's causality statistical technique which has certain advantages over those that have been used in all the other previous studies on the subject. Their results cast some doubt on the efficacy of export promotion in fostering economic growth. The essence of Granger's causality is that a variable X causes a variable Y if taking account of past values of X leads to improved predictions for Y. In other words, X (the right-hand-side independent variable) causes Y (the left-hand-side dependent variable) in a regression equation, if the part of current Y that cannot be explained by the past values of Y is explained by the past values of X. These causality tests have certain advantages over the simple contemporaneous correlation-based tests that have been employed to investigate the export promotion hypothesis in that their use of information about temporal precedence enables them to say something about the direction of causation. It is well known that two variables may be correlated yet not causally related because they are both associated with other factors. By including lagged values of the dependent variables and by paying attention to the time-series properties of the residuals, the Granger test removes several sources of spurious correlation. The question of causality is not the only important issue at stake in such an investigation as the sign of the effect is of some importance as well. For example, if one finds that export growth causes output growth, but also that a steady state increase in export growth would eventually decrease output growth, one would hardly be justified in inferring that the export promotion hypothesis finds support.

Jung and Marshall performed causality tests and F tests for the sign of the effect for each of 37 developing countries. The 37 countries were chosen from the International Financial Statistics published by the IMF, with no country having fewer than 15 observations, for the period 1950-81. Their results were remarkable for their lack of support for the export promotion hypothesis. Only Indonesia, Egypt, Costa Rica and Ecuador passed the causality test from export growth to output growth and had export growth coefficients that were significantly positive. Fewer countries supported the export promotion hypothesis than supported the export-reducing growth hypothesis (South Africa, Korea, Pakistan, Israel, Bolivia and Peru). Almost as many countries (Iran, Kenya, and Thailand) provided evidence in favour of the internally generated export (IGE) hypothesis as those that provided evidence in favour of the EP hypothesis. Greece and Israel supported the growth-reducing exports hypothesis. More interestingly, many of the countries most famous for the miraculous growth rates that appeared to arise from export promotion policies (e.g. Korea, Taiwan, Brazil) provided no statistical support for the export promotion hypothesis. This means that factors other than export promotion were more important in promoting growth in these countries, which is consistent with what we saw in Chapter 2 that the state played an active interventionist role in some of these countries.

The reason why these results are obtained when other studies have uniformly tended to support the export promotion hypothesis is that most of the other studies were international cross-section regressions, while the tests here are based on the comparison of each individual country's time series. Cross-sectional tests suffer from the dubious assumption of structural stability of coefficients across countries. The Jung and Marshall tests are preferable, not only because they ask the important question about the direction of causation, but also because they do not presume the strong similarity of different countries. Finally, the theoretical structure might not imply a Granger causal relation. For example, export promotion policies which make a country more creditworthy, enabling it to import more capital goods and grow faster, may only increase exports several years, after additional borrowing begins.

Following the pioneering work of Jung and Marshall, a few researchers have attempted to incorporate the ideas of direction of causation in examining the relationship between exports and economic growth. For example, in a study of eight NICs, Chow (1987) tried to investigate the causal relationship between export growth and industrial development, but using the Sim's causality test technique. According to this technique, if the causality runs one way from current to past values of some list of exogenous variables to a given endogenous variable, then in a regression of the endogenous variable on future, current and past values of the exogenous variables, the future values of the exogenous variables should have zero coefficients. In other words, one can regress Y on past and future values of X, and if causality runs from X to Y only, future values of X in the regression should have coefficients which are insignificantly different from zero, as a group.

Chow's results supported the hypothesis of reciprocal causality, i.e., that the growth of exports causes the growth of manufacturing industry and the growth of manufacturing industry causes the growth of exports. However, Chow misinterpreted its policy implication as being that export growth can cause industrial growth, either uni-directionally or bi-directionally, by influencing the development of manufacturing industries. Strictly, the proper interpretation of Chow's result is that the growth of manufacturing industry leads to the growth of exports and the growth of exports also helps manufacturing industry to grow. This has a different policy implication from Chow's interpretation in that it says that policy can either be to encourage exports or manufacturing industry and not that it should only encourage exports, as concluded by Chow.

However, some critics have expressed doubts about the validity of Chow's method. For example, Sephton (1989) has argued that Chow did not provide a rigorous nor an adequate description of the causal link and that he made errors common to those who are unfamiliar with the econometric pitfalls of testing causality. The reservations which have been cited on Chow's study are the following:

1. there are too few observations to undertake the analysis and so the statistical tests have low power;

2. no tests for serial correlation and stationarity were performed to determine whether the "own-lag" was correctly chosen in the specification of the model and that an ad hoc length of three years was chosen without providing any convincing rationale for doing so; and

3. it is not possible to know whether Chow's results are free from autocorrelation, heteroscedasticity, or whether they are temporally stable.

Therefore, Chow's work can only be regarded as tentative at best and certainly not evidence of a rigorous investigation into the relationship between exports and industrial output.

Hsiao (1987) also investigated the relationship between exports and growth, taking into account the Jung-Marshall ideas. However, he used both Sim's uni-directional exogeneity test and Granger's causality test. His two tests yielded different causal implications for each of the four rapidly developing Asian countries covered in his study, i.e., Hong Kong, South Korea, Singapore and Taiwan. This suggests that the outcome of statistical tests depends on the methods used. The Sim's test indicated a feedback relationship while his Granger's test indicated no causal relationship between exports and GDP, except for Hong Kong which both tests indicated a uni-directional causality from GDP to exports without feedback. Thus, his two tests indicated that the rapid economic growth of the Asian NICs is not only achieved with the export promotion policy, but also derived from the domestic growth of industries and import-substitution. This is consistent with the Jung-Marshall results we have already referred to.

However, the studies by Jung and Marshall, Chow and Hsiao, although they tried to deal with the problem of simultaneity bias, also suffer from the weakness that they relied on the use of ordinary least squares in the estimation of their equations. Ordinary least squares are not efficient parameter estimators and give rise to relatively large unequal disturbance variances the implication of which is that the individual observations on the dependent variable are not of equal reliability. If the variance of one particular disturbance is relatively high, there is a correspondingly greater probability of finding a value of that disturbance which is well away from zero. This means that the corresponding value of the dependent variable is more likely to contain a relatively large random error. In this sense, an observation associated with a relatively high disturbance variance contains less information about the underlying relationship between the variables in the model. Thus, the results of Jung and Marshall, Chow and Hsiao can only be regarded as tentative.

All in all, the many empirical studies that have been undertaken by the proponents of outward orientation on the relationship between trade regime and economic growth have not provided conclusive evidence that export promotion is superior to import substitution. This is because of the flaws in the methodologies they used to prove their case. The few studies undertaken by other researchers who have attempted to challenge the export promotion hypothesis have suffered from a few short-comings in that, although they utilised better statistical methods, the econometric technique of ordinary least squares used in estimation of their models is not a very efficient estimator and their results are also subject to doubt.

This seems to suggest that we are landed with Karl Popper's problem of induction which hold that any attempt to prove a theory or hypothesis is always fallacious. But as also argued by Popper, one theory can be preferable to another in terms of what tests and trials it has withstood, i.e. how far it has been able to prove its fitness to survive by standing up to tests or how far it has been "corroborated". However, this is not to say that such a theory would also continue to stand up to tests in the future (see, for example, Popper, 1972).

3.4 Trade regime bias and economic integration

At the regional level, it is interesting to investigate whether trading blocks, such as the PTA, promote economic growth. Much of the theoretical literature (for example, Lipsey, 1960; Krugman, 1991) focus on the welfare effects of discriminatory tariff cuts in static environments; this literature does not predict large changes in welfare. Yet Harris (1984), who stresses the role of economies of scale and imperfect competition, and Brade and Mendez (1988), who emphasizes the impact of trading blocks on domestic savings and investment, show that regional trade reforms can have substantial dynamic effects.   Dinopoulos and Syropoulos (1996) reinforce the argument that substantial dynamic effects are associated with an outward-looking trade regime, especially if the possible impacts on innovativons and technological change are integrated into the analysis.   A generalization of the noe-Schumpeterian model of growth and trade is applied.   In the model, the Schumpeterian long-run growth rate is described by the growth rate (g) of the export sector as follows:

$$g = \ln(\mu)\left(R/(1+\lambda R)\right) \tag{3.18}$$

where *ln (μ)* = exogenous increase in labour productivity following a process of innovation; R = a country's steady-state R & D investment services; λ = a parameter for the magnitude of instateneous diminishing returns to industry-wide R & D. Equation (3.18) is utilised to illustrate the magnitude of growth effects due to outward-oriented trade policy reform:

$$\hat{g} \equiv dg/g = \left[\frac{\partial g}{\partial R} \cdot \frac{R}{\partial}\right]\left[\frac{\partial R}{\partial \phi} \cdot \frac{\phi}{R}\right]\left[\frac{\partial \phi}{\partial \tau_k} \cdot \frac{\tau_k}{\phi}\right]\left(-\hat{\tau}_k\right) \tag{3.19}$$

where a hat denotes percentage change; $\phi \equiv \sum_k (1+\tau_k)^{-1}$ and τ_k is a non-negative ad-valorem tariff on imports of good k. In equation (3.19), the first term represents the elasticity of Schumpeterian growth with respect to R & D investment. Dinopoulos and Syropoulos (1996) guestimate it at 0.85. The second term is the elasticity of R & D investment with respect to trade policy reform; the estimate was about 2. The third term in equation (3.19) is the responsiveness of the trade reform measure (ϕ) to a particular tariff; this is also estimated at about 2.

The above analysis represents a pre-integration scenario. Suppose now that a trading block is formed in the form of a custom's union or a free-trade area that leads to dismantling of internal tariffs without changing the external tariffs. The conventional welfare effects will be attained: trade creation; trade diversion; and terms-of-trade effects. In addition, Dinopolous and Syropoulos (1996) suggest that a trading block may raise the expected utility of consumers located outside as well as inside the block. In a world of 30 countries and 30 traded commodities, with 25 percent tariff on all imported goods, it is shown that if 10 countries form a trading block the growth rate (*g*) of each member increases by about 10 percent, and the long-run growth rate of global GNP increases by 100 percent, suggesting that all economies in the world experience a doubling in the growth of real income.

3.5   Conclusion

The many empirical studies that have been undertaken on the relationship between trade regime and economic growth have not provided conclusive evidence that export-orientation is superior to import-substitution. This is because of flaws in the methodologies they have used.

The few recent studies, that have tried to correct some of the flaws in the previous studies (i.e. the studies undertaken by Jung and Marshall and Chow) have indicated that no such conclusive evidence can be reached. Indeed, they have pointed to the possibility that import-substitution could very well be superior to outward-orientation. Therefore, the controversy about import-substitution versus export-promotion has not been resolved empirically.

A very comprehensive survey of the measures that have been used in recent literature to shed further light on the trade and growth debate is given by Harrison (1996). In a brief review of the literature on openness and growth, Harrison (1996) identifies four main types of measures that have been used: measures based on trade shares; price-based and administrative measures; micro and productivity studies; and causality tests. These measures, and the related studies and findings are summarised in Table 3.4 (adopted from Harrison, 1996; Table 1). Some main conclusions emerge from the information in the table; in particular, it is found that the debate on openness and economic growth remains unresolved, notwithstanding the large volume of literature on this issue. While methodological problems make it difficult to investigate directly the link between trade policy (in its open form) and economic growth, many studies show a positive relationship.

Table 3.4

Summary evidence on openness and growth according to the Harrison (1996) classification

Openness measure	Countries	Period	Impact	Source
I. *Measures based on trade shares*				
			Coefficient on openness	
Deviation from predicted trade	45	1973-78	Significant > 0	Balassa (1985)
Deviation from predicted trade (Leamer, 1988)		1982	Significant > 0	Edwards (1992)
II. *Price-based and administrative measures*				
Relative domestic price of investment goods to international prices	98	1960-65	Raises GDP growth per capital	Barro (1991)
Relative price of traded goods	95	1960-85	Raises GDP growth per capita	Dollar (1991)
Effective rate of protection in manufacturing	47	1950-80	Lower protection raises GDP growth	Heitger (1986)
Trade liberalization index		1978-88	Trade reform positively affects GDP growth	Thomas and Nash (1992)

Table 3.4 (concluded)

III. *Micro and productivity studies*

Description	Number/Country	Result	Period	Author
Deviation from predicted export share	108	Positive	1960-82	Syrquin and Chenery (1989)
Export growth	4	Positive	1955-78	Nishimizu and Robinson (1984)
Export growth	17	Positive	1950-80	Nishimizu and Page (1990)
Export growth	4	Positive	1976-99	Tubout (1992)
Import penetration	17	Ambiguous Negative	1950-73 1973-85	Nishimizu and Page (1990)
Import substitution (IS) (1 - Import penetration)	4	IS negatively affects TFP	1955-78	Nishimizu and Robinson (1984)
Import substitution	4	IS positively affects TFP	1976-88	Tybout (1992)
Effective rates of protection and domestic resource costs	Turkey	Ambiguous	1963-76	Krueger and Tuncer (1982)
Change in import shares	UK	Ambiguous	1976-79	Geroski (1989)
Tariffs and import penetration	Ivory Coast	Positive	1975-87	Harrison (1994)

IV. *Causality tests*

Methodology		*Exports cause growth?*		
Granger tests	37	For only 4 countries	1950-81	Jung and Marshall (1985)
White specification test	73	Yes	1960-77	Ram (1985)
Granger, Sim tests	4 (Asian NICs)	Sometimes		Hsiao (1987)
Granger tests	Austria	No, but productivity growth causes exports	1965	Kunst and Marin (1989)

Source: Harrison (1996, p.422-3) Table 1.
Note: Studies based on working papers are excluded from this table.

4 Empirical evidence on ten African economies

4.1 Introduction

In the previous chapter, it was concluded that although many empirical studies have been undertaken on the relationship between trade regime and economic growth, there is no conclusive evidence that export-orientation is superior to import-substitution. The conclusion arises from flaws in the methodologies used in most empirical studies, especially flaws arising from the problem of simultaneity bias. The few recent studies that have tried to correct such flaws have yielded evidence which points to the possibility that import-substitution could very well be superior to outward-orientation. Consequently, the controversy about import-substitution versus export-promotion remains an important empirical and policy issue.

Therefore, a more efficient estimating technique to dispel the doubts that still surround the empirical studies that have so far been undertaken is required. This is what this chapter is motivated to do in order to contribute meaningfully to the on-going controversy. Innovative econometric techniques are used to examine the direction of causation between exports and growth. Moreover, unlike other studies which have concentrated on the newly industrialising countries and semi-industrialised countries, this chapter focuses on a sample of ten African countries. The sample countries are at lower levels of development than countries in other regions of the world.

As it has been argued above, to demonstrate the superiority of export promotion over import substitution requires the fulfilment of three conditions:

(a) outward orientation should be clearly distinguishable from non-outward orientation; (b) a causal link between outward orientation and export performance should be established; and (c) a causal link between export performance and economic growth should be established. To meet all these conditions, which none of the previous studies has attempted to do with the exception of the Krueger study, the analysis is supplemented by applying the Granger causality test to two countries, one of which has persistently pursued an export oriented strategy and another country which has experimented with both types of trade regimes. This analysis will also benefit from the use of long series of observations which most of the previous studies did not have.

In general, the relationship between export promotion and economic growth has been investigated using four main approaches. In the first approach, bivariate testing of the correlation between exports and economic growth has been conducted in levels form as well as in growth rate form (for example, Jung and Marshall, 1985). In the second approach, a production function is used to put forward the main factors such as land and labour that account for growth in total exports; the specification then provides a platform for investigating the link between exports and economic growth (for example, Kavoussi, 1984). The third approach implicitly tests for the critical minimum effort hypothesis, by considering the differential impacts of exports on economic growth conditional on the level of industrial development (or economic growth) of the country (for example, Moschos, 1989). In the fourth approach, causality between export growth and economic growth is investigated in order to confirm or reject the export-led growth hypothesis; recent work in this approach has utilised the recent developments in econometrics especially testing for non-stationarity and cointegration, and the use of the error-correction form (for example, Bahman-Oskoee and Alse, 1993). Most of the above studies conclude that the causality tests offer weak support for the alternative notions of trade as an "engine" of growth and trade as a "handmaiden" of growth.

The remainder of this chapter is structured as follows. Section 4.2 reports on the main econometric procedures and results relating to the linkage between export growth and economic growth; the work applies some recent econometric procedures in the literature on non-stationarity, cointegration and error-correction. Further econometric procedures and results are reported in Section 4.3 for standard Grainger-causality testing using a bivariate vector autoregression (BVAR) model. Section 4.4 concludes.

4.2 Econometric testing of the linkage between export growth and economic growth: non-stationarity, cointegration and error-correction

We call upon recent innovations in econometric techniques to further test for the linkage between export growth and economic growth in a sample of African economies. Specifically, we do not ony rigorously test for non-stationarity, but we find it necessary to test for cointegration. We are also able to extend the time series used in previous work on these confines, by taking the period 1965-95. This allows us to work with a large sample, and to obtain more degrees of freedom.

We conduct tests of non-stationarity (unit roots) using levels and first differences of the logarithmic transformation of the series. In most of the existing literature, testing for non-stationarity is based on the Dickey-Fuller tests (see Dickey and Fuller, 1979). However, these tests have been criticised on the grounds that, among other problems, they assume an error structure that is an independently and identically distributed (iid) $(0, \sigma^2)$ Gaussian process. Recent literature suggests that many economic time series exhibit time-dependent heteroskedasticity; and rather than being pure Autoregressive Integrated Moving Average (ARIMA: 1,0,0) processes, most economic variables are characterised by random walks with a moving average (MA) component (see Phillips and Perron, 1988). For this matter, we rely on the Phillips-Perron (hereafter, PP) test. Moreover, the PP test is robust to autocorrelated errors in the sense that it allows greater general dependence including conditional heteroeskedasity. Fortunately, the asymptotic critical values of the PP tests are the same as those tabulated by DF.

In setting up the two-step PP method, we first calculate the DF statistic assuming ARIMA (1,0,0). We then adjust the DF statistic using autocovariances of the error process. Specifically, we obtain residuals, $\hat{\varepsilon}_t$, by regressing the series, say y_t, on its lagged value, y_{t-1}, as follows:

$$y_t = \hat{\mu} + \hat{\beta}(t - \frac{T}{2}) + \hat{\alpha} y_{t-1} + \hat{\varepsilon}_t \qquad (4.1)$$

One the basis of the above equation, we compute S_t^2 and S_k^2 as follows:

$$S_t^2 = \frac{1}{T} \sum_{t=1}^{T} \hat{\mu}_t^2 \qquad (4.2)$$

and:

$$S_k^2 = \frac{1}{T}\sum_{t=1}^{T} \hat{\mu}_t^2 + \frac{2}{T}\sum_{s=1}^{T} w_s \sum_{t=s+1}^{T} \hat{\mu}_t \hat{\mu}_{t-s} \qquad (4.3)$$

where k = lag structure that whitens the error term; and $w_s = 1-s/(k+1)$. To render further robustness to our testing procedure with regard to the non-stationarity status of our series, we use the method proposed by Kwiatkowski, Phillips, Schmidt and Shin (1992). In this method, the series is decomposed into a deterministic trend, a random walk and a stationarity error, as follows:

$$y_t = \alpha + \mu_t + v_t \qquad (4.4)$$

where α = unknown constant; $\mu_t = \mu_{t-1} + e_t$ and e_t = iid $(0, \lambda \sigma_v^2)$ errors; v_t is a stationarity ARIMA process whose variance is σ_v^2; v_t, which represents the deviations from trend, is I(0); and μ_t is I(1).

Hence, the unit-root testing procedure employed here relies on three techniques namely the Dickey-Fuller (DF), the Phillips-Perron (PP) and the Kwiatkowski, Phillips, Schmidt and Shin (KPSS) methods.

The data for export growth and real growth were retrieved from the International Financial Statistics Yearbook published by the IMF, initially for the period 1961 - 1989 and later updated up to 1995. Preliminary overview of the data was aimed at determining the comparability of series across the countries in order to minimise the problems associated with outliers if certain definitions of exports and economic growth were adopted. The initial diagnostics (not reported here for brevity) showed that these countries do not necessarily have good quality data; however, we were satisfied to work with the best data we could obtain.

The results are reported in Table 4.1 for Botswana, Burundi, Ethiopia, Kenya, Malawi, Mauritius, Rwanda, Tanzania, Zambia, and Zimbabwe for non-stationarity in annual data for real gross domestic product (GDP) and real exports (EXP) for the period 1967-95.

The results reported in Table 4.1 suggest that the null hypothesis of non-stationarity (unit root) for real gross domestic product and real export variables cannot be rejected for almost all the sample countries at the 1 percent level. However, at the 5 percent level the results for all the three tests with respect to the two variables and 10 countries are rather mixed. Non-stationarity for GDP as well as EXP is rejected for some countries in the sample. Nonetheless, on the basis of the 1 percent level of significance, it is reasonable to assume that the null hypothesis of a unit root is supported for GDP and EXP for all the sample countries.

Table 4.1

Test results for non-stationarity (unit root) in real gross domestic product (GDP) and real exports (EXP) for 10 African economies, 1967-95

Sample country	Variable and test GDP			EXP		
	DF $(Z_\tau \hat{\beta}_2)$	PP (Z_t)	KPSS $(L=2)$	DF $(Z_\tau \hat{\beta}_2)$	PP (Z_t)	KPSS $(L=2)$
Botswana	-1.23	-0.84	0.89	-3.01	-0.11	0.79
Burundi	-1.74	-2.13	1.06	-1.47	4.86	1.05
Ethiopia	-2.95	1.94	0.94	-1.13	2.65	1.04
Kenya	-1.08	0.13	1.04	-0.93	4.43	0.88
Malawi	-3.11	1.15	0.89	-2.41	1.20	0.92
Mauritius	-1.91	3.16	1.03	-2.78	3.09	1.14
Rwanda	-1.29	-1.83	1.05	-1.53	-1.04	1.07
Tanzania	0.73	-0.19	1.31	-1.67	-0.49	1.43
Zambia	1.21	4.87	0.76	1.36	7.53	0.91
Zimbabwe	-3.47	-1.67	1.33	-1.19	-2.35	1.29

Notes: DF is the Dickey-Fuller test based on Dickey and Fuller (1979, 1981) with critical value at the 5 percent significance level for sample size 50 of - 3.50; $(Z_\tau \hat{\beta}_2)$ tests the null hypothesis that the series is I(1). PP is the Phillips-Perron test based on Phillips and Perron (1988); (Z_t) is the t-statistic for the hypothesis B = 1; the critical values are 3.18, -3.50, and -4.15 at the 10 percent, 5 percent and 1 percent significance levels, respectively. KPSS is the Kwiatkowski, Phillips, Schmidt and Shin (1922) test, where $(L=2)$ is the lag length of the autocorrelation function and the critical values are 0.463 and 0.739 at the 5 percent and 1 percent level, respectively. Although some countries had series going as far back as 1960, a uniform sample size of 1967-95 was imposed for all the 10 countries.

On the basis of the results on unit root properties of the data, we move to test for the cointegration properties of the two variables, GDP and EXP, using the Engle and Granger two-step cointegration procedure. The idea is to establish whether (or not) growth in exports and economic growth are cointegrated such that they are able to demonstrate some causality (or otherwise). Given that the series are individually I(1), we are interested in the stationarity properties of the linear combination of the two series i.e. it is expected that if the variables are cointegrated, their linear combination will be I(0). In the first step, we therefore run the following regressions:

$$y_t = \alpha_1 + \Psi_1 x_t + s_{1t} \tag{4.5}$$

$$x_t = \alpha_2 + \Psi_2 y_t + s_{2t} \tag{4.6}$$

where y_t = log of real gross domestic product; x_t = log of real exports; s_{1t} = error term. We pursue the above idea that if y and x are cointegrated, their linear combination $(y_t - \psi_1 x_t)$ and $(x_t - \psi_1 y_t)$ would be a stationary process i.e. I(0). We refer to (4.5) as the direct regression, and (4.6) as the reverse regression.

In the second step of the Engle-Granger cointegration procedure, we test for stationarity of the error process. Given the error structure in equations (4.5) and (4.6), we regress the first difference of the residuals (ΔS_t) on a time trend (t) and lagged residuals (s_{t-1}) as follows:

$$\Delta s_{1t} = s_{1t} - s_{2(t-1)} = \alpha_3 + \Psi_3 t + \phi_1 s_{2(t-1)} + w_{1t} \tag{4.7}$$

$$\Delta s_{2t} = s_{2t} - s_{2(t-1)} = \alpha_4 + \Psi_4 t + \phi_2 s_{2(t-1)} + w_{2t} \tag{4.8}$$

The null hypothesis is: $H_0 = Z(\theta) = (\alpha, \psi, \phi) = (\alpha, 0, 1)$. The results are reported in Table 4.2.

Table 4.2
Results of the Engle-Granger two-step cointegration test for exports and growth in 10 African economies

Country	Direct regression $Z(\theta)$	Reverse regression $Z(\theta)$
Botswana	6.814*	10.193
Burundi	3.196	4.109
Ethiopia	5.693	5.701
Kenya	1.672	1.428
Malawi	2.539	2.616
Mauritius	7.952*	6.89*
Rwanda	3.470	3.582
Tanzania	4.195	4.283
Zambia	6.144	5.290
Zimbabwe	5.014	3.180

Note: The critical value at the 5 percent significance level for sample size 50 is 6.73.

The results in Table 4.2 suggest that cointegration does not hold for eight out of the ten countries in our sample. Cointegration only holds for Mauritius and Botswana i.e. there is some indication of a possible causal relationship between export growth and economic growth; however, we do not know the direction of causality. To obtain further information on the direction of causality for all the ten sample countries, we take a two pronged attack. First, for the eight countries, which do not exhibit evidence of cointegration, we proceed to test for causality using a standard Granger-causality procedure (see Lyons and Murinde, 1994 and Murinde and Eng, 1994). Second, for Mauritius and Botswana, which exhibit cointegration between x and y, we search for the direction of causality using an error-correction model (ECM). The idea is that the ECM incorporates errors from a cointegrating regression, and this characteristic of ECM makes it possible to trace temporal causality. It is hypothesized that if the series x_t and y_t are cointegrated, they may be generated by an ECM whose form is given by:

$$\Delta y_t = -\lambda_1 Z_{t-1} + A(L)\Delta y_t + B(L)\Delta x_t + e_{1t} \tag{4.9}$$

$$\Delta x_t = -\lambda_2 Z_{t-1} + C(L)\Delta x_t + D(L)\Delta y_t + e_{2t} \tag{4.10}$$

where λ_1 or λ_2 are non-zero, and $Z_{t-1} = x_{t-1} - Ay_{t-1}$, depending on the direction of causality; and e_{1t} and e_{2t} are finite order moving averages. Two possible sources of causality are implied by the ECM. First, changes in x_t or y_t or both are partly driven by Z_{t-1}; this term is a function of the linear combinations of x_{t-1} and y_{t-1} as well as lagged values of these variables. Thus, in order to make inference regarding causality between x and y, we need to check the statistical significance of λ_1 and λ_2 as well as the elements of $B(L)$ and $D(L)$. There are a number of possible results. If λ_2 and $D(L) = 0$, then y does not Granger-cause x. If, however, λ_1 and $D(L) \neq 0$, then y Granger-causes x. Similar interpretations can be made for Granger-causation from x to y.

The results for equation (4.9) are reported in Table (4.3) while those for equation (4.10) are given in Table (4.4).

Table 4.3

Results for the error-correction model (ECM) for

Granger-causality from exports to growth

Country[+]	t-statistic Z_{t-1}	F-statistic $A(L)y_t$	F-statistic $B(L)\Delta x_t$
Mauritius	-2.463*	7.514*	7.170*
Botswana	-0.798	1.712	1.902

Note: [+]The rest of the sample (i.e. eight countries) are excluded from the ECM as they did not exhibit cointegration. Critical values of $Z_{t-1} = -2.02$. The critical values of the F-statistic for sample size 40 is 2.84 at the 5 percent significance level. *Indicates significance at the 5 percent level.

Table 4.4

Results for the error-correction model (ECM) for

Granger-causality from growth to exports

Country[+]	t-statistic Z_{t-1}	F-statistic $C(L)\Delta x_t$	F-statistic $D(L)\Delta y_t$
Mauritius	-1.42	0.62	0.58
Botswana	-1.38	2.17	1.94

Note: [+]The rest of the sample (i.e. eight countries) are excluded from the ECM as they did not exhibit cointegration. Critical values of $Z_{t-1} = -2.02$. The critical values of the F-statistic for sample size 40 is 2.84 at the 5 percent significance level. *Indicates significance at the 5 percent level.

The results for equation (4.9), with respect to the export-led growth hypothesis, are reported in Table 4.3. These results support the hypothesis for Mauritius only; the hypothesis is rejected for Zimbabwe. We are therefore in a position to conclude that export growth leads to economic growth in the sense of Granger in only one of the ten sample economies. The results for equation (4.10), reported in Table 4.4, are inconclusive on the strength as well as the directions of causality from economic growth to export growth for Mauritius and Botswana. In general, while we acknowledge that the export growth and economic growth linkage tends to be country-specific, we find that both the standard Granger-causality test and the ECM (following non-stationarity tests and the Engle-Granger two-step procedure) yield results which indicate that the export-led growth hypothesis is not consistent with the experience of the sample African economies (with the exception of Mauritius).

4.3 Further empirical procedures and results: standard Granger-causality testing in a BVAR model

This section applies standard Granger causality tests to eight African countries, namely Zimbabwe, Burundi, Ethiopia, Kenya, Malawi, Rwanda, Tanzania and Zambia. In the empirical procedures and results reported in Section 4.2, these eight countries did not exhibit evidence of cointegration. As Lyons and Murinde (1994) and Murinde and Eng (1994) have shown, it is preferable to test for causality for the eight countries using a standard Granger-causality procedure. More specifically, the approach we adopt in this section follows the study of Jung and Marshall (1985). The reason for the preference of the use of Jung-Marshall causality test rather than Sim's causality test is that the Granger ideas employed have more intuitive philosophical appeal. The Sim's causality idea sounds perverse as future events seem to be taken to predict the present or the past, whereas the Granger method uses the past to predict the present. The sample countries are Botswana, Burundi, Ethiopia, Kenya, Malawi, Mauritius, Rwanda, Tanzania, Zambia and Zimbabwe. The choice of these countries is dictated by the fact that they are in a quite different group and cannot be compared to the NICs but have more or less similar economic conditions, production technology, and social and cultural background. Since the causality tests we have referred to applied mainly to the NICs, our objective here is to test whether the same kind of results would also be obtained. This has important policy implications for African countries as they are always advised that foreign trade is even more important for them and that if they are to achieve fast economic growth, they should pay special attention to export promotion which requires trade liberalisation. The data for the growth rates of real exports and real GDP have been obtained from the IMF (1986, 1988) with no country having less than 14 observations and some countries having as many as 24 observations. The growth rates of real GDP have been calculated directly from the GDP figures given at 1980 prices while the growth rates of real exports have been arrived at after deflating the export values by the unit value of imports or, where this is not available, by the GDP deflator to obtain the values of real exports. In what follows, X stands for the rate of growth of real exports and Y for the rate of growth of real GDP.

To carry out the Granger causality test, the following bivariate vector autoregressive (BVAR) model for each of the ten countries in the sample is estimated:

$$X_t = \sum_{i=1}^{m} a_i X_{t-i} + \sum_{j=1}^{m} b_j Y_{t-j} + \mu_t \qquad (4.11)$$

$$Y_t = \sum_{i=1}^{r} Y_{t-i} + \sum_{j=1}^{s} d_j Y_{t-j} - v_t \qquad (4.12)$$

where (μ_t, v_t) is a serially independent random vector with mean zero and finite covariance matrix. The causality tests to be performed are stated as:

(a) X causes Y if H_o: $d_j = 0$; and $b_j \neq 0$ can be rejected

(b) Y causes X if H_o: $b_j = 0$; and $d_j \neq 0$ can be rejected

Feedback occurs if both (a) and (b) hold. The question of causality is not the only interesting issue at hand. The sign of the effect is also important. The sign of the effect of the causal variable can 4be checked by using an F test to see whether $\Sigma s_{j-1} d_j$ is positive or negative. For each country Y is regressed on past values of itself, on past values of X and on a constant. X is regressed on the same variables. An autocorrelation test is carried to ensure that in all the regressions the residuals are white noise (unpredictable from their own past and, therefore, not significantly autocorrelated). The estimation technique used in all our regressions is the two-stage least squares.

The results after performing all these procedures for the ten countries in our sample are as follows:

Burundi:

$$Y_t = \quad -0.333 \ Y_{t-1} + \quad 0.067 \ X_{t-1} + 4.44$$
$$ (-1.698) (1.966)$$

$A_{t20} = 2.845$ at 1 percent level
  2.086 at 5 percent level
  1.725 at 10 percent level
$t(b) = 1.966$, significant at 10 percent level.
i.e. $Ho : d_j = 0$, is rejected
This implies that X causes Y or that real exports growth causes real GDP growth.
F (2, 20) Crit. val. = 3.49.
F (2, 20) = 12.17 (significant)
Scaled residuals:
Sample size   = 23
Mean   = 0.000

Std. dvn.   = 1.022
Skewness   = 0.701
Excess kurtosis   = -0.724
$CHI^2(2)$ = 2.178
DW   = 2.02

$$X_t = -0.536 \, X_{t-1} + \; 0.630 \, Y_{t-1} + 13.76$$
$$\quad\;\; (-2.796) \qquad (0.574)$$

$t(d) = 0.574$, not significant.

$H_o : d = 0$ is accepted

This implies Y does not cause X or that real GDP does not cause real exports.

F (2, 20)   = 2.92 (not significant)

Scaled residuals:

Sample size   = 23
Mean   = 0.000
Std. Devn   = 1.022
Skewness   = 0.794
Excess kurtosis   = - 0.071
$CHI^2(2)$ = 2.210
DW   = 2.17

Ethiopia:

$$Y_t = \; 0.262 \, Y_{t-1} - 0.044 \, X_{t-1} + 2.61$$
$$\quad\;\; (1.159) \qquad (-1.306)$$

t_{24} = 2.797 at 1 percent
                = 2.064 at 5 percent
                = 1.711 at 10 percent
$t_{(b)}$ = -1.306 (not significant)
$H_o: d_j$ = 0 is accepted

This implies that X does not cause Y or that exports growth does not cause GDP growth.

F (2, 24) Crit. val. = 3.40
F (2, 24) = 1.55 (not significant)

Scaled residuals:

Sample size   = 27
Mean   = 0.000
Std.devn.   = 1.019
Skewness   = 0.167
Excess kurtosis   = -0.311
$CHI^2(2)$ = 0.218

CHI²(2) Crit. val.   = 5.990
DW   = 1.99

$X_t =$ $-0.404 X_{t-1} + 0.631 Y_{t-1} + 1.88$
   (-1.836)   (0.427)
$t_{(d)} = 0.427$ (not significant)
$H_o : b_j = 0$ is accepted
This implies that Y does not cause X or that real GDP growth does not cause real exports growth.

   F(2, 24)   = 0.63 (not significant)
   Scaled residuals:
   Sample size   = 27
   Mean   = 0.000
   Std. devn.   = 1.019
   Skewness   = 0.212
   Excess kurtosis   = 0.102
   CHI²(2)   = 0.199
   DW   = 2.12

Kenya:

   $Y_t = -0.152 Y_{t-1} + 0.062 X_{t-1} + 6.36$
      (-0.572)   (0.758)

   t_{17} = 2.898 at 1 percent
            = 2.110 at 5 percent
            = 1.740 at 10 percent
   $t_{(b)}$ = 0.758 (not significant)
   $H_o: d_j$ = 0 is accepted
This implies that X does not cause Y or that exports growth does not cause GDP growth.
   F (2, 17) Crit. val. = 3.59
   F (2, 17) = 0.27, not significant
   Scaled residuals:
   Sample size   = 20
   Mean   = 0.000
   Std.devn.   = 1.026
   Skewness   = 1.061
   Excess kurtosis   = 1.563
   CHI²(2)   = 5.211

CHI²(2) Crit. val.   = 5.990
DW   = 1.68

$X_t =$ 0.030 X_{t-1} - 0.691 Y_{t-1} + 3.48
　　　(0.107)   (-0.768)
$t_{(d)}$ = -0.768 (not significant)
$H_o : bj$ = 0 is accepted
This implies that Y does not cause X or that real GDP growth does not cause real exports growth.
F(2, 17)   = 0.28 (not significant)
Scaled residuals:
Sample size   = 20
Mean   = 0.000
Std. devn.   = 1.026
Skewness   = 0.120
Excess kurtosis   = -0.530
CHI²(2)   = 0.254
DW   = 1.85

Malawi:

$Y_t =$ -0.097 Y_{t-1} +   0.039 X_{t-1} + 4.13
　　　(-0.541)   (0.643)

t_{28} = 2.763 at 1 percent
           = 2.048 at 5 percent
           = 1.701 at 10 percent
$t_{(b)}$ = 0.643 (not significant)
$H_o: dj$ = 0 is accepted
This implies that X does not cause Y or that exports growth does not cause GDP growth.
F (2, 28) Crit. val. = 3.34
F (2, 28) = 0.19 (not significant)
Scaled residuals:
Sample size   = 31
Mean   = 0.000
Std.devn.   = 1.016
Skewness   = 0.337
Excess kurtosis   = 0.899
CHI²(2)   = 1.526
CHI²(2) Crit. val.   = 5.990

DW   = 1.98

$X_t =$ 0.011 X_{t-1} +   0.626 Y_{t-1} - 1.01
         (0.062)   (1.142)
   $t_{(d)}$ = 1.142 (not significant)
   $H_o : b_j$ = 0 is accepted
This implies that Y does not cause X or that real GDP growth does not cause real exports growth.
   F(2, 28)   = 0.79, not significant
   Scaled residuals:
   Sample size   = 31
   Mean   = 0.000
   Std. devn.   = 1.016
   Skewness   = 0.389
   Excess kurtosis   = 1.035
   CHI²(2)   = 2.027
   DW   = 2.01

Rwanda:

$Y_t =$ 0.450 Y_{t-1} -   0.040 X_{t-1} + 3.04
          (1.954)   (-2.083)

   t_{14} = 2.977 at 1 percent
              = 2.145 at 5 percent
              = 1.761 at 10 percent
   $t_{(b)}$ = -2.083, significant at 10 percent.
   $H_o:d_j$ = 0 is rejected.
This implies that X causes Y or that real exports growth causes real GDP growth.
   F (2, 14) Crit. val. = 3.74
   F (2, 14) = 2.35 (not significant)
   Scaled residuals:
   Sample size   = 17
   Mean   = 0.000
   Std.devn.   = 1.031
   Skewness   = -0.635
   Excess kurtosis   = -0.477
   CHI²(2)   = 1.250
   CHI²(2) Crit. val.   = 5.990
   DW   = 1.77

$$X_t = -0.446\, X_{t-1} + 4.315\, Y_{t-1} + 1.41$$
$$\quad\ (-1.797) \qquad\ (1.452)$$

$t_{(d)}$ $\qquad$ = 1.452 (not significant)

$H_o : b_j$ $\quad$ = 0 is accepted.

This implies that Y does not cause X or that real GDP growth does not cause real exports growth.

$F(2, 14)$ $\qquad\qquad$ = 1.87, not significant.

Scaled residuals:

Sample size	= 17
Mean	= 0.000
Std. devn.	= 1.031
Skewness	= 1.225
Excess kurtosis	= 1.321
$CHI^2(2)$	= 4.843
DW	= 2.05

Tanzania:

$$Y_t = 0.165\, Y_{t-1} + 0.044\, X_{t-1} + 2.73$$
$$\quad\ (0.794) \qquad\ (0.760)$$

t_{15} $\qquad$ = 2.947 at 1 percent

$\qquad\quad$ = 2.131 at 5 percent

$\qquad\quad$ = 1.753 at 10 percent

$t_{(b)}$ $\qquad$ = 0.760 (not significant)

$H_o: d_j$ $\quad$ = 0 is accepted.

This implies that X does not cause Y or that real exports growth does not cause real GDP growth.

F [2, 15] Crit. val. = 3.68

F (2, 15) = 1.29 (not significant)

Scaled residuals:

Sample size	= 18
Mean	= 0.000
Std.devn.	= 1.029
Skewness	= 1.022
Excess kurtosis	= 0.501
$CHI^2(2)$	= 2.955
$CHI^2(2)$ Crit. val.	= 5.990
DW	= 1.84

$X_t = 0.269 X_{t-1} + 1.460 Y_{t-1} - 9.84$
        (-1.174) (1.787)

$t_{(d)}$ $= 1.787$, significant at 10 percent level.
$H_o : b_j$ $= 0$ is rejected.

This implies that Y causes X or that real GDP growth causes real exports growth.

$F(2, 15)$ $= 1.34$ (not significant)
Scaled residuals:
Sample size $= 18$
Mean $= 0.000$
Std. devn. $= 1.029$
Skewness $= -0.639$
Excess kurtosis $= -0.218$
$CHI^2(2)$ $= 1.119$
DW $= 1.65$

Zambia:

$Y_t = 0.262 Y_{t-1} - 0.073 X_{t-1} + 2.20$
        (1.480) (-1.125)

t_{29} $= 2.756$ at 1 percent
              $= 2.045$ at 5 percent
              $= 1.699$ at 10 percent
$t_{(b)}$ $= -1.125$ (not significant)
$H_o : d_j$ $= 0$ is accepted.

This implies that X does not cause Y or that real exports growth does not cause real GDP growth.

$F(2, 29)$ Crit. val. $= 3.33$
$F(2, 29) = 0.60$ (not significant)
Scaled residuals:
Sample size $= 32$
Mean $= 0.000$
Std.devn. $= 1.016$
Skewness $= 0.252$
Excess kurtosis $= 0.002$
$CHI^2(2)$ $= 0.317$
$CHI^2(2)$ Crit. val. $= 5.990$
DW $= 1.63$

$$X_t = -0.042 \, X_{t-1} - 0.193 \, Y_{t-1} + 4.63$$
$$\quad\quad (-0.219) \quad\quad (-0.365)$$

$t_{(d)}$ $\quad = -0.365$ (not significant)

$H_o : b_j \quad = 0$ is accepted.

This implies that Y does not cause X or that real GDP growth does not cause real exports growth.

$F(2, 29)$ $\quad\quad\quad = 1.47$ (not significant)

Scaled residuals:

Sample size	= 32
Mean	= 0.000
Std. devn.	= 1.016
Skewness	= 0.234
Excess kurtosis	= -0.287
$CHI^2(2)$	= 0.377
DW	= 1.99

Zimbabwe:

$$Y_t = 0.002 \, Y_{t-1} + 0.036 \, X_{t-1} + 4.51$$
$$\quad\quad (0.010) \quad\quad (0.216)$$

t_{17} $\quad = 2.898$ at 1 percent
$\quad\quad = 2.110$ at 5 percent
$\quad\quad = 1.740$ at 10 percent

$t_{(b)}$ $\quad = 0.216$ (not significant)

$H_o{:}d_j \quad = 0$ is accepted.

This implies that X does not cause Y or that real exports growth does not cause real GDP growth.

$F(2, 17)$ Crit. val. $= 3.59$

$F(2, 17) = 0.72$ (not significant)

Scaled residuals:

Sample size	= 20
Mean	= 0.000
Std.devn.	= 1.026
Skewness	= -0.206
Excess kurtosis	= -0.894
$CHI^2(2)$	= 0.727
$CHI^2(2)$ Crit. val.	= 5.990
DW	= 1.89

$$X_t = -0.208\,X_{t-1} + 0.844\,Y_{t-1} - 0.02$$
$$ (-1.093) \qquad (3.123)$$

$t_{(d)} \quad = 3.123$ (significant at 1 percent level)

$H_o: b_j \quad = 0$ is rejected.

This implies that Y causes X or that real GDP growth causes real exports growth.

$F(2, 17)$	$= 4.89$ (significant)
Scaled residuals:	
Sample size	$= 20$
Mean	$= 0.000$
Std. devn.	$= 1.026$
Skewness	$= 0.008$
Excess kurtosis	$= -1.042$
$CHI^2(2)$	$= 0.815$
DW	$= 2.32$

Table 4.5 gives a summary of the findings of the Granger causality test carried out for each of the ten countries in the sample using standard econometric technique to examine the question of causality between exports and economic growth. It will be observed from this table that there are two cases where the export promotion hypothesis is supported, two cases where GDP growth gives rise to growth of exports; and four cases where there is no relationship between exports and GDP. The two cases where the export promotion hypothesis finds support are Burundi, and Rwanda. The evidence suggests that for these countries export promotion brings positive real growth results. However, the results for Rwanda are are not robust in that their associated F-tests are not significant. Thus, it is only for Rwanda that we find support for the export-led growth hypothesis.

The two cases where GDP growth causes exports growth are Tanzania and Zimbabwe. Measures aimed at raising GDP would result in growth of exports in these countries. Growth in exports would not induce growth in lead GDP. The finding in respect of Zimbabwe are particularly evealing. Following the Unilateral Declaration of Independence by the White Regime of Ian Smith in 1965, the international community imposed economic sanctions against that country. As the goods she used to import from abroad were no longer available through this means, Zimbabwe was forced to produce them herself on an import substitution basis. As a result, Zimbabwe is now one of the most industrialised country and the largest exporter of manufactured goods in Sub-Saharan Africa, excluding South Africa. Tanzania's case is, however, doubtful as its associated F-test is not significant which means that the result is not of much economic meaning. Ethiopia, Kenya, Malawi and Zambia provide no evidence of causality between exports and economic growth. The possibility of bidirectional causality between export growth and economic growth does not arise according to the evidence in Table 4.5.

Table 4.5
Summary results of causality tests

Country	Real export growth causes real GDP growth			Real GDP growth causes real export growth		
	Causation	F	Chi-squared	Causation	F	Chi-squared
Burundi	yes*	12.17***	2.178	no	2.92	2.210
Ethiopia	no	1.55	0.218	no	0.63	0.199
Kenya	no	0.27	5.211	no	0.28	0.254
Malawi	no	0.19	1.526	no	0.79	2.027
Rwanda	yes	2.35	1.150	no	1.87	4.483
Tanzania	no	1.29	2.955	yes*	1.34	1.119
Zambia	no	0.60	0.317	no	1.47	0.377
Zimbabwe	no	0.72	0.727	yes***	4.89**	0.815

*** Significant at 1 percent level.
** Significant at 5 percent level.
* Significant at 10 percent level.

4.4   Conclusion

For the ten countries in the sample, the hypothesis of export-led growth as a development strategy is not supported by the evidence in such a manner that a generalisation can be formulated. Policies of export promotion may not be helpful in bringing about economic growth in some of these countries. Thus, the results of the econometric tests suggest that even for countries in Africa, the export promotion hypothesis is not of general applicability. Some countries would be helped by export promotion to achieve economic growth but other countries may not benefit from such a strategy. For some of these countries, a strategy of import substitution may well be helpful in bringing about economic growth. This is an issue we will take up in respect of Zambia and Malawi in the next two chapters.

5　The experience of Zambia

5.1　Introduction

In terms of economic geography, Zambia is a large land-locked country, covering an area of about 753,000 square kilometres. It shares borders with Zaire and Tanzania in the North, Malawi and Mozambique in the East, Zimbabwe and Botswana in the South, Namibia in the South-west and Angola in the West.[1] The population of Zambia was recorded at 5.66 million in the 1980 Census, which showed an increase of 39.6 percent since 1969.[2] The average annual growth rate during the intercensal period was 3.1 percent, compared to a growth of 2.5 percent during the period 1963-69.[3] The estimated population size by mid-1987 was 7.27 million. About 45 percent of the population lives in a 40 kilometre-wide urbanised zone (Livingstone-Lusaka-Ndola), along the line of rail. Most of the country is sparsely populated.[4]

At the time of independence in 1964, Zambia was, by Sub-Saharan Africa standards, relatively well-off. Although it inherited a single-product economy, this was based not on an agricultural crop, as it is usually the case with most developing countries, but on copper, a mineral that was in high demand in the dynamic world economy of the 1960s and one that in consequence enjoyed buoyant prices and large profits.

5.2 Evolution and phases of trade and payments restrictions

One may delineate the following phases of trade and payments restrictions which Zambia may be said to have gone through since gaining her political independence in 1964. The classification below follows the chronology of events in Zimbabwe, but the phases are named as per the Bwagati and Krueger nomenclature of trade regime bias (hence BK) rather than the sequence regime switching in Zambia.

5.2.1 Phase 5 of BK: 1964-68 liberal period

The period between 1964 and 1968 marks Phase 5 during which Zambia pursued a relatively liberal trade policy. During this period, most imports were allowed into the country without restrictions. There was no licensing for all imports except for oil products, coal and coke, personal and household items and goods of less than K50 in value as well as goods of Kenyan, Tanzanian or Ugandan origin which were allowed under the open general license (OGL).[5] There was no restriction on imports by country of origin although there were some restrictions by commodity in respect of clothing, unmanufactured gold, sugar, wheat, flour, flick knives, explosives, cement, radios, matches, 4-wheel drive vehicles and some footwear. Foreign exchange for imports was granted freely on production of import documents (Gulhati, Bose, Swadesh and Vimal, 1985).

The Zambian Kwacha was pegged to the Pound Sterling (UK £) up to 1966 and then to the US Dollar from 1967 to 1975. It should be noted that, by and large, the late 1960s and early 1970s was a period of domestic price and exchange rate stability in the world economy and no African government looked upon the exchange rate as a major instrument for economic management. Thus, although Zambia changed the peg of its currency to the Dollar in 1967 from the British Pound Sterling, it maintained more or less the same value of the Kwacha in terms of other foreign currencies.

5.2.2 Phase 2 of BK: 1968-76 trade and exchange controls

Following the achievement of political independence, one of the first tasks of the new government was to weld into a single nation-state what had been rather disparate collections of ethnic and tribal groups. In addition to this, the new government sought to develop the country's economy, which was until then controlled by expatriates. It was, therefore, logical for the new government to try to match political independence with increased economic independence.

To promote the process of indigenization and development of the economy, the government adopted the following three approaches:

(i) Creation of parastatal companies to acquire a controlling interest in existing activities and to initiate new activities The economic reform programmes for the attainment of this objective were launched in 1968 and 1969 at Mulungushi and Matero (O'Neil, 1987). These programmes attempted to "Zambianise" the economy and give the state a major role in running it. Parastatal corporations were to constitute the instruments for implementing the programmes.

The Industrial Development Corporation (INDECO) was already in existence as a state-run agency, having been acquired by the government in 1964 from its private (expatriate) shareholders.[6] Formed in 1951 by the colonial government of Northern Rhodesia as a credit board to finance the establishment of businesses by expatriates, INDECO later became a private limited-liability company. In 1968, INDECO's operational structure was changed following the State's acquisition of a controlling interest in more than twenty companies in a variety of such areas as brewing, transport, chemicals, building, supplies, hotels, and finance. INDECO's job was to combine these companies into a coherent group and to ensure that each of them operated according to official policy on industrialisation. In 1969, again in the spirit of the economic reform programmes, the Zambia Industrial and Mining Corporation (ZIMCO) was formed, and INDECO, together with the Zambia Consolidated Copper Mines Limited (ZCCM), became subsidiaries of it. Since then, INDECO has acquired or set up many more companies, and ZIMCO has grown into a giant holding company owning or controlling 119 subsidiaries in such diverse industries as mining, manufacturing, tourism, commerce and marketing, transport, posts and telecommunications, energy, finance, and agribusiness. Taken together, these subsidiaries produce more than three-quarters of Zambia's GDP (Chanthunya, 1991).

(ii) National planning In order to guide the new republic's economy, the government instituted a system of national economic and social planning. In addition to a transitional plan covering the period immediately after independence (1965-66), there have been four national five-year plans (1966-70, 1972-77, 1980-84, and 1989-93). All of these plans have had two central objectives, namely: to diversify the economy away from copper towards agriculture and industry and spread economic activity to the areas of the country off the line-of-rail.

(iii) Controls The new government chose not to leave the allocation of economic resources to the market but rather to rely on administrative mechanisms involving a huge collection of subsidies and price controls. Some so-called "essential" consumer goods and some agricultural inputs (especially fertilizers) were subsidized. The prices of most goods were controlled. These controls were intensified following the Unilateral Declaration of Independence by Southern Rhodesia (now Zimbabwe) in 1965 and the subsequent closure of the border with Zambia in 1973 which led to a severe disruption of Zambia's trade patterns. In order to protect low-income consumers and minimise monopolistic profits, the existing system of price controls was considerably extended and developed. The basis for establishing prices was a cost-plus (mark up pricing) approach,[7] which was consistent with the imperfect competition market structures.

Foreign exchange rationing was also subject to administrative control, especially in the aftermath of the foreign exchange crisis that began in the mid-1970s. Importers were required to go through a two-stage process. First, they had to receive approval for their application for an import license. Second, they had to obtain the actual foreign exchange allocation.

To handle the first stage, an interministerial import licensing committee, chaired by a representative of the Ministry of Commerce and Industry, was established. This committee set sectoral priorities for allocating anticipated foreign exchange resources among competing demands. The priorities corresponded closely with those reflected in the tariff structure; essential consumer goods ranked above intermediate goods and capital goods for strategic and import substituting industries; in turn, intermediate and capital goods for strategic and import substituting industries ranked above imports for the transport, communications, and tourism industries. Public and private non-essential consumer goods had the lowest priority.[8]

Therefore, the period from 1968 to 1976 was characterised by the imposition of protective high tariffs on imported consumer goods in support of an import-substitution strategy adopted by the Government in an attempt to diversify Zambia's economy. The protection to import-substitution industry was supplemented by support given to domestic industries by exempting them from the payment of customs duties on imported machinery, spare parts and raw materials. These measures were reinforced by the imposition in 1972-73 of import controls which were aimed at controlling the level of imports as well as the type of imports. Alongside these measures, a fixed exchange rate policy, through which the Kwacha was pegged to the US Dollar at the same level, was maintained and domestic prices were also tightly controlled. Thus, Zambia moved directly to Phase 2 without passing through Phase 1 by imposing stiff controls immediately in her efforts to diversify her economy.

5.2.3 Phase 3 of BK: 1976-82 discrete devaluation with trade and import controls

The period between 1976 and 1982 marks Phase 3. During this period, the import control regime of the second phase was maintained. However, this phase was accompanied by discrete devaluations of the Kwacha. The Kwacha was devalued in 1976 and in 1978. In 1976, it was devalued by 20 percent and in 1978 by 10 percent. These devaluations came as part of the IMF stabilization programme and were, therefore, accompanied by restrictive monetary and fiscal policies.

5.2.4 Phase 4 of BK: 1982-85 trade liberalization efforts

Phase 4 is the period from 1982 to 1985. This was a phase of relatively less restrictive economic policies, paving the way for the introduction of liberal economic and trade policies. In 1982 the price control regime was abandoned and industries were allowed to determine their own prices, depending on their cost structures; although price controls on a few essential commodities such as maize meal remained in force. The fore-runner to this pricing policy change was the livestock industry which had its prices liberalized as early as 1978. The apparent success of the livestock industry since 1978 was quite encouraging. Zambia, although endowed with a wetter climate, had for a long time been dependent on beef imports from Botswana, a country with a semi-arid climate. With the 1978 livestock price changes, Zambia subsequently became self-sufficient in livestock products. The high success of the new livestock pricing policy change placed high hopes on the new general price policy change. The under-lying principle behind the general pricing policy change was the belief in the efficiency of market forces in allocating resources optimally.

The move to liberal policies came in as part of an adjustment programme agreed with the IMF under which the IMF was to provide Zambia with K325 million (SDR317 million) on the basis of a stand-by credit arrangement. The conditions attached to this stand-by arrangement aimed at restraining domestic demand by limiting the budget deficit through wage restraint, limiting government borrowing from the domestic banking system and limiting overall domestic credit extended by the banking system. Zambia was also required to take steps to reduce her payments arrears as the IMF argued that these inhibited the flow of imports and as such contributed to inflation and foreign exchange shortage through high interest rates.

The currency was devalued by 20 percent against the Special Drawing Right in January 1983. In the same year, July 1983, the Kwacha which had been linked to the Special Drawing Right since July 1976, was pegged to its own basket of currencies and the Bank of Zambia adopted a managed flexible exchange rate regime which entailed small but frequent downward adjustments of the currency.

In 1983 prices were further decontrolled and producer prices, especially those of agricultural products, were increased. During 1983-84 prices were further liberalised when the authorities decontrolled most wholesale and retail prices of consumer goods, including those of wheat and wheat products, and significantly reduced budgetary subsidies on basic foodstuffs and fertilizer through sharp price increases. Most agricultural producer prices were also adjusted upwards. Due to these measures, the prices of a wide range of commodities, including politically-sensitive products such as cooking oil, beer, sugar and washing powder rose sharply. In September 1985, consumer prices for mealie meal, the staple food, were raised by 38 to 50 percent.

Interest rates were also further liberalized. During 1983-84, the authorities adjusted upwards the administrative ceilings on interest rates by 4.5 percentage points, with the maximum lending rate being moved to 17.5 percent and the treasury bill rate to 9.5 percent, while short-term deposit rates were raised to 11 percent. Wage increases were limited to 5 percent per annum.

However, imports continued to be restricted. Most imported goods were subject to a sales tax of 12.5 percent of taxable value. Except for those items for which no foreign exchange was required, all imports were subject to a foreign exchange constraint. In addition, all letters of credit had to have a minimum 90- day term. Importers also had to have licences approved by a ministerial foreign exchange committee before approval by the Bank of Zambia, and subsequently the commercial bank had to issue the letter of credit. If authorised foreign exchange was not used, permission from the Bank of Zambia had to be obtained before applying for a "no currency" import license.

5.2.5 *Phase 5 of BK: 1985-87 liberal period*

The period from 1985 to 1987 also marks Phase 5. This was a phase of complete liberalization and full currency convertibility and came about with the introduction of a freely floating exchange rate system determined through auctioning of foreign exchange. The mechanics of auctioning entailed the Bank of Zambia making a public announcement through the media about the amount of auctionable foreign exchange available each week. Anybody in need of foreign exchange submitted his requests for foreign exchange through his commercial bank indicating the type of foreign currency required, the amount requested, the Kwacha/US Dollar rate that he was willing to pay and deposited the Kwacha equivalent of that amount together with his bid. Commercial banks consolidated the bids and submitted them to the Bank of Zambia with necessary authority to debit their accounts with the consolidated Kwacha to cover all the bids. These submissions had to reach the Bank of Zambia by 9.00 hours each Friday. The Foreign Exchange Management Committee assisted by the Secretariat processed the bids by arranging them in a descending order, starting with the highest bid rate and ending up with the lowest. At its meeting on Saturday morning, the Foreign Exchange Management Committee struck the marginal rate which was that rate at which the auction funds offered got exhausted. This was technically termed the "marginal rate" and constituted the base rate that was used in purchasing of all foreign exchange by all the successful bidders and it was also the rate at which all foreign exchange transactions for the week beginning the following Monday were made. Any administrative allocations for the exempted categories of economic agents such as the oil companies, Zambia Airways, the Zambia Consolidated Copper Mines Limited and the Government were allocated by the Committee using the same rate.[9]

A key element of the free trade regime was the liberalization of the import licensing system. Import licenses were now to be issued freely without restriction. A licence accompanying an unsuccessful bid at the foreign exchange auction could be used again at any subsequent auction. Thus, administrative restrictions were removed from being used to contain the volume of imports or to protect local producers. Import prohibition for balance of payments reasons, which covered about 50 items, was abolished and was to be replaced by appropriate tariffs. In addition, the authorities introduced a policy whereby the source of foreign exchange earnings was no longer subject to declaration, in order to encourage capital inflows. Furthermore, in order to re-direct clandestine exports into official channels, the exchange control regulations were modified to permit the inflow of capital without declaration.

Another important measure to enable market forces to play a more important role in the allocation mechanism was the further liberalization of prices which started in 1982 with the decontrol of industrial prices, except for wheat flour, maize flour, candles and oil. It was felt that while the previous policy of controlling prices was justified by the desire to protect consumers from exploitation by producers, it had led to economic consequences far beyond what had originally been foreseen or intended. In particular, it had reduced the profitability of firms and their ability to re-invest. In November/December 1986 consumer prices for mealie meal were raised by as much as 120 percent, after eliminating the subsidy completely which would lead to eventual decontrol of agricultural prices as well.

Interest rates were also liberalised through the establishment of a daily treasury bill auction. Treasury bill rates consequently rose steadily from a pre-auction regulatory ceiling of 9.5 percent to 24 percent by end-November, 1985. By end-1986, lending interest rates had risen to as high as 32 percent and deposit rates to as high as 20 percent.

Accompanying the decontrol of prices was also the liberalization of the agricultural marketing system. This was aimed at dismantling the monopoly of the National Agricultural Marketing Board (NAMBOARD) in the marketing of agro-inputs and produce. The marketing arrangement included the provision of subsidies to support agricultural development efforts. These subsidies were intended to cover the costs of the new marketing board in areas where the volume of surplus production offered for marketing was too small to support the cost of full scale marketing service. The marketing subsidy for the uneconomic maize growing areas was, therefore, provided as an incentive for the promotion of agriculture in less developed areas. In 1986 the government reduced the subsidy provision both on fertiliser distribution and maize marketing and the fertiliser trade was liberalized and NAMBOARD's monopoly in the importation and internal distribution of fertilisers and other inputs was reduced. The fertiliser prices were raised to import parity and anyone could import and sell fertilisers to farmers. Later in the year the subsidy on maize marketing was also to be completely withdrawn and everybody was to be allowed to buy maize from farmers and sell it to consumers (Banda, 1987).

5.3   Economic performance under the different phases of trade and payments restrictions

It is useful to examine the performance of the Zambian economy during each different phase of trade restrictions and exchange controls. Table 5.1 contains selected economic indicators, namely real growth of Gross Domestic Product (GDP), growth of manufacturing output, real growth of exports, savings ratio, incremental capital - output ratio, foreign exchange reserves and inflation rate, which summarise the performance of the Zambian economy in each different phase. It is shown that during the period 1964 to 1968, i.e. the phase of liberalisation (Phase 5), the annual real growth rate of GDP averaged as high as 13.98 percent. Manufacturing output grew at an annual average high rate of 17.72 percent. National savings, as a percentage of GDP, averaged as high as 24.4 percent per annum. End-of-year foreign exchange reserves averaged high enough to cover imports for 9 months and 25 days. The domestic rate of inflation, as measured by the GDP deflator, averaged relatively low at 5.9 percent per annum. The incremental capital-output ratio averaged relatively low at 1.60 in each year which indicates that investment resources were used relatively efficiently. However, the average real growth rate of exports (value of exports deflated by the unit value of imports) was negative at -6.81 percent per annum.

It is interesting to note that during this phase of liberal trade regime, the economy performed impressively well in terms of growth rate of real GDP, growth rate of manufacturing output, savings, use of investment resources, foreign exchange reserves, stability of prices; although real exports were declining. Since real exports were declining and growth of exports is taken to represent the pursuit of liberal policies, this seems to suggest that the good performance of the economy during this phase probably had little relationship with the liberal trade policies being pursued during the period. It also suggests that liberal trade policies do not necessarily facilitate the growth of exports.

During the period 1969 to 1976, i.e. the phase of trade and exchange controls (Phase 2), the average real growth of GDP fell to 2.94 percent per annum; a fall of 11.04 percentage points from the average annual rate for the period between 1964 and 1968. The average growth rate of manufacturing output dropped by as much as 15.09 percentage points to 2.63 percent per annum. The average savings ratio, as a proportion of GDP, decreased by 7.9 percentage points to 16.5 percent. Foreign exchange reserves dropped to cover only 5.41 months of imports on average compared with 9.83 months of imports during the period 1964 to 1968. The rate of inflation fell slightly by 0.3 of a percentage point to an average annual rate of 5.6 percent. The use of investment resources was relatively inefficient as the incremental capital-output ratio averaged 2.92 compared to 1.60 during 1964 to 1968. However, the average real growth rate of exports was positive, at 1.32 percent per annum during this phase of trade and exchange controls.

It is also interesting to note that although the country achieved a positive real growth of exports during this period, the economy performed relatively worse than during the period 1964 to 1968. It is of further interest to note that the country performed better in terms of exports against a background of a host of quantitative restrictions (QRs). This seems to suggest that the good performance of exports did not have much influence on the rest of the economy. It also suggests that QRs do not necessarily act as an obstacle to the development of exports. Therefore, one cannot discern any relationship between the performance of the economy and the trade policies that were pursued during this phase.

In the period 1977 to 1982, the phase of discrete devaluations with trade and import controls (Phase 3), real GDP declined by 0.05 percent annually, on average. Manufacturing output also declined in this period by an average rate of 1.40 percent per year. Real exports declined by a high average rate of 8.29 percent yearly while national savings, as a percentage of GDP, averaged -4.9 percent annually. There was no improvement in the efficiency of investment as the incremental capital-output ratio averaged 2.76 yearly which is only 0.16 below that for the period 1969-76. Interestingly enough, there was an improvement in the foreign exchange reserve position as the end-of-year foreign exchange reserves averaged 6.62 months of imports; but the average rate of inflation was double that for the period 1969-76.

An interesting observation from the performance of the economy in this period is that the discrete devaluations seem to have only helped to improve the foreign exchange reserves position, but this was at the expense of suffering declines in GDP, manufacturing output, real exports, savings and an increase in domestic prices. To be sure, the improvement in the foreign exchange reserves position was due to drawings of the IMF loan under the stabilisation programme.

During the period from 1982-85, i.e. the phase of gradual trade liberalization (Phase 4), economic performance worsened in terms of GDP, national savings, foreign exchange reserves position and the rate of domestic inflation. Real GDP declined by an average of 0.27 percent per year. National savings, as a percentage of GDP, averaged -5.3 percent per annum. Foreign exchange reserves were very much reduced to cover only 1.87 months of imports. The rate of inflation increased to an average of 26.1 percent per year. Economic performance only improved in terms of growth of manufacturing output and real exports and the use of investment resources. After suffering an average annual decline of 1.40 percent in the period between 1977 and 1982, manufacturing output grew at an average rate of 1.43 percent per year during the period 1982-85. Exports seem to have responded to the liberal measures that were instituted as real exports grew by an impressive average rate of 22.65 percent per year over this period. The efficiency with which investment resources were used improved considerably as the incremental capital-output ratio reduced to a yearly average of 0.74.

What is worth noting about the performance of the economy over this period is that although real exports grew substantially, real GDP declined even more and the foreign exchange reserves position worsened compared to the period between 1977 and 1982.

During the period 1985 to 1987, i.e. the period of trade liberalization and full currency convertibility (Phase 5), real exports grew even more, by an average rate of 35.21 percent per annum and the efficiency of investment improved, with the incremental capital-output ratio having been reduced to an average of 0.31 per annum. However, real GDP only grew marginally by an average of 0.20 percent, manufacturing output by an average of 0.65 percent and national savings, as a percentage of GDP, averaged -10.8 percent. End-of-year foreign exchange reserves were at a very low level, only enough to cover 1.50 months of imports. Domestic prices rose considerably as the rate of inflation accelerated to an average rate of 60.8 percent per year. Again, it would seem that the growth of exports and the trade policies employed did not have a positive effect on the rest of the economy.

The rest of this chapter is devoted to an examination of the economic policies that prevailed before the adoption of the liberal economic and trade policies, how the economy of Zambia performed against the background of these policies, the factors that prompted the authorities to adopt the liberal economic and trade policies and the appropriateness of the liberal policies that were pursued within the context of the working of the Zambian economy.

5.4 Economic and trade policies prior to the adoption of liberal economic and trade policies

After gaining her political independence on 24th October, 1964 Zambia sought to diversify her economy from one that was predominantly copper mining and copper exporting to a more diversified and relatively self-sufficient economy in basic manufactured products. Table 5.2 shows that at the time of Independence, mining was the mainstay of the economy, contributing over 47 percent of the country's GDP. Table 5.3 shows that mining also accounted for almost all of the country's total exports in 1964. Of the ZK335,518,000 value of total exports in 1964, ZK312,862,000 (or 93.2 percent) were mineral exports. Of this, copper alone accounted for ZK296,800,000 (or 88.5 percent of total exports). The balance of ZK16,062,000 (4.8 percent) was accounted for by zinc, lead, manganese ore and cobalt. Thus, copper was both the strength and weakness of Zambia's economy. If the production and prices of copper were high, the country's economy was in a healthy state. On the other hand, if copper production and copper prices tumbled, their shock waves permeated all the sectors and the whole economy was adversely affected and put in danger of collapse.

Due to this overdependence on copper, the government took deliberate policy measures to diversify Zambia's economy. In particular, the government sought to increase the size of the manufacturing sector which was only 6.1 percent of total GDP in 1964 as shown in Table 5.4. To do this, the government adopted an import-substitution industrialisation strategy. In support of this strategy, the government took measures aimed at protecting domestic industries through the imposition of high tariffs on imported consumer goods. At the same time, the government provided support to domestic industries by exempting them from the payment of customs duties on imported machinery, spare parts and raw materials. These measures were reinforced by the imposition in 1972-73 of import controls which aimed at controlling the level of imports as well as the type of imports. Under the import control regime, the licensing of imports and the allocation of the requisite foreign exchange to successful applicants was done by the Ministry of Commerce and Industry and the Bank of Zambia (Zambia's Central Bank).

Table 5.1
Selected economic indicators

	1964-68 Phase 5	1969-76 Phase 2	1977-82 Phase 3	1983-85 Phase 4	1986-87 Phase 5
Average real GDP growth rate	13.98	2.94	-0.05	-0.27	0.20
Average growth of manufacturing output	17.72	2.63	-1.40	1.43	0.65
Average real growth rate of exports	-6.81	1.32	-8.29	22.65	35.21
Average savings ratio (percent of GDP)	24.40	16.50	-4.90	-5.30	-10.80
Average incremental capital-output ratio	1.60	2.92	2.76	0.74	0.31
Average foreign exchange reserves (in months of imports)	9.83	5.41	6.62	1.87	1.50
Average inflation rate	5.90	5.60	11.50	26.10	60.80

Sources: Monthly Digest of Statistics, various volumes from 1969 to 1988 issued by the Central Statistical Office, Lusaka.

Table 5.2
Sectoral GDP shares (in percent)

	1964	1970	1976	1982
Agriculture, Forestry, Fishing & Hunting	11.5	13.6	11.0	14.0
Mining & Quarrying Manufacturing	47.5	27.3	33.3	10.4
Electricity, Gas & Water	6.1	9.7	10.0	20.0
Construction	1.1	1.9	3.5	3.6
Wholesale & Retail Trade, Hotels, Bars & Restaurants	4.3	6.1	6.6	4.0
Transport & Communication	9.8	12.1	8.4	11.1
Financial Institutions, Insurance, Real Estate & Business Services	4.4	4.7	4.4	5.7
Community, Social & Personal Services	2.4	6.5	9.0	0.9
Import Duties	13.0	15.2	12.5	18.9
	-	2.9	1.3	1.3
Total	100.0	100.0	100.0	100.0

Source: Monthly Digest of Statistics, various volumes from 1969 to 1986 issued by the Central Statistical Office, Lusaka.
Note: Percentage sectoral GDP shares are calculated on constant values of the respective GDP shares.

In order to accelerate the development of the manufacturing sector, the government itself decided to invest in manufacturing industry. For this purpose, it created the Industrial Development Corporation (INDECO) to act as the government's arm for investing in manufacturing industry. Alongside these measures, a fixed exchange rate policy was adopted while domestic prices were also tightly controlled.

5.5 Performance of the economy under import-substitution policies

Following the adoption of the above measures, the manufacturing sector grew very rapidly. Table 5.4 shows that from 1964 to 1974, the index of manufacturing output rose from 124.4 to 311.7, representing an impressive average growth rate of 9.6 percent per annum. Consequently, the share of the manufacturing sector in total GDP rose from 6.1 percent in 1964 to 12.0 percent in 1974. Manufacturing output continued to grow rapidly so that by 1982, its share in total GDP had risen to 20.0 percent, although after 1974, it grew at a slower rate.

Table 5.3
Composition of exports in 1964 (Kwacha)

Copper	296,800,000
Zinc	9,730,000
Lead	2,274,000
Manganese ore	564,000
Cobalt	3,494,000
Tobacco	5,664,000
Timber	816,000
Others	16,176,000
Total	335,518,000

Source: Monthly Digest of Statistics, Vol. VIII, No. 4 April, 1972 issued by the Central Statistical Office, Lusaka, Government of Zambia.

During the ten-year period between 1964 and 1974, real GDP grew at an average rate of 6.3 percent per annum. With a population growth rate of almost 2.5 percent per annum over the period, real GDP per capita grew at 3.8 percent per year between 1964 and 1974. Between 1975 and 1981, real GDP grew only marginally at about 0.5 percent per annum. Thereafter, real GDP declined in each of the following three consecutive years up to 1984. The decline was 2.7 percent in 1982, 2.2 percent in 1983 and 0.2 percent in 1984. Real GDP seems to have picked up thereafter, growing at 3.4 percent in 1984. As shown in Table 5.4, the most significant structural change that took place between 1964 and 1984 involved the sectors of mining and quarrying, manufacturing and that of the group for financial institutions, insurance, real estate and business services. It will be observed that the mining and quarrying sector decreased its share from 47.5 percent in 1964 to 9.9 percent in 1984. On the other hand, the manufacturing sector increased its share from 6.1 percent in 1964 to 19.2 percent in 1984 while that of the group for financial institutions, insurance, real estate and business services increased its share from 2.4 percent in 1964 to 11.9 percent in 1984. The other sectors maintained more or less the same shares as in 1964.

Table 5.4

Index of manufacturing output (1961 = 100)

Year	1964	1968	1974	1980	1982	1985	1986	1987
Index	12.4	236.7	311.7	259.1	262.0	271.7	268.9	275.0

Source: Monthly Digest of Statistics, Vol. VIII, No. 4, April, 1972 and Vol. XXII No. 5 to 8 May/August 1986 issued by the Central Statistical Office, Lusaka, Government of Zambia and information provided by the Central Statistical Office.

Regarding the mining and quarrying sector, it is of important significance to note from Table 5.4 that its share in total GDP decreased not only because the other sectors increased their outputs but, more importantly, also because the output of the mining and quarrying sector decreased over the period. Thus, the relatively poor performance of the economy from 1975 which worsened in 1982 was largely the result of the poor performance of the mining and quarrying sector whose production was almost wholly for export. Therefore, the import-substitution policies which were introduced and put in place in support of the import-substitution industries may not have been the cause of the poor economic performance of the economy. Indeed, it could be argued that had it not been for the import substitution industries, real GDP could have declined even more.

Admittedly, the manufacturing sector stagnated after 1974. But this was due to a shortage of foreign exchange required for imports of intermediate products and spare parts in the import-substitution industries. The shortage of foreign exchange resulted from the poor performance of the mining and quarrying sector which could no longer earn as much foreign exchange from the export of copper and other minerals as before.

5.6   Factors prompting economic reform

However, the continued poor performance of the economy as reflected in low rates of growth of real GDP between 1975 and 1981 and in the declines of real GDP from 1982 to 1983 prompted the government to adopt new policy measures. Also of grave concern to the government was the deterioration of the balance of payments position.

As Mwananshiku (1985) pointed out, several factors contributed to the deterioration of the balance of payments position. The first was a reduction of export earnings from copper due to decreased production and a fall in the

143

prices of copper. Since the 1980s copper production has been falling as shown in Table 5.5.

Prices of copper fell from an average of US$0.93 per pound in 1974 to US$0.56 per pound in 1975. Except for a short-lived rally in 1979-80, when prices reached US$0.99 per pound, the world copper market remained depressed until 1986. The average price was US$0.60 in 1986 and was expected to remain the same during 1987. The fall in copper production and in prices resulted in reduced exports earnings.

Table 5.5
Copper production (Tonnes)

Year	1976	1978	1980	1982	1984	1986
Output	712000	651000	612000	584000	525000	459000

Source: Zambia Consolidated Copper Mines Limited (ZCCM).

The second factor was the oilshock of 1973 and 1979-80. The 1973 oilshock increased oil prices four-fold. The oilshock of 1979-80 pushed up crude oil prices even much higher. Consequently, Zambia had to spend nine times more on crude oil imports in 1980 than she did in 1973. Thirdly, the oil price explosion set off an upsurge in inflation in both the industrialised and developing countries. Given her heavy dependence on foreign goods, Zambia's import bill increased considerably as the industrialised countries passed on the higher prices to their trading partners. For land-locked Zambia, the high import bill was exacerbated by high transportation costs which also added to high costs of production. The fourth and final factor was the rise in international interest rates. Unfortunately enough, this occurred at a time when Zambia was borrowing relatively large amounts of money from abroad in order to minimise the disruptive effects of declining mineral export earnings on the economy. The high international interest rates made debt servicing very high and difficult. Table 5.6 shows the amount of debt service from 1981 to 1986. As a result of these debt service payments, the country accumulated substantial external payments arrears, including commercial arrears, estimated at US$540 million as at the end of 1985.

The combined effect of all the four factors cited above was high deficits in the balance of payments as shown in Table 5.7 below. However, it should be noted from this Table that of the four factors cited, the first three were not the main causes of the worsening balance of payments situation as the trade balance was positive in most years. This suggests that the balance of payments problems mainly emanated from the other items of the current account balance, particularly debt service in the form of high interest payments.

Table 5.6
Debt service payments (US$ million)

	1981	1982	1983	1984	1985	1986
Principal	135	54	46	282	267	283
Interest	75	72	65	119	209	103
Total	210	126	111	401	476	386
Debt Service Ratio	19.5	12.3	13.3	59.1	60.0	53.9

Source: Bank of Zambia and Ministry of Finance.

Table 5.7
Balance of payments (ZK million)

	1980	1981	1982	1983	1984	1985
Trade Balance	270.5	-60.1	-51.8	308.9	542.0	756.0
Current Account Balance	-490.3	-648.5	-573.7	-244.6	-218.1	-317.0
Overall Balance	-214.1	-341.4	-287.8	-126.1	-141.1	-66.7

Source: Bank of Zambia 1985 Report.

The economic problems resulting from these developments had far reaching consequences on the rest of the economy. These consequences were ably explained by the then President Kenneth Kaunda at a press conference in Lusaka on 4th October, 1985 where he announced the introduction of auctioning of foreign exchange. As Kaunda put it, "the overall result of these problems is that production in the economy and especially in the industrial sector has fallen. The poor performance of agriculture over the last three years due to the drought has worsened the situation" (see Zambia Daily Mail, October 9, 1985).

This general lack of growth resulted in falling GDP per capita. For example, in 1969, GDP per capita at 1980 prices was ZK758. In 1975 this had

145

fallen to ZK614. In 1980 GDP per capita fell to ZK539 and by 1984 it had fallen to ZK481.

The shortage of foreign exchange led to a dramatic fall in the level of imports. In 1985, imports were less than half of their level in 1974. This fall in imports meant that domestic industries did not have enough raw materials to continue operating normally as before. For instance, it was estimated that the industrial sector was operating only at about 30 percent of capacity.

At the individual company level, the situation became so critical that some companies were even forced to close down for lack of raw materials, laying off great numbers of workers in the process. In addition, the shortage of essential spares made it increasingly difficult to maintain capital equipment, rolling stock and the general infrastructure. The nation's capacity to provide such essential services as road transport had also been reduced.

Table 5.8
All items consumer price indices (1975 = 100)

	High income	percent Change	Low income	percent Change
1980	189.4	-	202.9	-
1981	209.1	10.4	231.3	14.0
1982	236.6	13.2	260.2	12.5
1983	278.6	17.8	311.2	19.6
1984	336.4	20.7	373.5	20.0
1985	446.6	32.8	513.3	37.4
1986	707.2	58.4	778.4	51.6
1987	1092.6	54.5	1113.1	43.0

Source: Monthly Digest of Statistics, January-April, 1988, Central Statistical Office, Lusaka.

All these problems, in industry and commerce, adversely affected the employment situation. With a population growth of over 3.0 percent per annum, the country faced the most serious unemployment situation since independence. The shortage of foreign exchange also affected the availability of ordinary consumer goods which the country had been used to. Even the availability of such commodities as drugs and educational materials was threatened. The result was a high rate of inflation. As shown in Table 5.8, between 1983 and 1984, the all items consumer price index for the high income group rose by 20.7 percent. In 1985, this rose by 32.8 percent and in

1986 this rose by 58.4 percent over the 1985 level. For the low income group, the all items consumer price index rose by 20 percent between 1983 and 1984. It rose by 37.4 percent in 1985 and by 51.6 percent in 1986 over the 1985 level.

Another consequence of the lack of foreign exchange was the development of a "black" or parallel market for foreign currency. This took some of the foreign exchange held by residents and visitors out of the official channels and resulted in a growing divergence between the official exchange rate and the exchange rate on the parallel market. For example, in 1983, one United States Dollar was equal to ZK1.19 on the official foreign exchange market. On the black market, it was equal to about K3.00. In 1985, before the introduction of the auction, the official exchange rate was ZK2.42 to US$1.00 while the parallel exchange rate was ZK9 to US$1.00.

The problems resulting from the deterioration of the external payments position may be summed up as a fall in GDP and in GDP per capita; a fall in imports; a fall in capacity utilisation; closure of production units; loss of employment; fall in government revenue; inadequate maintenance of existing infrastructure; debt service difficulties; accumulation of external payments arrears; shortage of consumption goods; high inflation rate; and, development of a parallel market for foreign exchange and a growing divergence between the official exchange rate and parallel market rate and the consequent channelling of foreign currency into the parallel market.

5.7   The introduction of liberal economic and trade policies

In order to deal with these problems and reverse the trend of economic decline and resuscitate the economy into viability once again, the government adopted new measures aimed at reforming domestic economic policies. Reformation of the domestic policies essentially involved liberalisation of the economic system. The introduction of the liberal economic system started in 1982 when the price control regime was abandoned and industries were allowed to determine their own prices depending on their cost structures. However, price controls on a few essential commodities, such as mealie meal, remained in force.

The move to the liberal policies came in as part of an adjustment programme agreed with the International Monetary Fund (IMF) under which the IMF was to provide Zambia with ZK325 million (SDR 317 million) on the basis of a standby credit arrangement. The conditions attached to this standby arrangement aimed at restraining domestic demand by limiting the budget deficit through wage restraint, limiting government borrowing from the domestic banking system and limiting overall domestic credit extended by the banking system. Zambia was also required to take steps to reduce her payments arrears as the IMF argued that these inhibited the flow of imports and as such contributed to inflation and foreign exchange shortage through high interest rates. The currency was devalued by 10 percent in March, 1978 (in addition to the 20 percent devaluation of 1976) and producer prices, especially those of agriculural products, were increased. Subsidies on essential items were tightened and were to be gradually phased out and sales taxes were increased. Interest rates were adjusted upwards.

However, the adoption of these measures did not improve the performance of the economy. On the contrary, economic performance worsened. The government budget deficits continued on an upward trend. The balance of payments deficits also continued to rise, growing from ZK247 million in 1981 to a record level of ZK561 million in 1982. Real GDP remained stagnant and the rate of inflation accelerated. Export proceeds decreased and so imports declined, too. The country also accumulated even more external payments arrears.

Because of the failure of the standby credit arrangement of 1978, Zambia concluded with the IMF an Extended Fund Facility of SDR800 million for a period of three years, beginning in May 1981. Under the Extended Fund Facility, Zambia was required to restrain domestic demand, again by limiting overall domestic credit, domestic credit extended by the banking system to the government and the government budget deficit from 12 percent to 7 percent of GDP. Other measures to be taken included the elimination of financial imbalances and diversification of the economy. In this regard, the government was to re-orient expenditure from infrastructure to agricultural and industrial projects under a World Bank sponsored three-year investment programme.

Again, the adoption of these measures failed to improve the performance of the economy. Export proceeds fell due to a fall in copper prices. Consequently, the balance of payments deficit rose and the country accumulated even more and more external payments arrears.

The facility was cancelled in July 1982 because the ceiling that was placed on overall domestic credit was overshot as a result of credit which was extended to transport and agricultural sectors in order to have and store bumper crop.

In 1983, the government negotiated a standby arrangement with the IMF under which the latter was to provide Zambia with SDR270 million for one year from April 1983. Again, the conditions attached sought to contain domestic demand by limiting money supply, overall domestic credit and credit to the government and a reduction of the government budget deficit to 5.6 percent of GDP. Other measures which were to be taken were aimed at addressing imbalances emerging from the breakdown of the 1981 Extended Fund Facility and establishing conditions for promoting economic diversification. In this respect, a 20 percent devaluation was effected in January 1983; a new exchange rate system was introduced in July 1983 by which the Kwacha was pegged to a basket of currencies of Zambia's major trading partners and a crawling peg exchange rate system was adopted; prices were further decontrolled and agricultural producer prices and interest rates were increased and wage increases were to be limited to 5 percent per annum.[10]

Economic performance continued to worsen. Export earnings fell mainly as a result of disruptions in copper shipments. Higher than expected cash payments to external creditors due to rescheduling of loan repayments led to a reduction in imports. This gave rise to a slack in industrial production and to lower national output. Low export earnings and high debt service payments led to a worsening of the balance of payments position. Consequently, external payments arrears rose.

In view of the failure of all these programmes, the Zambian government thought of taking more drastic economic policy reform measures. The government presented the new drastic economic policy reform measures to the international donor community at a Consultative Group Meeting in Paris which was convened and chaired by the World Bank in May, 1984 in order to solicit international donor community support. The report which the Government submitted to the Consultative Group was titled "Restructuring in the Midst of Crisis". There could perhaps not have been a more appropriate title than this to reflect, on the one hand, the determined efforts of the Government to restore the economy to vitality through various policy reform measures and, on the other hand, the grim picture of the Zambian economy which was characterised by, *inter-alia,* an acute balance of payments crisis. The report outlined a development strategy for reversing the trend of economic decline through:

1. diversifying the productive structure so as to reduce dependence on the mining sector;

2. increasing the efficiency of use of resources; and

3. promoting growth with equity.

Naturally, the strategy gave priority to the agricultural sector and in this regard resources were to be concentrated on smallholder farmers. Additional measures included reform of incentive structures to ensure better prices; making marketing systems more open and competitive; getting the most out of existing capacity in the commercial subsector through the provision of critically needed inputs; and, increasing the availability of consumer or wage goods in rural areas.

For long-term growth, the strategy recognised that the mining industry, which was the major source of foreign exchange, had to play an important role. In this respect, the strategy sought to restore the industry to previous levels of efficiency in order to make it profitable, once again, and competitive in world markets. The strategy also recognised that the resumption of economic growth required attention to other sectors as well, particularly industry which faced serious problems, the most pronounced manifestation of which was the severe under-utilisation of productive capacity. Given the prevailing circumstances in the industrial sector, it was imperative to concentrate efforts on strengthening the industries that already existed. This involved making them qualitatively better in their output and technical performance, more competitive against foreign products, more supportive of one another and of other economic sectors, a better training ground for management and skilled manpower, and more efficient in their use of scarce resources.

Since lack of budgetary funds and foreign exchange had impaired the maintenance and effective utilisation of existing infrastructures, an essential aspect of the strategy was to ensure that existing facilities worked better. In this regard, special emphasis was placed on the rehabilitation of existing infrastructure.

Recognising that social progress was an important and necessary component of economic development, the strategy also aimed at developing human skills intensively through education for maximum contribution to economic development; to improve standards of health as much as possible with the available resources; and, to ensure that economic development resulted in an equitable distribution of social services.

Furthermore, the strategy stressed the importance of macroeconomic policies, including exchange rate and budgetary policies, in ensuring the efficient allocation and use of scarce resources; the need to ensure that parastatals operated efficiently within a commercial environment to the maximum extent possible; and the importance of institutional changes to upgrade economic management.

However, the economy continued to deteriorate mainly because prices of copper declined further instead of recovering modestly as had been anticipated and external inflows did not materialise as was hoped for at the time. Consequently, the foreign exchange constraint became more binding. The response from the initiatives that had been taken on the policy and institutional front was threatened by the shortage of foreign exchange that limited Zambia's ability to produce goods and services. The prospects for recovery and future growth, therefore, appeared grimmer.

In view of the continued deterioration of the economy and the fact that the Zambian economy had been almost totally dependent on the mining industry, an industry that was rapidly approaching its demise as copper reserves were estimated to be completely depleted in less than 20 years' time, the government thought of intensifying and accelerating the policy of economic reform. To implement the necessary measures the government felt that this would require a quick injection of resources into the directly productive and major supporting sectors of the economy.

Since it was recognised that the implementation of the new measures for accelerated recovery and growth would bring hardships on the population, the government sought to reach a national consensus in support of the required measures. Kaunda led the effort to introduce the new policy environment to the masses. He consistently delivered the message that "the days of high copper prices are over and that Zambians must for many years to come accept a lower standard of living". In this regard, he drove home the point that business needed to be profitable in order to expand and that in order to survive in the long run, new types of production and exports had to be developed. The efforts in persuading the nation to accept economic policy reform culminated in the convening of the Third National Convention in July, 1984, the objective of which was to discuss the economic crisis facing the country, and, in the words of the President, "to cause the economic problems to be understood by everyone here ...". The Convention was attended by delegates representing the ruling Party (UNIP), trade unions, the Chamber of Commerce, the Commercial Farmers Bureau, commercial banks, senior government and parastatal officials, and provincial and district leaders. The resolutions passed at the Convention covered the need for the mobilisation of revenue resources; reduction of subsidies; fiscal measures to discourage reliance on imported raw materials and encourage utilisation of local raw materials; and improvement in the management of public enterprises and the possible closure of uneconomic mining operations and other production units.

The new economic measures were worked out and presented in a report to a meeting of the Consultative Group in June 1985. The report identified a number of sectoral programmes which were considered critical for a resumption of economic growth through the improved utilisation of existing capacities and the promotion of non-traditional exports and efficient import substitution. Since the implementation of these measures needed substantial financial resources, donors were requested to support the programmes in the form, principally, of quick-disbursing input support. The report also outlined the measures which the government intended to undertake over the next two or so years in continuation of the substantial progress that had been made in the last few years in economic policy reform.

In devising the new policy measures for accelerated recovery and growth, the government's aim was to remove the principal policy deficiencies which had been in operation and had also contributed to the country's economic ills, namely:

1. pricing and subsidy policies favoured the urban consumer at the expense of the agricultural producer, depressing the latter's income and incentive to produce for the market;

2. controlled industrial prices led to low profitability in the manufacturing sector and a decrease in the resources for reinvestment;

3. tax incentives and controlled interest rates led to a pattern of capital-intensive investment; and

4. exchange rate and tariff policies encouraged the use of artificially cheap imported raw materials and other inputs and discouraged the use of local raw materials. As a result, a highly capital and import-intensive production structure was created which proved to be very vulnerable to prolonged declines in the availability of foreign exchange.

In the last few years, the government had made major changes in economic policy to reduce or eliminate the above policy biases. It was now considered necessary to take additional measures in conformity with Zambia's development objectives as reflected in the resolutions of the Third National Convention and the Nineteenth Council, namely:

1. to diversify away from copper through new forms of exports and import substitution;

2. to economise on the use of foreign exchange and reduce import intensity;

3. to make better use of existing capacity; and,

4. to relieve the long-term constraints to growth, particularly by improving health services and family programmes.

To achieve the first two objectives listed above, the exchange rate, trade and pricing policies were considered to be among the most powerful instruments that could be used. Let us now turn to the considerations which the authorities took into account in opting for these policy instruments.

5.8 Trade and exchange rate policy

The authorities noted that although Zambia's industrial sector was relatively large and advanced compared to that of other African countries, its manufactured exports were exceptionally small. This was attributed to the existence of serious constraints which in the past included quantitative export controls administered through the export licensing system which imposed administrative burdens on potential exporters; lack of foreign exchange to import raw materials and other inputs; the absence of effective institutional arrangements to support exporters; an over-valued exchange rate which made Zambian goods uncompetitive in world markets; and, a foreign exchange control system that offered strong incentives for producing for the domestic market.

In an attempt to remove some of these obstacles, the government took some important measures. For example, in May 1982 a foreign exchange retention scheme was introduced which enabled exporters to retain 50 percent of their export receipts in foreign currency for meeting their import requirements as a way of providing an incentive to exporters. Secondly, an operational framework for an Export Credit Revolving Fund was developed, the purpose of which was to provide immediate, guaranteed foreign exchange for imports needed to meet a firm export order and working capital for the production cycle. Thirdly, legislation was passed for the setting up of a semi-autonomous Export Promotion Board, with a full-time secretariat, with the overall objective of encouraging, promoting and developing exports of goods from Zambia through the provision of services and support to exporters and potential exporters. Fourthly, the Industrial Development Act was replaced by an Investment Code which defined the incentives and legal and policy framework within which the business sector could operate and gave specific incentives for non-traditional exports such as a drawback of all import duties, excise tax and sales tax paid on inputs.[11]

However, in order to achieve meaningful diversification of exports, the exchange rate was considered to be the most powerful instrument of general economic policy that could be used. Indeed, the exchange rate was regarded to be even more appropriate in that the high cost of domestic production and the over-valuation of the Kwacha had made Zambian exports uncompetitive in world markets. For example, two important export commodities, tobacco and cotton, required export subsidies in the past as the cost-price of Zambian tobacco in 1981, for instance, was 15 percent higher than the price in neighbouring countries; while cotton could only be produced in Zambia at a price that was more than twice the world market equivalent price. It was felt that without a realistic exchange rate such cost-price relationships would not enable Zambia to diversify her export base. In view of these considerations, the government devalued the Kwacha by 20 percent in January 1983. In July 1983 the Kwacha was linked to a special basket of currencies and a flexible exchange rate system, namely a crawling peg, was adopted. Following the adoption of the crawling peg the Kwacha depreciated further and by June 1985 it was 50 percent lower, in real terms, than at the end of 1982.

In order to cope with the severe shortages of foreign exchange that had characterised the economy during the past several years, a centralised system of foreign exchange budgeting and allocation was instituted. This system required an import licence to have foreign exchange backing prior to importation of any item. However, the system proved cumbersome and costly to administer as foreign exchange allocation decisions had to be made on a firm-by-firm and product-by-product basis. Furthermore, foreign exchange budgeting became problematic, with the result that a considerable over-hang of import licences issued without sufficient foreign exchange backing developed.

The structure of nominal protection had included high tariffs on final consumer goods and low tariffs or zero duties on capital and intermediate goods. For example, the average import duty collected in Zambia during 1972-78 was a very low six percent of import value, compared to a simple average of 20 percent for 31 African countries. The low level of duty collection was due to the low level of consumer goods imports and to the low or zero duties on a majority of imported inputs. The system of low protection on capital and intermediate goods and high protection of import competing consumer goods had induced resources into highly protected activities and allowed inefficient firms to exist. The foreign exchange control and import licensing systems, by excluding a wide range of competing imports of consumer goods from the domestic market, provided high protection to import substituting activities and reinforced the protection effects of the tariff structure.

The tariff system and the foreign exchange allocation and import licensing systems, therefore, substantially influenced decisions regarding capacity expansion, new investment, production for the domestic or export market and the choice of techniques. In this respect, the government recognised that the structure of protection accorded by the existing trade regime had resulted in severe inefficiencies in the allocation of resources. It had, specifically, encouraged import-intensive industry and discouraged the development of domestic industries that utilise local raw materials and labour. The existing trade regime had also favoured packing or assembly-type industries, which conferred very few benefits on the economy either in foreign exchange, employment or skill development. Furthermore, the trade regime had impeded the growth of factor productivity.

Because of these perceived shortcomings of the existing system of foreign exchange controls, the government searched for a formula that would permit attainment of two policy objectives, namely:

1. ensuring that in the allocation of scarce foreign exchange, firms and activities that were most beneficial and profitable to society as a whole would be given priority; and

2. minimising the incidence of inefficient allocations and make the allocation mechanism less subjective and less dependent on the human factor.

The government was convinced that such an allocative formula should embrace the following elements:

1. increasing the reliance upon market forces rather than on administrative mechanisms for allocating resources. This implied the gradual dismantling of the foreign exchange controls, import and export licensing and interest rate regulations;

2. restoring balance and increasing the uniformity of the incentive system, particularly between exports and import substitutes, as well as between agriculture and industry. This implied a major reform in the trade regime with greater reliance on the exchange rate as a mechanism for allocating foreign exchange, elimination of import restrictions, rationalisation of the tariff structure and review of incentives; and

3. introducing greater automaticity into the determination of the exchange rate consistent with the long run prospects for exports and terms of trade.

To bring into existence an enabling policy environment for the achievement of an allocative formula on the above lines, the government took a number of important measures. For example, in October 1984, a 10 percent minimum duty on intermediate goods and raw materials was introduced in order to increase the incentive for domestic production of inputs that were currently being imported and reduce the effective protection on assembly-type industries. Secondly, the basis for levying import duties was changed from free on board (fob) to cost insurance freight (cif) so as to increase government revenue while at the same time reduce somewhat the excess demand for foreign exchange. Further changes in the trade regime and sales tax were introduced in the 1985 Budget which were aimed at reducing the overall level

155

and wide dispersion of effective rates of protection in order to encourage efficient allocation of resources to industry, besides raising additional government revenue. In specific terms, most of the manufacturers' rebate under which given subsectors were exempted from duties on imports of industrial inputs were abolished. In addition, the existing rate of sales tax of 12.5 percent on imports was raised to 15 percent and the sales tax on locally produced goods and services was increased from 10 percent to a uniform rate of 15 percent.

In order to make tariffs the sole source of import protection in the fiscal structure, further actions were planned which included the unification of the domestic and import sales tax rates so that the sales tax would apply uniformly to all goods in the same category, whether of imported or domestic origin. It was hoped that such action would facilitate further work on tariff reform by permitting, among other things, the abolition of quantitative restrictions. In this regard, the government was convinced that further adjustment of the exchange rate was required to ensure that the tariff-inclusive prices of importables would rise to levels which would eliminate excess import demand. The national tariff schedule was to be reviewed and modified in order to achieve greater uniformity of incentives between import substitution and exports and between industry and other sectors of the economy.

In view of the need to introduce some measure of centralised allocation of foreign exchange, the government felt that it was imperative to reduce the gap between the supply of and the demand for foreign exchange. To achieve this, the government was convinced that the exchange rate was the most effective instrument that should be used. Currently, the excess demand was being suppressed by import-licensing and foreign exchange allocation systems which created serious distortions. In this respect, it was felt that a further real depreciation of the Kwacha would help in relieving pressure on the allocation system. To this end, various options were considered with a view to introducing a fundamental change in the exchange rate system in order to reduce excess demand for foreign exchange and lessen the reliance on administrative controls. It was also hoped that this change would ensure that the exchange rate would be maintained at a level consistent with the long run prospects for exports and terms of trade. The government was convinced that such an exchange rate should be market determined. Hence on 4th October, 1985 the government delinked the Kwacha from the special basket of currencies and a freely floating exchange rate system determined through auctioning of foreign exchange was introduced.[12]

The rationale for the auctioning of foreign exchange was that the use of market forces would result in striking an exchange rate that would bear a proper relationship to the underlying strength of the economy; otherwise the country would obtain foreign goods in excess of its means to pay for them. Indeed, Zambia had already lived beyond its means and had for some long period of time recorded substantial deficits in its external payments position. It was thought that this was the result of the fact that the exchange value for the Kwacha had been pegged at an unrealistic level.

It was believed that the discrete devaluations effected over the past years did not correct the long term imbalance which existed in the demand for and supply of foreign exchange. The problem of determining an exchange rate for the Zambian Kwacha was compounded by the generalised floating of all the major currencies of the world. Any fixed peg chosen for the domestic currency would be prone to induce a revaluation of the exchange rate through the movements of the exchange rates of the major currencies over time and any exchange rate changes instituted through discrete devaluation would be, under the circumstances, arbitrary. A fundamental adjustment requires that whatever exchange rate changes are effected, fully reflect the underlying economic conditions in the country. This was the justification for the adoption of a freely floating exchange rate.

The authorities were convinced that a freely floating exchange rate would enable the exchange rate to adjust sufficiently enough to a level that would be commensurate with the strength of the Zambian economy; as opposed to the fixed exchange rate system of the past where adjustments to the rate were normally infrequent and the magnitudes of the adjustments were discretionary and imprecise.

The previous foreign exchange allocation system hinged on the subjective decisions of those who were charged with the responsibility of allocating foreign exchange among the many competing users. Through the new system of auctioning, the allocative function would be left to the inter-play of the forces of demand and supply in the market. In this process, the element of subjectivity in the allocation of foreign exchange would be minimised as foreign exchange would be distributed impartially on the basis of underlying forces of effective demand, given a fixed supply. This was a necessary mechanism through which the exchange value of a freely floating local currency would be established. This was considered essential in view of the fact that the Kwacha is a non-tradeable currency. Its value on the international markets can only be expressed through some internationally traded medium of exchange such as the US Dollar. But since the supplies of such foreign exchange currencies to the country were severely limited, some appropriate mechanism had to be evolved and auctioning was that mechanism.

The liberalisation process constituted a carefully worked out adjustment programme for the achievement of economic recovery and growth that was consistent with balance of payments equilibrium. In order to achieve such an equilibrium, the liberalisation measures included the implementation of demand management programmes, which sought to control the money supply by limiting total domestic credit and government expenditure, and the institution of liberal measures that were designed to bring about structural adjustments in the economy in order to increase the volume of real goods and services supplied by the domestic productive sector.

5.9   The end of the liberal trade regime

The liberal trade regime was put to an end by Kaunda on 1st May, 1987. In a speech broadcast to the nation on both TV and radio, he announced the scraping of the auction system of foreign exchange and with it the end of the liberal trade regime. The reason for abandoning the liberal trade regime was that rather than improving the economy, this had exacerbated the already worsened economic situation. Thus, the President told the nation:

> After four years of these experimental programmes per capita income has fallen from the equivalent of US$630 in 1981 to less than US$200 in 1987. We have observed, with growing alarm, a situation where escalating unemployment is becoming a permanent feature of our economy. Galloping inflation has set in which has pushed the prices of basic essential commodities beyond the reach of our people especially the low income groups who are in the majority. Cases of malnutrition are on the increase everyday.

The result of this outcome was a deteriorating social and political environment which the leadership recognised as politically very dangerous. In his speech of 1st May, 1987, Kaunda stated:

> We are witnessing a situation where our social fabric is slowly disintegrating thereby sowing seeds of unrest and undermining the peace and unity of the Nation. This situation cannot and will not be allowed to continue.

Having abandoned the liberal trade regime, the government replaced it by a "New Economic Recovery Programme" which, according to the President's address of 1st May, 1987 comprised the following elements:

1.   Manufacturers of industrial goods and producers of agricultural commodities would recommend the maximum wholesale and retail prices of their products in conjunction with the Prices and Incomes Commission;

2. in the case of imports, other than capital equipment, intermediate inputs and raw materials, the importer and the Prices and Incomes Commission would recommend the maximum wholesale and retail prices;

3. an immediate price freeze on all products;

4. ban on imports of luxury products;

5. a fixed exchange rate system at which the Kwacha was pegged at K8.00 to one US Dollar;

6. fixed interest rates at 15 percent, allowing a margin of 5 percent;

7. collective bargaining as a means of determining wages and conditions of service and establishment of a minimum living wage;

8. limit on external debt service to 10 percent of net export earnings, after allowing for foreign exchange requirements of ZCCM, the oil companies, Zambia Airways and fertilizer imports and ploughing the balance into productive ventures to reactivate the economy;

9. establishment of an Export-Import Bank to finance activities for diversifying the economy;

10. establishment of a Revolving Fund Facility to support small scale entrepreneurs including those in agriculture and industry;

11. injection of resources into the expansion of public works schemes for temporary employment generation for the unemployed;

12. increasing public expenditure on capital projects, particularly investment projects which are low-cost with short maturities; and

13. improvement of Government's Capacity for Economic Management.

Under the "New Economic Recovery Programme", import licensing, including "No Funds Involved Import Licences", was subject to a bi-weekly foreign exchange allocation by the Foreign Exchange Management Committee (FEMAC). The Secretariat of FEMAC comprised staff from the Bank of Zambia and officials from the Ministry of Commerce and Industry. FEMAC comprised persons drawn from the private sector, parastatals and Government but the identity of such persons and of persons comprising the Secretariat were not disclosed to the public. All applications for import licences were submitted to the Permanent Secretary, Ministry of Commerce and Industry. The Secretariat of FEMAC processed the applications for import licences by verifying whether they were in the proper form as required by the rules and if they were supported by required documentation. On the basis of published criteria approved by FEMAC, the Secretariat made recommendations to FEMAC for allocation of foreign exchange and/or authority to obtain import licences.

The success of the new set of policies under the "New Economic Recovery Programme" remained to be seen. But one thing was certain: auctioning of foreign exchange and liberal trade regime were gone. What went wrong?

Too few statistical data exist to analyse the impact of the various liberalisation measures on the Zambian economy and the industrial sector, in particular. However, information from a number of informed sources suggested that the measures immediately worsened some problems and also led to new ones. Price decontrol stepped up inflation. Official sources put the inflation rate in mid-1986 at around 57 percent, though casual empirical evidence suggested a much higher rate. The high inflation rate pushed the prices of all commodities, including essential commodities, beyond the reach of most of the people and this led to rioting in November/December 1986 the country had ever seen. At least 15 people lost their lives and hundreds others were seriously injured. In addition, property worth ZK80 million was destroyed. The rioting was in protest against increases in the prices of maize meal (the country's staple food) and other essential commodities, following the government's decision to withdraw subsidies on these commodities, as part of the liberal trade regime arrangement.

The commercial banks' lending rates shot up to 30-33 percent, making it virtually impossible for small businessmen to borrow money. In the first week after the introduction of auctioning, the value of the Kwacha fell from 2.42 to 5.01 to the US Dollar, and the rate steadily declined since. On 12 July 1986, the Kwacha fell to what was considered as its lowest value at that time (8.07 to the US Dollar) although in the following week it recovered dramatically to 5.03 to the US Dollar. The general feeling was that the Zambian Kwacha had overshot its true value. But it is difficult to tell at what rate it would have stabilized in the long run had not the auctions and the liberalisation measures been discontinued in May 1987.

There is general agreement that the auction system produced two benefits. One, it facilitated a regular flow of foreign exchange to all sectors for legitimate imports. Two, it eliminated the corruption that existed in the previous regime when no objective criteria existed for allocating a limited supply of foreign exchange.

Some firms seem to have obtained more foreign exchange after the auctioning started. During an interview in July 1986, an officer of Refined Oil Products (1975) Limited (a parastatal under INDECO that produces cooking oil, soaps, and detergents) stated that since auctioning began the company had obtained imported packaging materials and spares more quickly and smoothly.

Whereas earlier 50 percent of management time was reportedly spent on financial and foreign-exchange matters, most management time was subsequently devoted to the operation of the plant.

For the industry as a whole, however, the story was not such a happy one. The Managing Director of INDECO stated in July 1986 that foreign-exchange allocations to the INDECO group of companies dropped by 40 percent after auctioning was introduced due to their liquidity problems. Because of the highly depreciated value of the Kwacha, a firm had to pool much more domestic currency to obtain a given amount of foreign exchange. All but the large firms lacked that amount of cash. Zambia Steel Building Supplies (ZSBS) was at one time one of Zambia's best performing companies and had no liquidity problem. But since auctioning began, the excessive quantity of Kwacha the company had to put up for its foreign exchange bids created cash-flow problems, including the payment of salaries to its staff.

A big drop in demand was one of the most serious problems the manufacturing industry faced. Although in 1986, firms had the freedom to charge economic prices, the tremendous increase in production costs, especially when inputs were imported, pushed prices far beyond what the market could bear. Mansa Batteries Ltd., for instance, was able to sell only 1.2 million out of the 3 million batteries it produced during April-June 1986. ZSBS also had K1 million worth of unsold doors in the Copperbelt. The firms were faced with a dilemma: unless they sold their products they could not earn the Kwacha to bid for foreign exchange. They could not sell their products unless they lowered prices. If they lowered their prices to sell the products, production costs would not be covered. As Phiri, the former General Manager of Mansa Batteries, stated (in Sheshamani, 1988):

> We get into a vicious circle. If we cannot sell more batteries, then we cannot have enough Kwacha with which to bid. We may not resort to borrowing from banks as interest rates were liberalised and have gone sky high. If no Kwacha, then no foreign exchange, and then we are back to the pre-auction problem of lack of foreign exchange and, therefore, stock outs of raw materials and then complete closure. The threat is as serious as that.

One of the measures that led to the hike in costs and prices is the change from fob to cif basis for the levy of duty and sales tax on imports. Duty and sales taxes equaled 40-45 percent of the cost of pumps, sprinklers, and tractor engine spare parts imported by the Agricultural Farm Equipment Company (AFE) in 1986. On higher-valued capital goods, this percentage reached 60-65 percent. Such a high percentage of duty and sales tax levied on the total cif cost of inputs valued in a highly depreciated Kwacha greatly affected prices.

Even goods exempt from duty were no longer affordable for a common man. A tractor, for instance, cost nearly K200,000, a price no small farmer could afford. Companies therefore shifted their imports from high-cost capital goods to spare parts. While this might be a wise strategy for an enterprise in the short run, in the long run it would inhibit the development of key sectors in the economy, such as agriculture.

The liberalisation measures by the government also generated serious- and often unwholesome - competition among local firms, especially among parastatals. Along with the introduction of auctioning, the government revived a holiday allowance of five hundred US Dollars per annum and liberalised the issue of import licences not requiring foreign exchange. Zambian residents could use their foreign-exchange holdings abroad with no questions asked. These measures resulted in a flood of imported consumer goods, particularly from South Africa. This further depressed demand for locally produced goods. For instance, the market was full of tinned beer from South Africa while several thousand crates of beer produced by Zambia Breweries lay unsold. Such competition with imported finished goods posed a threat to firms striving for genuine import substitution.

Auctioning increased competition by breaking the monopoly of some companies in importing goods. For example, before auctioning, ZSBS had a virtual monopoly in importing steel. All construction companies in Zambia had to buy steel from ZSBS. Since the auctioning began, several companies obtained licenses to import steel. A giant company such as Lewis Construction could then import its steel directly from South Africa instead of buying it from ZSBS. In the long run, such competition could prove healthy; large firms such as ZSBS would be roused from the lethargy and complacency induced by monopoly and instead become effective and dynamic. In the short run, however, survival of such companies, due to loss of their hitherto assured markets, posed a critical problem.

The economic liberalisation measures virtually destroyed small-scale industry. With few Kwacha reserves of their own and an inability to obtain bank loans due to high interest rates, the small businessmen were in no position to bid for foreign exchange. Furthermore, a large part of the available foreign exchange was allocated to large multinational firms. Had this continued, very soon the bulk of the economy would have become foreign based. If this had happened and the foreign investors were later to move out of the country due to the increasing threat of economic sanctions in the region, the domestic industrial base of Zambia would have been left extremely weak. The government had to prevent this eventuality. It is partly for this reason that in May 1987, Zambia discontinued the package of economic liberalisation measures that had been urged upon it by the World Bank and the International Monetary Fund.

Thus, by all accounts, the liberalisation measures destroyed Zambian industry. This is an unfortunate result in view of the importance of manufacturing industry in the country's economic growth. As it has been seen, following the measures which the government took on attaining independence to diversify away from copper, the manufacturing sector grew very rapidly, rising from 6.1 percent of GDP in 1964 to 20 percent by 1982 and this contributed greatly to the country's economic growth. Our examination of the country's economic performance suggests that the manufacturing sector played a key role in the growth of its GDP. Use of the Granger causality test, as shown below, indicates that the growth of the manufacturing sector was a signicant factor in the growth of the GDP and that the causality relationship between manufacturing and GDP was uni-directional, i.e. running from manufacturing to GDP. This implies that while the growth of Zambia's GDP did not lead to the growth of the manufacturing sector, the growth of Zambia's GDP depended to a very significant degree on the growth of manufacturing output. In other words, Zambia's import substitution industry is an important cause of the country's economic growth, a result which is contrary to the view of the proponents of outward orientation.

$$Y_t = \quad 0.033\ Y_{t-1} + \quad 0.409\ MX_{t-1} + 1.26$$
$$\qquad\quad (0.180) \qquad\quad (2.775)$$

A_{t20} = 2.845 at 1 percent level
     = 2.086 at 5 percent level
     = 1.725 at 10 percent level

$t(b)$ = 2.775 , significant at 5 percent level.

Therefore, $H_o : b = 0$, rejected.

This implies that manufacturing growth causes GDP (MX) growth.

F(2, 20) Crit val. = 3.49 at 5 percent.
          = 2.59 at 10 percent.

F(2, 20)   = 3.36, significant at 10 percent.

Scaled residuals:

Sample size	= 23
Mean	= 0.000
Std devn	= 1.022
Skewness	= 0.304
Excess kurtosis	= -0.399
$CHI^2(2)$	= 0.463
DW	= 2.87

$$X_t = 0.118\ X_{t-1} + 0.540\ Y_{t-1} + 1.20$$
$$(0.617)\qquad (2.309)$$

$t(d) = 2.309$, significant at 5 percent level.

Therefore, $H_o{:}b = 0$ is rejected.

This implies that Y causes X; in other words, real GDP growth causes manufacturing output growth.

$F(2, 20)$	$= 2.41$, not significant.
Scaled residuals:	
Sample size	$= 23$
Mean	$= 0.000$
Std devn	$= 1.022$
Skewness	$= 0.784$
Excess kurtosis	$= -0.170$
$CHI^2(2)$	$= 2.179$
DW	$= 2.24$

Taking the two equations together and considering that the F-test statistic associated with the second equation is not significant, the causality relationship is uni-directional and runs from manufacturing to GDP growth. Considering this result, it can be said that the liberalisation measures did not achieve their main intended objective which was to restore the country's growth. Instead, they produced the unintended opposite result of killing the very source of growth of the country's economy and, therefore, accelerating the rate of economic decline and producing other undesirable side effects such as inflation.

But even if exports were an important causal growth factor, devaluation did not really succeed to promote exports. In 1986, non-mineral exports constituted only 5 percent of the country's total exports in that year. It is this sector which holds the key to the country's improved export performance as mineral deposits are nearing depletion and it is estimated that these will be completely exhausted within a few years' time. Therefore, devaluation should have aimed at increasing non-mineral exports but, as pointed out above, this was not achieved.

The other undesirable consequence of the liberalisation policies was rising debt service payments which the government found increasingly difficult to honour. It has been pointed out that in order to minimise the disruptive effects of declining mineral export earnings on the economy, the government borrowed large sums of money from abroad. As this was denominated in foreign currency, the repayments in Kwacha which the government had to produce to the Bank of Zambia in order to get the required foreign currency increased with the devaluation. But government revenue did not rise *pari passu* with the rate of devaluation. Government revenue, including grants, increased by 42 and 103 percent in 1985 and 1986, respectively, while expenditure went up by 76 and 197 percent in the same years. The huge increase in expenditure was mainly due to foreign debt service payments in local currency by the government which rose, principally because of the devaluation of the Kwacha. The effect of the devaluation in increasing debt service payments is quite significant given the fact that the government secured debt relief through rescheduling under the Paris Club in 1983, 1984, and 1986.

Nonetheless, growth factors must prevail. One of the primary objectives of Zambian policy since Independence has always been the achievement of high living standards for its people. A clear manifestation of this objective has been a series of development plans, starting with an emergency plan (1964-65) and then a transitional plan (1965-66). This was followed by the First National Development Plan, covering the period 1966-70. The year 1971 was a year of consolidation and the Second National Development Plan which lasted up to 1976 was launched in 1972. There was no national plan for the period 1977-78. The Third National Development Plan was launched for the period 1979-83. Since the Government entered into a structural adjustment programme agreement with the World Bank/IMF, there was no National Development Plan for the intervening period up to 1987. After abandoning the World Bank/IMF adjustment programme in 1987, the Government launched the Interim National Development Plan for the period 1987 to 1988, pending the preparation of the Fourth National Development Plan which was launched in January 1989 for the period up to December, 1993.

The primary aim of all these national plans, except the interim national development plan, has always been to achieve a significant growth rate of the GDP in order to enhance the living standards of the people. For example, in launching the Third National Development Plan, President Kaunda stated, "this marks another milestone in our march towards our cherished goal of achieving economic independence and enhancing the welfare of the masses of the people of Zambia."[13] But even the Interim National Development Plan, whose principal objective was to stabilise the economy by controlling inflation, sought economic growth as its ultimate objective. By stabilising the economy,it was hoped that a firm foundation would be laid from which economic growth could take place.

However, the ambitious statements of intentions have not always been matched with performance. Table 5.9 shows GDP at current prices, GDP at 1980 prices, population and real GDP per capita for the period 1964-87. It will be observed that real GDP per capita rose steadily from 1964 to 1969. In the following two consecutive years real GDP per capita declined. From 1971 to 1975 real GDP per capita rose and declined every other year. Thereafter, it decreased continuously up to 1979. In 1980 there was no change in real GDP per capita. In 1981 real GDP per capita rose; but from 1982 real GDP per capita declined in each of the following consecutive years so that by 1987, real GDP per capita was lower than in 1964, the year Zambia attained her Independence. Nonetheless, Zambia has something to be proud of as a nation. Life expectancy at birth has risen from forty-four to fifty-two years, while infant mortality has fallen from 123 to 85 per 1,000 live births. Progress in the field of education has been remarkable. Enrolment in primary school as a percentage of the relevant age group has risen from 53 to 94, while the increases for secondary and tertiary education have been from 7 to 17 and from 0 to 2 percent, respectively. On the economic front, the country has become one of the most urbanised and industrialised in Sub-Saharan Africa, and the manufacturing sector now produces 21 percent of the GDP compared to 6 percent in 1964.

5.10   Saving and investment performance

Capital occupies a dominant position in the theory of economic growth. For example, Rostow (1956) specified a rise in the rate of productive investment to over 10 percent of national income as a pre-condition for a country's take-off. An important ingredient of the preconditions for take-off was the effort expended in building up a capital base. Take-off, once achieved, had to be sustained as the economy strives to attain high mass consumption. Similarly, Sir Arthur Lewis (1954) argued that the central problem in the theory of economic development was to understand the process by which a community which was previously saving and investing 4 or 5 percent of its national income or less, converted itself into an economy where voluntary saving was running at about 12 to 15 percent of national income or more and that this was the central problem because the central fact of economic development was rapid capital accumulation.

Essentially, these arguments may be interpreted to emphasise the concept of incremental capital stock in which capital in the present period comprises capital in the previous period (adjusted for depreciation at a given depreciation rate) plus investment in the present period. Hence, in this context the secret of building up the country's capital base involves a sustained effort to make investment outlays.

Table 5.9

GDP, population and real GDP per capita

Year	GDP at current prices (K mil)	Real GDP at 1980 prices (K mil)	Mid-year population (mil)	Real GDP per capita at 1980 prices (K)	Percent Change
1964	502	1618	3.61*	448	n.a.
1965	711	1915	3.71*	516	+15.2
1966	848	2172	3.81*	570	+10.5
1967	957	2449	3.92*	625	+9.6
1968	1062	2632	4.01*	656	+5.0
1969	1314	3123	4.12*	758	+15.5
1970	1269	2695	4.24*	636	-16.1
1971	1181	2697	4.40*	613	-3.6
1972	1348	2962	4.53	654	+6.7
1973	1591	2934	4.68	627	-4.1
1974	1888	3132	4.83	648	+3.3
1975	1583	3056	4.98	614	-5.2
1976	1896	3187	5.14	620	+1.0
1977	1986	3049	5.20	586	-5.5
1978	2251	3067	5.36	572	-2.4
1979	2660	2973	5.52	539	-5.8
1980	3064	3064	5.68	539	0.0
1981	3485	3253	5.87	554	+2.8
1982	3595	3161	6.05	522	-5.8
1983	4181	3099	6.22	498	-4.6
1984	4931	3087	6.42	481	-3.4
1985	7072	3136	6.72	467	-2.9
1986	12954	3155	6.95	454	-2.8
1987	18080	3149	7.27	433	-4.6

Source: Monthly Digest of Statistics, December 1978, 1980, 1986, Central Statistical Office, Lusaka, and IMF (1995).

*Estimates based on GDP and GDP per capita in National Accounts.

An important aspect of Table 5.9 is that it focuses on nominal and real GDP, population and real GDP per capital in Zambia in the period 1964 - 1987, precisely during the post-independence era in which the government's favoured trade policy regime was interrupted by the trade liberalisation policies popularised by multilateral organisations (mainly the World Bank and the IMF) in the 1980s. Most of the story relating to this period has already been detailed in the previous sections of this chapter; the period from 1987-97 does not offer a reversal of the gloomy scenario depicted by the declining percentage change in real GDP per capital during 1982 - 87.

Table 5.10
Savings, gross fixed capital formation, import surplus, stocks
(Kwacha million), incremental capital-output ratio and discount rate

Year	Savings	GFCF	Import surplus	Stocks	Incremental capital output ratio	Discount rate
1964	96.8	76	-198.6	9	0.93	4.50
1965	187.6	138	-162.3	-19	0.66	4.50
1966	243.2	198	-209.9	36	1.42	4.50
1967	233.2	246	-168.6	50	2.26	5.00
1968	244.1	288	-128.8	49	2.74	5.00
1969	465.8	277	-551.2	56	1.10	5.00
1970	301.4	372	-344.3	-39	-8.27	5.00
1971	90.9	393	-101.7	-12	-4.47	5.00
1972	133.0	445	-183.5	47	2.66	5.00
1973	331.2	423	-433.1	31	1.74	5.00
1974	483.7	502	-437.4	42	1.69	5.00
1975	-63.2	602	22.6	185	-1.97	5.00
1976	249.3	445	-363.2	40	1.42	5.00
1977	-9.0	483	-252.7	7	5.37	6.00
1978	-29.0	437	-262.2	7	1.65	6.00
1979	-4.7	450	-614.1	100	1.10	6.50
1980	-116.1	558	-391.3	74	1.38	6.50
1981	-358.6	610	-73.6	155	1.45	7.50
1982	-473.8	618	-63.0	63	5.62	7.50
1983	-149.7	615	-387.8	-15	1.05	10.00
1984	-157.9	623	-699.3	-4	0.83	14.50
1985	-637.9	725	-1129.9	55	0.34	25.00
1986	-1652.4	1385	-979.9	n.a.	0.24	30.00
1987	-1591.9	1929	-1880.1	n.a.	0.38	14.00

Source: National Accounts and Input-Output Tables 1969, 1973, 1980; National Accounts Statistical Bulletin No. 1, February 1987; Monthly Digest of Statistics December 1980 and May/August 1986; IMF (1995).

The presumption in the foregoing discussion is that growth hinges on capital accumulation, and that additional capital would either provoke or facilitate a more rapid rate of economic growth. The accumulation of capital requires the mobilisation of an economic surplus. If investment is to increase, there must be a growing surplus above current consumption that can be tapped and directed into productive investment channels. An economic surplus develops where GDP grows more rapidly than the growth of consumption. Therefore, any trade regime that promotes rapid growth of GDP would be said to facilitate more capital accumulation through higher savings which are made possible.

It is, of course, recognised that capital accumulation, although very important, is just one of the many factors for rapid economic growth. Other things such as entrepreneurship, human skills and technology are needed in addition to capital accumulation. Therefore, a generally necessary but by no means sufficient condition for growth in the productive capacity of an economy is accumulation and efficient use of capital. For this reason, Zambia's savings and investment performance will be reviewed. The nature of the relationship between the trade regime and the processes of saving and investing will then be examined. Finally, the specific growth-related responses of economic units to the trade regime will be looked at.

Table 5.10 shows savings, gross fixed capital formation (GFCF), import surplus, stocks, incremental capital - output ratio and the discount rate for the period 1964 to 1987. In terms of casual inspection if one relates these magnitudes to output, one does not see any clear relationship between the growth of factor supplies and the growth of output. In this regard, it is pertinent to investigate the question: "what effect, if any, did the trade regime have on the factors directly influencing economic growth?"

From 1964 to 1974, Zambia generated positive savings in each year. In 1975 Zambia had negative savings and in 1976 positive savings. From 1977 to 1987, Zambia had negative savings with the situation deteriorating every year. Yet, Zambia continued with the process of investment. Where did the resources come from? With negative savings one would think that the investment was maintained via an import surplus. But this was not the case since the import surplus was negative throughout the period from 1964 to 1987, with the exception of 1975 when the import surplus was positive. Thus, except for 1975, Zambia was exporting rather than importing capital during this period. This, then, might be the reason for the poor savings performance given inadequate domestic resources. Zambia, therefore, had to borrow from abroad in order to invest. This proved very costly as time went by.

It is worth noting that during the pre-restriction period (1964-68) savings were positive. This is also the case during the period of quantitative controls (1969-76) except in one year (1975). Thereafter, during the periods of discrete devaluations (1977-82) and liberalisation (1982-86), savings were negative.

On the side of investment, no pattern is discernible. Gross fixed capital formation rose steadily from 1964 to 1987, at least in current prices. However, if one looks at the more interesting aspect of the response of output to additions to the stock of capital, one gets a different picture. The incremental capital-output ratios in the pre-restriction period show that capital was more efficiently used than in the period of quantitative restrictions. Capital was also

169

more productively used in the period of discrete devaluations and liberalisation.

5.11 Responses to the control system

This section examines the effect the controlled trade regime had on other factors such as overbuilding of plant, low capacity utilization and excessive inventories and allocation of resources which are often said to arise from a control regime.

Regarding the allocation of resources, a question which requires examination is whether the controlled trade regime played an important role in resource allocation by pulling resources into inefficient sectors away from efficient ones, thereby retarding or reducing the growth rate. It has been stated in the section on the economic and trade policies prior to the adoption of the liberal economic policies that after gaining her political independence in 1964, Zambia sought to diversify her economy. In this regard, the government took deliberate policy measures in order to increase the size of the manufacturing sector. It was observed that following the adoption of these measures, the manufacturing sector, which accounted for only 6.1 percent of GDP in 1964, grew at a very fast rate and by 1982 its share in GDP had reached 20 percent. On the other hand, the share of agriculture and mining fell. Was this due to the system of incentives offered to the manufacturing sector and was this done at a great price of retarding the growth process as a whole?

To answer this question one needs to look at the structure of protection that was given to manufacturing industries by the system of incentives provided. In Zambia, the most important incentives given to manufacturing industries have been the tariff structure and the working of the foreign exchange allocation system which modified the incentives provided by the structure of tariff protection through direct quantitative restrictions on imports.

The role of the tariff structure in promoting industrial growth and development depends on its effectiveness in providing incentives to industrial producers. Quantitative restrictions limit the volume of imports and this also provides protection to producers of import - controlled goods. When the two are employed together, the resulting level of incentives can exercise substantial influence over decisions made by the private sector regarding capacity expansion, new investment, production for the domestic or export markets and the choice of technology. In the public sector, they can determine the financial viability of existing enterprises and of proposed investments.

From the time Zambia attained political independence through the mid-1970s, the principal intervention by the Government in the foreign trade sector was through the structure of tariff protection. Beginning in the second half of the 1970s, however, the Government placed increasing reliance on the use of import licenses, prohibitions, and the allocation of foreign exchange, both to control the overall use of foreign exchange and to protect domestic industry.

To examine the effect of protection in this situation, it is necessary to take into account both the tariffs and the quantitative restrictions by translating the quantitative restrictions into their tariff equivalents and adding this to the tariffs. However, in practice it is extremely difficult to translate the effect of quantitative restrictions into their tariff equivalents and the only practical way of measuring the effect of both tariffs and quantitative restrictions is to measure how much the prices of locally produced goods exceed the prices of similar goods on world markets. This requires a direct comparison of the domestic and c.i.f. prices of similar products in order to determine the nominal protection. This, of course, requires the availability of the necessary data which, in Zambia's case, is simply unavailable.

The structure of tariff protection only establishes the base line of incentives conferred by the trade regime. The net effect of tariffs, import sales taxes and other trade interventions on the structure of incentives and on the ensuing pattern of allocation of resources for industrial production can be assessed by the use of the concept of effective protection. This measures the degree to which domestic value added in any industry or sector differs from the corresponding level of value added which would exist in the absence of trade interventions. The concept of effective protection goes beyond the simple examination of nominal tariff rates in the sense that it explicitly attempts to reflect the net incentives to producers resulting from tariffs on both output and inputs. For any economic activity, the trade regime affects not only the price of output and revenues but also the prices of inputs and costs. High nominal protection on output can be wholly or partly offset by high tariff rates on imported inputs. The effective protective rate (ERP) for a sector or industry is given by the percentage by which value added at domestic prices (VADP) exceeds value added at world prices (VAWP):

$$ERP = (VADP - VAWP)/VAWP \times 100. \tag{5.1}$$

An example may be helpful here. Suppose that an industry has a gross output of 200 and the cost of all inputs, excluding payments to factors, is 100. Assume that there are no restrictions on trade. If now a tax of 20 percent ad valorem is levied on imports of the final goods, the bundle of goods which previously sold for 200 can now sell for 240. Value added, therefore, has risen from 100 to 140, an increase of 40 percent. If, however, a tax of 40 percent ad valorem is levied on imported inputs, then the cost of inputs would rise to 140.

There are many examples to illustrate this theory worldwide; for example in the motor-car industry, the manufacture of motor-cycles (UK versus Japan) and in the manufacture of bicycles (UK versus China). In the context of trade regimes for African economies, this theory suggests that African economies would imitate the technological content of their imports at time t_1; however, they would not be in position to implement the technology until time t_2. Import substitution industrialization would then begin, perhaps facilitated by some form of protectionism of the infant industries, until time t_3, when an open trade regime is adopted and domestically produced goods would be able to compete with imports.

and value added would be 100, which is exactly what it was in the situation with no restrictions on trade.

Corden (1966), who is one of the orginators of the concept of "effective rate of protection", has provided a formula for working out the effective protection rate given to an industrial activity by the system of tariffs as follows; taking into account more than one importable input:

$$g_j = \left[\left(\sum_{i=1}^{m} a_{ij} t_i \right) / \left(1 - \sum_{i-1}^{n} a_{ij} t_j \right) \right] \tag{5.2}$$

where g_j = effective protective rate for importable j; a_{ij} = share of importable input i in the cost of j in the absence of tariffs; t_j = tariff rate on j; t_i = tariff rate on i.

Using data obtained from National Accounts and Input - Output Tables 1980 published by the Central Statistical Office, Lusaka derived data for the structure of imports and duty on imported inputs; Table 5.11 reports the data. We also derived the data on imports of final products and duty paid in all the manufacturing categories; Table 5.12 reports the data. From the data given for imports for final use and imports for intermediate inputs and the respective duties paid, the respective nominal tariff rates have been calculated.

We then applied equations (5.1) and (5.2) to the data reported in Tables 5.11 and 5.12. The results of the computations using the Corden formula are shown in Table 5.13. Ideally, these calculations should have taken into account the trade restrictions in place in 1980. In other words, the quantitative restrictions should have been translated into their tariff equivalents and added to the tariff rates. As pointed out, a practical way of taking into account the effect of both tariffs and quantitative restrictions is to measure how much the prices of locally produced goods exceeded the prices of similar goods on world markets. But it has not been possible to do this due to lack of the required data. This is not a terrible drawback. What it means is that the results should be interpreted with caution. However, the results indicate the orders of magnitude of the effective protection given to Zambian manufacturing industries in 1980. It may also be safely assumed that this level of effective protection was given to manufacturing industries in the years before and after 1980.

It will be observed that it is Textiles and Leather industries followed by Food Manufacturing and then Beverages and Tobacco industries that received effective rates of protection which were higher than the nominal tariff rates. Textiles and Leather received the highest effective rate of protection, 98.4 percent higher than the nominal tariff rate. Food Manufacturing industries received an effective rate of protection which was 25.4 percent higher than the nominal tariff rate and the Beverages and Tobacco industries were accorded effective protection 20.2 percent higher than the nominal duty rate.

Most of the industries received effective protection that was lower than the nominal tariff rates. In the case of two types of industries, Wood and Wood Products and Basic Metal Products, the effective protection given was negative. It must also be noted that the nominal tariff rates were very low, most of them below 10 percent.

Table 5.11
Intermediate inputs and duty on imported inputs
(Kwacha million)

	Total Inputs	of which imported inputs	percent share of imported inputs	Duty on imported inputs	percent rate of duty
Food manufacturing	207.7	65.2	31.4	5.7	8.7
Beverages & tobacco	63.5	10.9	17.2	0.9	8.3
Textiles & leather	114.1	65.9	57.8	5.7	8.6
Wood & wood products	16.1	7.5	46.6	0.7	9.3
Paper & printing	30.8	17.6	57.1	1.5	8.5
Chemicals & rubber	222.9	82.8	37.1	7.2	8.7
Non-metallic mineral Products	43.2	19.7	45.6	1.7	8.6
Basic metal products	8.6	7.6	88.4	0.7	9.2
Fabricated metal Products	122.9	107.2	87.2	9.3	8.7
Other Manufacturing	3.3	0.6	18.2	0.1	16.7

Source: Computed by data reported in National Accounts and Input-Output Tables 1980, Central Statistical Office, Lusaka.

Although, these effective rates of protection do not take into account the effect of quantitative restrictions, they seem to suggest that the Zambian system of tariffs was not very protective, although this was the objective of the authorities. In other words, it is possible that Zambian industries, with the exception of Textiles and Leather, Food Manufacturing and Beverages and Tobacco, did not flourish behind high protective tariff walls.

Table 5.12
Imports of final products and duty paid (Kwacha million)

	Imports cif	Import duties	Nominal tariff rate
Food manufacturing	42.2	8.3	19.7
Beverages & tobacco	2.5	7.1	284.0
Textiles & leather products	96.4	29.5	30.6
Wood & wood products	9.6	0.3	3.1
Paper & printing	29.1	2.1	7.2
Chemicals & rubber	397.5	29.2	7.3
Non-metallic mineral products	33.9	1.5	4.4
Basic metal products	10.1	0.6	5.9
Fabricated metal products	398.4	31.0	7.8
Other manufacturing	24.2	2.3	9.5

Source: Computed by data reported in National Accounts and Input-Output Tables 1980, Central Statistical Office, Lusaka.

Table 5.13
Structure of protection

Industry	Nominal tariff rate (percent)	Effective protective rate (percent)
Food manufacturing	19.7	24.7
Beverages & tobacco	284.0	341.3
Textiles & leather	30.6	60.7
Wood & wood products	3.1	-2.1
Paper & printing	7.2	5.5
Chemicals & rubber	7.3	6.5
Non-metallic mineral products	4.4	0.9
Basic metal products	5.9	-19.2
Fabricated metal products	7.8	1.7
Other manufacturing	9.5	7.9

Source: As Table 5.12 above.

Thus, the resource - allocational effect of the restrictive trade regime may not have been all that harmful for economic growth. Therefore, the fact that mining and quarrying and agriculture sectors suffered declines in output might not be because resources were diverted away from them to the manufacturing sector.

As it has been pointed out, overbuilding of plant, low capacity utilization, excessive inventories, limited technical progress, and diversion of entrepreneurial talent are some of the problems which are commonly cited as arising from a control system. In individual cases, such problems have arisen during both the control and liberal periods. Thus, the case against controls may not be proven. In the case of Zambia, the problems which may be associated with her industrialisation might have stemmed from factors other than the control system itself. Soon after attaining Independence, the Government pursued a policy of Zambianisation and most of the managerial posts in parastatals and government were taken over by inexperienced Zambians. Hence, inexperienced management and labour might have been responsible for Zambia's poor economic performance rather than the controls per se.

Nonetheless, an examination of whether liberalisation of the trade regime made a significant difference to industry performance is required. In this regard, the question of investigation is whether Zambian industries improved their capacity utilisation rates following liberalisation. Table 5.14 shows capacity utilisations for the 15 INDECO Group of Companies which were mostly dependent on imports of raw materials for the period October 1984 to September 1985, before the introduction of auctioning of foreign exchange, and October 1985 to September 1986, during the period of foreign exchange auctioning. It will be observed that following liberalisation and auctioning of foreign exchange, capacity utilisation dropped in general. The main reason is that in the majority of cases companies did not get sufficient foreign exchange because the amount of foreign exchange made available for auctioning was not sufficient to meet the demands of Zambian industries. It was, therefore, expecting too much in supposing that liberalisation and auctioning of foreign exchange would lead to improved capacity utilisation in the wake of inadequate foreign exchange to go round.

Another problem which is often cited as stemming from a control system is that the existence of a licensing system results in a diversion of investment flows into inventory holdings. To examine whether this phenomenon was true in Zambia, inventory holding as a percentage of GDP has been calculated for the period 1964 to 1987. The results are contained in Table 5.15. It will be observed that during the period of quantitative restrictions, i.e. 1969 to 1982, inventory holding as a percentage of GDP was on a declining trend whereas during the period of liberalisation, i.e. 1964 to 1968 and 1983 to 1987, the trend was upward. Since a controlled regime would normally be associated with a rising trend in inventory holding as a percentage of GDP, this result suggests that the control regime resulted in reduced stock holding while the liberal regime resulted in increased inventory holding.

Table 5.14

**Foreign exchange requirement/allocation and capacity utilization
for companies most dependent on foreign exchange (US $'000)**

Company	October 1984 - September 1985			October 1985 - September 1986		
	Requirement	Allocation	Capacity utilization %	Requirement	Allocation	Capacity utilization %
CTS	1968	654	38	1574	304	37
GPL	425	385	69	500	226	51
KIF	3687	1473	64	3840	2695	62
LENCO	3574	2276	50	3043	1193	35
LMA	10390	2057	16	4370	617	14
LIL	2620	1124	24	1577	147	18
MBL	1975	1119	34	1502	192	29
MONARCH	1959	611	36	1395	444	23
NMC	30732	19616	42	25565	14331	34
NGP	688	565	-	831	500	-
ROP	19779	14308	37	22380	14418	31
ZBL	8569	6095	51	8176	3649	69
ZAMOX	8309	5716	58	7256	3107	56
ZSBS	12522	2998	43	5506	2200	35

Source: INDECO.

5.12   Employment effect

Another aspect that merits investigation is the direction and the extent to which the trade and payments regime affected employment. One way of analysing this phenomenon is to use the techniques of the NBER project on alternative trade strategies and employment edited by Krueger, Lary, Monson, Akrasance, 1981). The project devised a methodology for analysing the relationship between trade regime and employment. This methodology first categorises commodities into tradable and non-tradable. Tradable goods are then classified into importables and exportables. For both of these, there is a further breakdown on the grounds that there is a great deal of evidence that the behaviour of tradable commodities that depend upon the local availability of natural resources for their production may be quite different, both in its determinants and in the likely supply response to altered prices, from the behaviour of the tradable commodities for which location is not contingent upon direct access to the source of the raw material.

Therefore, exportables and importables are divided into two groups of goods, namely:

1.   Natural resource based (NRB) goods and activities divided into agricultural, mineral, and other (including processing manufacturing industries); and

2.   H-O-S goods.

National resource base activities are those whose profitability depends basically upon the existence of some resource deriving a rent, such as land and mineral resources. While a change in the relative price of capital and labour might induce both substitution between these factors and perhaps also a change in the extensive margin of exploitation of minerals or cultivation of land, the industry's existence or absence, and hence the country's comparative advantage, is primarily the result of the presence of the natural resource whose exploitation is economic.

By contrast, H-O-S goods are those whose production location is not determined by the location of the resource to which rent accrues. For H-O-S sectors, profitability (and hence location) is primarily a function of the relative prices of labour (of various grades of skills) and capital goods and their services. Labour coefficients and effective protection rates are then calculated for NRB and H-O-S goods for both exportable and importable goods. From this a conclusion is then drawn as to whether a trade regime promotes or discourages employment. For example, in a study of the Côte d'Ivoire,

Monson (1995) calculated labour coefficients for Côte d'Ivoire exportables and importables and found that all exportables used unskilled and artisanal labour more intensively than importables and that for modern sector activities, importables were more capital-intensive and skilled-labour intensive than exportables. In addition, he found that labour-intensive exportables were discriminated against by receiving somewhat lower protection than less labour-intensive importables. From these results, it was concluded that Côte d'Ivoire export-oriented policies have generally encouraged employment because the country's comparative advantage lies in the export of labour-intensive commodities to developed countries.

Table 5.15
Inventory holding as a percentage of GDP

	Inventory holding (K million)	GDP (K million)	Inventory holding as percent GDP
1964	-19	502	-3.8
1965	36	711	5.1
1966	50	848	5.9
1967	49	957	5.1
1968	56	1062	5.3
1969	-39	1314	-3.0
1970	-12	1269	-0.9
1971	47	1181	4.0
1972	31	1348	2.3
1973	42	1591	2.6
1974	185	1888	9.8
1975	40	1583	2.5
1976	7	1896	0.4
1977	7	1986	0.4
1978	100	2251	4.4
1979	74	2660	2.8
1980	155	3064	5.1
1981	63	3485	1.8
1982	-15	3595	-0.4
1983	40	4181	1.0
1984	101	4931	2.0
1985	239	7072	3.4
1986	1701	12954	13.1
1987	768	18080	4.2

Source: National Accounts and Input-Output Tables 1969, 1973, 1980; National Accounts Statistical Bulletin No. 1, February 1987; Monthly Digest of Statistics December 1980 and May/August 1986; IMF (1995).

This study does not follow the above methodology for two reasons. First, it does not seem to be very appropriate for the subject of inquiry of the study, namely: how does one type of trade regime affect employment as opposed to one other type of trade regime, on the presumption that one is superior to the other in terms of overall economic performance? For if one strategy results in a higher rate of economic growth of the overall economy owing to superior resource allocation, the faster growth would presumably entail more employment growth.   And, within one strategy, there are both import-competing and export activities.   If in either strategy export activities are found to be more labour using than import-competing ones, it cannot be justifiably concluded that one type of strategy is superior to the other.   In order to do this, one needs to compare labour coefficients for export activities in an open trade strategy with labour coefficients for export activities in a restrictive trade strategy or compare labour coefficients for import-competing activities in an open trade regime with labour coefficients for import-competing activities in a restrictive trade regime.   In other words, like ought to be compared with like for each different type of trade regime.   Secondly, the available statistics are not sufficiently disaggregated to get information on exports and imports within the same sector and as such deciding on the individual activities for analysis is not possible.   Neither is it possible with the available data to compute a "t-statistic" which can be used as a cut-off point between exportable and import-competing or non-import-competing so as to analyse each activity in the three categories.

Given the above considerations, the methodology to be used will be to look at what happened to employment during a given period when the country was pursuing a restrictive trade and payments strategy and compare this with the situation when the country was following an outward-oriented strategy. However, this will only focus at employment in the manufacturing industry. In a sense, this is tantamount to examining H-O-S goods and excluding NRB goods, such as copper, from the analysis.

The period for which statistics are available is from 1964 to 1980 with gaps in between. During this period, manufacturing accounted for 12 percent of total formal sector employment, with agriculture, forestry and fishing contributing 9 percent; mining and quarrying 17 percent; energy and water 2 percent; construction 13 percent; and the tertiary sector 47 percent.

Tables 5.16 and 5.17 show some important employment ratios, namely, value added per employee, employees per K1 million value added and capital employed per operative (defined to include all employees who are directly engaged in production or related activities, including any clerical or working supervisory personnel whose function is to record or expedite any step in the production process).

Table 5.16
Labour requirements in manufacturing industry

	Value added (K million)	Number of employees	Value added per employee (K)	Number of employees per K 1 million value added
1964	29.34	18492	1590	630.3
1965	53.07	26203	2030	493.7
1966	68.81	31467	2190	457.3
1967	83.27	33180	2510	398.5
1968	84.94	33299	2550	392.0
1969	95.85	36976	2590	385.8
1970	106.30	40604	2620	382.0
1971	127.14	43333	2930	340.8
1972	163.89	44479	3680	271.4
1973	184.11	47658	3860	258.9
1974	223.71	53849	4150	240.7
1975	226.59	55647	4070	245.6
1980	457.83	58153	7870	127.0

Source: Census of Industrial Production, 1972, 1973, 1974, 1975, 1980 - Central Statistical Office, Lusaka.

From these tables, the following are observed:

1. Value added per employee increased from K1,590 in 1964 to K7,870 in 1980;

2. The number of employees per K1 million value added decreased from 630.3 in 1964 to 127.0 in 1980; and

3. The capital employed per operative, deflated by the GDP deflator, rose from K10,650.5 in 1972 to K13,359.0 in 1980.

This suggests that less and less labour was required and that more and more capital was required in the production process per unit of output. Therefore, it could be argued that the production process became more and more capital-intensive and that the restrictive trade and payments regime of the period exerted an adverse impact on employment. In other words, the restrictive trade and payments regime retarded the growth of employment.

Table 5.17
Capital-labour ratio

	Capital employed per operative (Kwacha)	GDP deflator 1980 = 100	Capital employed in constant Kwacha per operative
1972	4846	45.5	10650.5
1973	5828	54.2	10752.8
1974	5643	60.3	9358.2
1975	6318	51.8	12196.9
1980	13359	100.0	13359.0

Source: Census of Industrial Production - 1972, 1973, 1974, 1975, 1980, Central Statistical Office, Lusaka.

Absence of data precludes examination of the situation following liberalisation of the economy from 1982 to 1987. However, Muchelemba (1988) points out that the trend of relatively high employment growth rates of the period from 1964 to 1974 was reversed during 1974 to 1987 period. There is thus no evidence to suggest that following liberalisation, the employment picture improved.

5.13   Conclusion

Zambia achieved better economic performance during periods when her export performance was poor; the country achieved poor economic performance when her export performance was good. In particular, the country achieved high rates of economic growth when she was pursuing an import substitution industrialisation strategy; and low or negative rates of economic growth when she was having good export performance. This suggests that economic growth and export performance had no relationship with each other and that import substitution manufacturing had some relationship with GDP. A Granger causality test between exports and GDP showed that the two did not bear any relationship. However, the same test carried out for manufacturing and GDP showed that there was a uni-directional causal relationship existed, running from manufacturing to GDP. This suggests that manufacturing was an important factor behind GDP growth. As it has been pointed out, manufacturing grew at an appreciable rate between 1964 and 1982, following the Government's measures to diversify the economy away from copper. Consequently, the share of manufacturing in total GDP rose from 6.1 percent in 1964 to 20 percent in 1982. The contribution of the mining and quarrying sector, i.e. the export sector, to GDP declined from 47.5 percent to 10.4

percent over the same period while that of the other sectors remained at more or less the same level as in 1964, or changed very little. This lends support to the Granger causality test result which suggests that manufacturing, rather than exports, was the main propelling force behind Zambia's GDP growth. Thus, import-substitution manufacturing via protection was a key factor in Zambia's growth performance. In this role, the growth of the manufacturing sector provided the dynamism for increasing productivity of the whole economy. It also provided the vital link between the primary producing sectors - agriculture and mining - and the consumer and, as pointed out in Chapter 2, helped to alter the structure of production of the economy in an important respect by laying the base for reducing the dependence on one export commodity, copper, for earning foreign exchange and by laying a foundation for the build-up of a capital and intermediate goods sector which will enable technological change necessary for the achievement of fast and self-sustaining economic growth to take place.

Liberalisation efforts implemented with a view to achieving improved export performance failed to restore growth. Instead, these measures destroyed the manufacturing sector which was an important source of the country's GDP growth. For example, the liberalisation measures stepped up inflation. This led to increased production costs and consequently to higher prices of final products which, in turn, resulted in a drop in the demand for these products. Together with increased competition from foreign products due to the import liberalisation, this threatened the survival of Zambian industries including genuine import-substitution industries.

The liberalisation measures also harmed domestic indusry including the agricultural sector. Prices of agricultural machinery and agricultural inputs went up and farmers found it very hard to raise the necessary financial resources to purchase such items and the output of the agricultural sector was therefore adversely affected. In addition, the development of small scale businesses and agriculture was thwarted by the high cost of borrowing which was brought about by the decontrol of interest rates. Many firms which had hitherto operated profitably found themselves producing at very low levels of capacity utilisation due to the fact that under the liberalised system of foreign currency auctioning, they could no longer obtain adequate foreign exchange needed for the importation of raw materials, spare parts and other intermediate inputs required in the production process. This contributed to the high cost of production and hence to the inflation which resulted in low demand for locally produced products. Furthermore, the liberalisation measures failed to boost the performance of other sectors such as savings, investment and employment creation. On the other hand, the pursuit of import substitution did not appear to have led to inefficient methods of production. The effective rate of protection and inventory holding were not significantly high.

All in all, import substitution helped the country to achieve better economic performance while trade liberalisation failed to resuscitate the economy from economic collapse and made things even worse.

Notes

1. See Zambia (1985b) for detailed country profile analysis. For more recent data, see the country profiles published in 1996.

2. Zambia (1985b) presents further data on these issues. Recent information is contained in the country profiles for 1995 and 1996.

3. See Zambia (1985b) on the climatic conditions, especially as the climate bears important implications for productivity in the agricultural sector.

4. See Zambia (1985b) for population data. The recent country profile for n1996 includes classification in skilled and unskilled labour.

5. For countries operating a licensing system for regulating imports because of foreign exchange constraints, OGL system provides a means of simplifying the rigour of an import licensing system; it avoids the delays and uncertainty connected therein and assumes the speedy availability of goods for the economy of the country. To be effective, foreign exchange availability must be assured and OGL licenses must be granted readily and as often as is required.

6. Economic Development Institute (1987), on these issues, especially on the first stage of Zambia's economic reform programme during 1982-86.

7. A detailed exposition is contained in World Bank (1984).

8. World Bank (1984) discusses the specifics of Zambia's industrial policy and performance.

9. These details were disclosed in an address, "Foreign Exchange Auctioning: How the System Works" by the ZCTU Executive Chairman during an Officials Seminar on *Trade Union Administration, Organization and Communication* at Kabwe in 1985.

10. See World Bank (1985) which reports the results of the consultative group for Zambia on progress towards economic restructuring.

11. See World Bank (1986) on Zambia's economic reforms during the early 1980s.

12. The auction system for foreign exchange was met with strong resistance among local economists; at least this was the general attitude during the Kabwe Seminar in 1985 (see endnote 9).

13. For further details see Zambia's *The Third National Development Plan*, for the period 1979-83, as in National Commission for Development Planning, (1985).

6 The experience of Malawi

6.1 Introduction

In terms of economic geography, Malawi is a small country occupying the southern part of the East African Rift Valley lying between 9 degrees and 17 degrees latitude south of the Equator and 32 degrees and 36 degrees longitude, east. It has an area of 119,140 square kilometres of which 20 percent is water. It is land-locked and bordered by Mozambique in the south east, Zambia in the west, and Tanzania in the east and north. The country exhibits wide ranges in climate, vegetation and economic activity.[1] Between the 1966 and 1977 censuses, Malawi's population grew at a rate of about 2.9 percent per annum, from a level of 4.0 million in 1966 to 5.5 million in 1977. In 1987, the total population was estimated at 7.5 million; hereafter it has growth at an annual rate of 3.2 percent. Some 11 percent of the population live in urban areas and the rest in rural areas where they depend on subsistence agriculture for their livelihood.

Malawi gained her political independence from the United Kingdom in 1964; the country became a Republic in 1966. At independence, Malawi was the poorest of the three territories of the Federation of Rhodesia and Nyasaland. Unlike Northern and Southern Rhodesia (Zambia and Zimbabwe), it possessed no significant mineral resources and, therefore, attracted little outside interest. Apart from the plantations of the southern region (mainly tea and tobacco), Malawi was largely a subsistence economy with non-monetary

185

output accounting for almost one-half of the gross domestic product. Population growth was relatively rapid and fertile land areas were already densely settled. Economic infrastructure was limited and almost entirely concentrated in the south.[2] GDP per capita was approximately US$60, half of which was accounted for by smallholder agriculture and the balance by some 100,000 in wage employment, largely on estates and in Government. Since the tax base was limited and domestic savings were virtually nil, most domestic capital formation was financed from abroad and government recurrent budget deficits were covered by U.K. grants-in-aid. Government economic and social services were limited, even by African standards. There were less than 5,000 hospital beds and the primary school system catered for less than half the relevant age group. Total secondary enrolment was only 4,000 students, about one percent of the relevant population, and total post-secondary vocational training enrolled less than 1,000 students. Only 33 Malawians had undertaken a university education.[3]

6.2   Evolution and phases of trade and payments regime

From the time of political independence to the present, Malawi may be said to have gone through three distinct phases of trade and payments regime (see Chapter 3) which are classired below according to the BK study; the years, however, are given in chronological order.

6.2.1   Phase 5 of BK: 1964-79, liberal period

From 1964 to 1979, Malawi did not impose any significant restrictions on imports, although some restrictions by origin and by commodity of import and those aimed at channelling some imports through parastatals were applied over this period.   Most commodities from Czechoslovakia, Japan, Rhodesia (Zimbabwe) and the non-contracting parties to the GATT and non-Commonwealth countries were restricted. The importation of products such as food and agricultural products, clothing, gold, sugar, wheat flour, cement, fertilizer, newsprint and paper, office equipment, knives, explosives, arms and ammunitions, game traps, wild animals, live fish, and cassava required licensing. This restriction was mainly for health and security purposes. Tariffs were, in general, low and quantitative restrictions on imports for protective or other purposes were largely avoided (Gulhati, Ravi, Swadesh and Vimal, 1985).

From 1964 to February 14, 1971, the Malawi Pound was pegged at par with British Pound Sterling, mainly as a colonial heritage. On November 14, 1967 the Pound Sterling was devalued by 14.3 percent and the Government devalued the Malawi Pound by the same amount. Malawi became a member of the Sterling Area Agreement which came into existence in 1968 under which Britain undertook to guarantee the U.S. Dollar value of reserves of Sterling Area countries on condition that they kept a certain proportion of their reserves in Sterling, in a bid to strengthen the Pound Sterling following the 1967 devaluation.

On February 15, 1971 Malawi changed to a decimal system of currency and introduced the Malawi Kwacha. The Kwacha was pegged to the Pound Sterling at MK2 = £1. Following the breakdown of the Bretton Woods system of fixed exchange rates, the United Kingdom floated the Pound Sterling. As the Pound Sterling depreciated, so did the Malawi Kwacha which became a cause of great concern to the Malawi authorities. Consequently, on November 19, 1973 the Kwacha was delinked from the Pound Sterling and pegged to a trade-weighted basket of the U.S. Dollar and the Pound Sterling. The value of the Kwacha was determined by the average of the US Dollar and the Pound Sterling as quoted daily by the Reserve Bank of Malawi. This did not help to achieve permanent stability for the Kwacha exchange rate due to the volatility of the major currencies. Thus on June 9, 1975 the Malawi Kwacha was pegged to the SDR at a rate of MK1.0541 = 1SDR. This rate was maintained until April 24, 1982.

It must be borne in mind that most countries in Africa, including Malawi, did not look upon the exchange rate as a major instrument for economic management for the most part of this period.

6.2.2   Phase 1: 1980-81, imposition of quantitative restrictions

Following economic downturn in 1979 the Malawi economy experienced, *inter alia*, balance of payments problems which led to a shortage of foreign exchange. The Reserve Bank of Malawi reacted to this situation by denying importation of certain items and allowing the importation of only those goods which it deemed essential, although the Ministry of Trade, Industry and Tourism pursued a liberal policy in the granting of import licences.

The peg of the Kwacha to the SDR at the rate of MK1.0541 = 1 SDR prevailed up to the end of this period.

6.2.3   Phase 3: 1981-87, Discrete devaluation and rationalisation with trade and import controls

While the Reserve Bank of Malawi continued with its policy of quantitative restrictions on imports through its system of foreign exchange allocation, the

Government, beginning in 1981, launched a broad-based structural adjustment programme which was aimed at restoring macro-economic stability and removing structural constraints to growth. The policy package of this programme comprised:

1. price reform and liberalisation, including agricultural price adjustments that would bring domestic producer prices in line with international prices, decontrol of most industrial prices, and gradual removal of fertilizer subsidies;

2. improved public sector resource management, including reduction of the government budget deficit, strengthening of government budgeting and planning operations, development of a rolling public sector investment programme and development of a tax reform programme;

3. external sector reforms, including exchange rate management and development of export promotion programmes;

4. parastatal reforms, including establishment of the Department of Statutory Bodies and restructuring of the Agricultural Development and Marketing Corporation (ADMARC) and the Malawi Development Corporation (MDC); and

5. restructuring of Press Holdings Ltd, a key private sector conglomerate.[4]

This reform programme was supported by three structural adjustment credits from the World Bank, with significant co-financing from the donor community, and successive stand-by arrangements and an extended facility from the IMF.

With this policy package, the government adopted an active exchange rate management policy. Noting that the Kwacha had appreciated with the SDR, the authorities devalued the Kwacha on April 24, 1982 by 15 percent against the SDR. This brought down the value of the Kwacha to MK1.2122 = 1SDR. The SDR continued to appreciate and so, too, did the Kwacha against the currencies of its major trading partners mainly because of the appreciation of the US Dollar which had a high weight in the SDR basket. Following this, the authorities again devalued the Kwacha by 12 percent on September 17, 1983. The authorities now realised that the strength of the US Dollar would make the SDR appreciate against other major currencies and along with it those currencies which were pegged to the SDR. Thus, on January 17, 1984 Malawi delinked the Kwacha from the SDR and pegged it to a weighted basket of currencies of its seven major trading partners (US Dollar, Pound Sterling, Deutschemark, Japanese Yen, South African Rand, French Franc and

Netherlands Guilder). Between then and January 1988 the Kwacha was devalued four times, by 15 percent on April 2, 1985, 10 percent on August 16, 1986, 20 percent on February 7, 1987 and 15 percent on January 17, 1988, in line with the Government's policy of flexible exchange rates.

Because Malawi pursued a liberal trade policy over a relatively long period of time, i.e. from 1964 to 1979, she had not yet passed through phases 2 and 4 by 1991.

6.3 Economic performance under the different phases of trade and payments restrictions

Table 6.1 below summarises the economic performance of the Malawi economy during the three different phases of trade and payments restrictions Malawi passed through in the period 1964 to 1987.

Table 6.1
Selected economic indicators

	1964-79 Phase 5	1980-81 Phase 1	1982-87 Phase 3
Average real GDP growth rate	5.1	-3.0	2.5
Average real growth rate of exports	4.6	0.7	-2.8
Average growth rate of manufacturing output	15.1	-3.1	4.2
Average savings ratio (as % of GDP)	9.1	11.4	13.7
Average iIncremental capital-output ratio	2.9	1.6	0.9
Average foreign exchange reserves position (in months of imports)	3.3	1.6	1.4
Average inflation rate	6.9	17.0	10.2

Source: Monthly Statistical Butlletin and National Accounts Reports - various issues by National Statistical Office; Financial and Economic Review - various issues by Reserve Bank of Malawi; and IMF (1995).

During the period 1964 to 1979, i.e. the period of liberalisation, real GDP grew at an average rate of 5.1 percent per annum. With an average population growth rate of 2.9 percent per year, real GDP per capita rose at an annual average rate of 2.2 percent over this period. Real exports (current value of exports deflated by the index of the unit value of imports) rose at an annual average growth rate of 4.6 percent. Manufacturing output rose rapidly at an average growth rate of 15.1 percent per year. Savings, as a percentage of GDP, averaged 9.1 percent. Foreign exchange reserves averaged high enough to cover imports for three months and ten days. The domestic rate of inflation, as measured by changes in the GDP deflator, averaged 6.9 percent per year. By and large, Malawi's economy performed relatively very well during this phase of liberal trade and payments regime.

In the period 1980 to 1981, the phase of the imposition of trade and payments controls, real GDP declined by 3.0 percent per year. The average growth rate of real exports decreased to 0.7 percent per annum. Manufacturing output decreased by 3.1 percent per annum, on average. Savings performance was relatively better than in Phase 5 as savings averaged 11.4 percent of GDP. The use of investment resources improved as the incremental capital-output ratio averaged 1.6 compared to 2.9 in Phase 5. Foreign exchange reserves declined to an average level that could only cover imports for one month and eighteen days. The inflation rate accelerated to an average rate of 17.0 percent. During this Phase of trade and payments controls, the economy performed relatively worse, except for savings performance and the use of investment resources.

During the period 1982 to 1987, the phase of discrete devaluations, rationalisation of economic policy but with the maintenance of quantitative restrictions, the Malawi economy performed relatively better compared to the period 1980 to 1981. Real GDP rose by 2.5 percent per annum, on average. Manufacturing output increased at an average rate of 4.2 percent per year. Savings, as a percentage of GDP, averaged 13.7 percent per year. Investment resources were used relatively more efficiently as the incremental capital - output ratio averaged 0.9. The inflation rate averaged 10.2 percent per year. However, real exports declined by 2.8 percent per annum, on average. Foreign exchange reserves fell to a level that was only high enough to finance imports for one month and twelve days.

This account of Malawi's economic performance over the three different phases that the country went through from 1964 to 1987 seems to support the thesis that economic performance is generally superior under a liberal trade regime than under a restrictive one. The question, however, is: why did the Malawi economy perform relatively poorly during the period 1980 to 1987, after doing so well in its first fifteen years of independence during which a liberal trade and payments regime was in force? Before tackling this question, it is necessary to examine the policies that were pursued, the factors that prompted the authorities to pursue those policies and how the economy performed generally against the backdrop of those policies.

6.4   Economic and trade policies: 1964-80

The declared aim of the government following political independence was to fight poverty, ignorance and disease. The economic policies to be pursued in order to wipe out these problems were spelt out in the 1965-69 Development Plan and in the Statement of Development Policies, 1971-80. The 1965-69 Development Plan and the Statement of Development Policies (DEVPOL), 1971-80 essentially contained the same development strategy. This development strategy was dictated by the pattern of economic activities among the population and by the nature and distribution of the country's economic resources. The vast majority of the population depended for its livelihood on peasant farming. Out of an economically active population of about 1.5 million, less than 150,000 were in paid employment inside the country and about 250,000 were working in neighbouring countries. Thus, over one million workers - and their dependents - derived their income solely from small scale agriculture. Land and labour were relatively plentiful but capital and high - level skills were in short supply. Moreover, there was no highly lucrative primary industry, such as copper in Zambia, which could have assisted in providing capital resources for financing development in other sectors. With a domestic market of only 3.9 million people, income growth was largely determined by the success achieved in increasing existing and developing new export cash crops. Except in very limited areas, industrial development, in particular import substitution, was not seen as offering any opportunity.

Given this situation, Malawi's development strategy sought to make maximum use of land and labour and economise on the use of capital and skills. The government was to rely on foreign capital to finance development in both the public and private sectors. The development strategy, therefore, focused primarily at developing agriculture. This involved a two-pronged attack, providing focal growth points in the forms of high-productivity projects - irrigation and settlement schemes - while attempting simultaneously to raise the general level of productivity through extension and marketing operations. Specific projects were to be sited at strategic points throughout the country and these were designed not only to achieve a high rate of direct return on the capital invested, but also to have a catalytic effect on the operations of peasant farmers in the surrounding area. The aim was to achieve self-sufficiency in food and generate enough agricultural output for export in order to earn foreign exchange. This involved the development of small scale agriculture and estate agriculture. For the small scale agriculture, the government was to undertake a number of rural development projects which were designed to increase productivity and augment cash incomes through the sale of surpluses in urban areas and export markets.

In time, concerned that intensive and costly capital investments could not be extended to the entire country quickly enough, the government developed the National Rural Development Programme (NRDP) which aimed at covering the entire agricultural sector within 20 years but with less intensive staffing and infrastructure. The NRDP emphasised increasing the productivity of land already under cultivation through the provision of agricultural services (most particularly extension, input supply, marketing and credit). The estate sector was to be developed in order to provide rural employment opportunities and generate foreign exchange earnings through the exports of tobacco, tea and sugar. This was to be done by improving the investment climate by limiting wage increases, making leasehold land available on very favourable terms and allowing considerable freedom in produce marketing.

In order to support the development of the agricultural sector by providing an outlet for marketing of agricultural produce, the development of transport was emphasized. As a result, the development of the transport infrastructure, particularly roads, was accorded priority and this took the lion's share of capital expenditure with the social sectors such as education, health and housing being tightly constrained in both capital and recurrent expenditure.

The development of manufacturing industry was, however, not ignored. The development strategy recognised that rising output in primary production would give rise to increasing opportunities for processing industries and that rising incomes derived from the sale of this output would open up the market for industries producing consumer goods and agricultural inputs. However, its emphasis on the development of small scale agriculture for food self-sufficiency and of the estate sector for export crops influenced its policies towards manufacturing as well as incomes policy. The growth of secondary industry was to be closely supervised. This was because it was believed by the authors of the development strategy that the establishment of capital-intensive industries by foreign capital would make little direct contribution to the elimination of poverty or even to aggregate domestic income, if they involved an increase in domestic prices as a result of over-protection or the closing down of existing labour - intensive Malawian enterprises such as brick-makers, carpenters and grain millers; their effect could only be to depress the standard of living of the people.

As a general rule, therefore, the development strategy ruled out the promotion of highly capital-intensive undertakings, unless their function was clearly essential and there was no choice of technology. It was thought that a high level of protective tariffs would lead to a serious rise in the prices of basic consumer commodities, which would depress real incomes and, probably, reduce the supply of agricultural products for export. The object of tariff policy was, therefore, only to provide a secure domestic market for internationally competitive producers and manufacturers and not to provide shelter for the inefficient or a stimulus to uneconomic investment. The same considerations applied in the case of supply - based industries processing local raw materials, in that these were only encouraged if they were able to pay export parity prices for their primary inputs. In this way, it was believed that industrial development would contribute to the fundamental economic objective and avoid the effect, noticeable in some other developing countries, of concentrating income in the towns at the expense of the rural areas. Thus, tariffs were, in general, low and quantitative restrictions on imports (for protective or other purposes) were largely avoided over the period 1964 to 1980.

Incomes policy took into account the distribution of income between urban and rural areas. Wage earners accounted for less than 10 percent of the economically active population. The strategy, therefore, sought to avoid the creation of a privileged position of urban wage earners by artificially inflating their incomes as such a situation would result in increased prices of manufactured goods and cause a reduction in real incomes of farmers which would act as a disincentive to increased effort in the agricultural sector and hence undermine the basic development strategy. Furthermore, the strategy sought to avoid encouraging the use of capital-intensive methods of production and also rural-urban migration. High minimum wages were not adopted in order to avoid the creation of a small privileged urban class whose consumption might become increasingly import-oriented, while leaving the total level of demand for domestic producers almost unchanged. Another consideration was the fact that the greater part of exports was made up of estate-grown crops and agricultural workers accounted for about 25 percent of total employment. It was believed that any rise in wage costs which were not related to productivity would adversely affect estate agriculture and jeopardise the chances of attaining the planned level of exports. Accordingly, a policy of adjusting wages only in response to changes in productivity and, in particular, avoiding actions which increase the income gap between urban and rural workers was adopted.

From the above description, it is quite clear that Malawi adopted an outward-looking, export-oriented development strategy based on agriculture. The economic policies which were adopted were influenced by the choice of this outward-oriented strategy.

6.5 Economic performance under export-oriented development strategy

According to DEVPOL, the main objectives of Malawi's development strategy were:

1. a rapid economic growth rate of 8 percent per annum;

2. an increase in agricultural productivity to improve rural living standards, provide employment opportunities and earn foreign exchange;

3. a better balance in economic development between the three regions, stimulated by public sector investment in the central and northern regions, in particular the relocation of the capital city from Zomba in the south to Lilongwe in the central region;

4. an increase in local participation both in semi-skilled and skilled employment and in the ownership of enterprises; and

5. elimination of dependence on foreign finance to cover government recurrent budget expenditures.

By and large, Malawi can be said to have achieved considerable success in attaining these objectives. Between 1964 and 1979, real GDP grew at an average rate of 5.1 percent per year, a respectable record even though below the planned target of 8.0 percent per annum. With a population growth rate of 2.9 percent per annum, real GDP per capita grew at an average rate of 2.2 percent per year. Foreign budgetary assistance for recurrent government expenditure was eliminated by 1972-73 and, in most succeeding years, modest recurrent surpluses were used to help to finance development expenditures. The capital city was moved to Lilongwe from Zomba in 1975. Many expatriate positions were localised. Agricultural output, particularly estate agriculture, expanded rapidly, generating employment and foreign exchange. Economic growth was widespread as all the sectors grew impressively. This is why in Table 6.2 on sectoral composition of output, it will be observed that structural shifts were not so pronounced over the period.

It is useful to note that most of the 1960s (post-independence era) and almost all the 1970s represent a period of rapid economic growth, symbolising the economic prosperity underpinned by the development strategies that were being pursued. Sectoral analysis helps to place emphasis on the intersectoral differences in economic prosperity, and any other patterns (say, similarities) that may be discerned in order to infer what arguably may be characterised as "pushing" and "pulling" sectors.

Table 6.2
Sectoral composition of GDP (%)

	1964	1968	1974	1978	1980	1982	1984	1986	1987
Agriculture, forestry and fishing	57.8	51.8	38.3	39.1	36.2	36.3	37.1	35.2	36.0
Manufacturing	8.3	11.2	11.6	11.2	11.3	12.0	12.2	11.4	11.4
Utilities	0.7	1.1	1.4	1.7	1.8	1.9	1.9	2.0	2.1
Building and construction	3.8	4.8	5.0	6.1	5.5	4.7	3.6	5.6	4.1
Distribution	8.1	9.1	14.7	13.9	14.1	12.6	12.6	12.2	12.4
Transport and communications	3.8	4.9	6.8	5.9	6.7	6.2	5.7	5.9	5.7
Financial and professional services	0.1	0.2	4.6	5.7	6.6	6.4	6.2	6.3	6.1
Ownership of dwellings	2.5	2.6	3.6	3.9	4.1	4.3	4.2	4.2	4.2
Private social services	5.4	6.0	4.4	3.6	3.7	4.1	4.2	4.1	4.2
Government	9.4	8.3	9.5	8.9	10.0	11.5	12.3	13.1	13.7
TOTAL	100.	100.	100.	100.	100.	100.	100.	100.	100.

Source: Monthly Statistical Bulletin and National Accounts Reports - various issues by National Statistical Office (Zomba); Financial and Economic Review - various issues by Reserve Bank of Malawi.

The only sector whose share in GDP declined over the period is agriculture, forestry and fishing whose share declined from 57.8 percent in 1964 to 36.2 percent in 1980. The shares of all the other sectors remained more or less constant or increased marginally. The economy also performed well in terms of investment levels, domestic savings and balance of payments. Overall, it was an economic success such that by 1979, the Malawian economy was considered by the international community as one of the few success stories in Africa.

6.6   Trade performance during economic stagnation

The economy's rapid growth ground to a halt in 1979. In 1979, the growth of real GDP decelerated to 3.3 percent from a rate of 8.3 percent in 1978. In 1980 real GDP fell by 0.7 percent and in the following year it dropped by 5.3 percent. The deterioration in production pervaded all sectors of the economy, except utilities. The sectors of agriculture, construction, manufacturing, transport and community and social services all registered declines in output. The fall in agricultural production was so large that it made it necessary to import maize in 1980-81.

Tables 6.3, 6.4, 6.5 and 6.6 show the terms of trade, the balance of payments, debt service and central government finance, respectively, during the period 1964 to 1987. of trade were on a downward trend and in 1980 they were 53 percent of their level in 1964. The trade balance was also negative throughout this period except in 1977. However, the negative trade balance was not that large but when combined with the balance on the services account, the current account balance registered high deficits which during the period 1978 to 1980 ranged from 17.8 percent to 24.0 percent of GDP. However, given the volumes of capital flows, the overall balance of payments position was positive throughout the period 1964 to 1975 except for 1966. From 1975, the overall balance of payments position began to worsen mainly because of increased deficits on the current account and the situation continued to deteriorate further until 1986, except for 1980 when a small positive balance was achieved.

The negative forces on the current account can be described as having arisen from four factors.[5] The first was the deterioration of the terms of trade. It has been stated that in 1980, the terms of trade were only 53 percent of their level in 1964, after having declined by a cumulative total of 47 percent. Owing to the importance of foreign trade in the economy, this exerted quite a significant adverse impact. Imports and exports constituted about 50 percent of GDP. Given the magnitude of the deterioration in the terms of trade, this resulted in loss of GDP equivalent to 23.5 percent between 1964 and 1980. The consequences of such a large fall in income are quite obvious and one need not enumerate them.

The second factor was the disruption in transport routes to the coast. Because of its geographical position, Malawi's traditional routes to the sea were by rail through Mozambique, one via Beira and another via Nacala. These routes carried more than 90 percent of the country's foreign trade. But these routes became unreliable due to insurgency and the deterioration of the Mozambican railway system. These routes were completely closed by 1984 and cargo had to be re-routed through the much more costly Durban route in South Africa. It cost almost seven times more to import petrol through Durban. It cost three times more to export tobacco or tea. The margin between imports fob and cif increased from the typical 16 percent to 25 percent by 1980, to 35 percent by 1982 and to over 40 percent by 1985. The additional foreign exchange cost as a result of the re-routing is estimated to amount to US$41 million in 1985; which is equivalent to 15 percent of exports of goods and services, excluding the extra cost of pilferage, spoilage and storage.

Thirdly, there was the increase in debt service payments mainly as a result of high interest payments. Malawi had borrowed substantially from abroad on a floating rate basis. Following the sharp rise in international interest rates, Malawi's scheduled interest payments to its creditors also increased considerably. Total interest payments on public debt rose from US$7 million in 1977 to US$24 million in 1979. As given by the estimates, about 11 percent of this increase was due to the rise in international interest rates.

The fourth factor was adverse weather conditions. Drought conditions in 1980 and 1981 reduced maize output considerably and imports of maize totalling 11,000 metric tons in the first year and 56,000 metric tons in the second year had to be made. The country received food aid which financed 43 percent and 30 percent of these imports, respectively, but the rest was paid for out of Malawi's foreign exchange earnings.

The combination of these four factors sent the current account of the balance of payments into large deficits which could not be offset to any significant degree by the positive balances on the capital account. The shock waves of these factors were very wide and exerted an adverse impact on the rest of the economy. However, the central government budgetary position did not weaken. The budget deficits from 1978 to 1986 were not larger than those during the period 1964 to 1977. For the period 1964 to 1977, budget deficits averaged 3.5 percent of GDP; whereas from 1978 to 1986 these averaged 2.7 percent of GDP.

Table 6.3
Terms of trade (1980 = 100)

	Unit values		Terms of trade
	Imports	**Exports**	
1964	29.9	39.4	131.8
1965	24.1	41.4	171.8
1966	24.9	40.1	161.0
1967	24.8	37.9	152.8
1968	26.5	42.2	159.2
1969	26.9	44.2	164.3
1970	26.6	47.0	176.7
1971	28.3	51.1	180.6
1972	29.5	48.7	165.1
1973	34.3	54.4	158.6
1974	46.4	69.1	148.9
1975	56.4	81.0	143.6
1976	64.5	90.5	140.3
1977	71.7	119.3	166.4
1978	72.1	107.3	148.8
1979	82.1	96.7	117.8
1980	100.0	100.0	100.0
1981	115.1	140.0	121.6
1982	124.4	153.5	123.4
1983	138.4	156.8	113.3
1984	164.2	193.9	118.1
1985	173.7	175.1	100.8
1986	223.2	195.9	87.8
1987	342.4	238.9	69:8

Source: IMF (1986) Financial and Economic Review, Volume XX - No. 1, 1988, Reserve Bank of Malawi; and Monthly Statistical Bulletin December 1975 and March 1988, National Statistical Office.

In order to overcome the economic problems, the Malawi government initiated from 1979 a number of short-term demand management measures which culminated in a standby arrangement with the IMF for the period from mid-1979 to 31 December 1981. However, transport dislocations at the end of 1979 led to the replacement of this arrangement with a new two-year standby arrangement covering the period 1 April 1980 to 31 March 1982 (drawing on the second through the fourth credit tranches and the supplementary financing facility for US $64.8 million).

Table 6.4
Balance of payments (Kwacha million)

	Trade balance	Current account balance	Overall balance
1964	-4.2	+1.5	+2.6
1965	-12.4	+2.2	+6.2
1966	-19.5	-17.1	-4.0
1967	-9.7	-9.7	+5.7
1968	-17.0	-21.0	0.0
1969	-17.0	-22.4	+2.8
1970	-18.7	-27.3	+6.8
1971	-16.0	-26.4	+2.6
1972	-24.8	-37.8	+1.1
1973	-19.2	-21.7	+23.9
1974	-37.7	-34.4	+29.0
1975	-71.0	-73.2	-11.6
1976	-14.5	-64.2	-56.6
1977	+15.1	-51.7	+35.1
1978	-68.5	-142.5	-19.8
1979	-71.7	-205.8	-71.2
1980	-27.4	-208.2	+6.6
1981	+26.7	-119.5	-34.9
1982	+46.6	-131.1	-66.4
1983	+37.8	-169.4	-123.5
1984	+211.8	-29.0	-52.2
1985	+134.2	-116.2	-116.4
1986	+175.3	-141.6	-115.0
1987	+218.5	-118.2	+35.6

Source: World Bank.(1982); Malawi: Growth and Structural Change - A Basic Economic Report. Washington, D.C.; and Economic and Financial Review, Vol.xx, No.1, 1988 and Vol. xviii; No.4, 1986 issued by Reserve Bank of Malawi.

The government's fiscal and financial austerity programme consisted of restraints on the expansion of recurrent and development account expenditures, measures to increase revenue (by raising excise and import duties) and increases in interest rates. The Government was also required to curb domestic credit and government borrowing of one to twelve year's maturity from both domestic and external sources.[6]

However, these measures did not seem to bear fruit as the economic situation continued to worsen. From 1981 the Government, therefore, launched a broad-based structural adjustment programme aimed at restoring macro-economic stability and removing structural constraints.[7] This programme was supported by three structural adjustment loans from the World Bank and successive stand-by arrangements with the IMF, and external debt rescheduling in 1982 and 1983. The adjustment package consisted of the following:

1. price rationalisation and liberalisation (including the use of agricultural prices to increase incentives to smallholder farmers), decontrol of most industrial prices, gradual removal of fertilizer subsidies and introduction of tariffs based on long-run marginal costs in public utilities;

2. improved public sector resource mobilisation and management, including strengthening of government budgeting and planning operations, development of a rolling public sector investment programme and development of a tax reform programme;

3. rationalisation of external sector policies, including active exchange rate management; and

4. restructuring of the parastatal sector, including parastatal divestiture and reorganisation, and introduction of a multi-channel marketing system for most agricultural commodities.

These measures appear to have brought about only limited results, and this only for a time. From 1982 to 1985 Malawi resumed growth and real GDP grew by 3.0 percent in 1982, 3.6 percent in 1983, 3.3 percent in 1984 and 2.8 percent in 1985. In 1986, real GDP fell by 0.3 percent, but in 1987 real GDP increase by 2.3 percent.

The terms of trade which had improved in 1981 and 1982 deteriorated considerably so that by 1987 they were only 37 percent of their level in 1964 or only 59 percent of their level in 1979. The balance of payments worsened so that by end-1986, international reserves were virtually depleted and Malawi accumulated external trade areas equivalent to 6 percent of GDP, although the current account deficit fell to 10.8 percent of GDP in 1981 and continued on the downward trend up to 1987 when it declined to 4.1 per cent of GDP. The central government financial situation did not improve and in 1985 the budget deficit rose to 5.4 percent of GDP from 0.8 percent in 1984. The rate of inflation was disturbingly high at 14.2 percent per annum.

Table 6.5
Debt service (Kwacha million)

	Loan repayments	Interest payments	Total	Total debt service as % of total export earnings
1964	4.4	2.1	6.5	26.6
1965	2.4	2.2	4.6	16.1
1966	1.7	2.2	3.9	11.3
1967	1.5	2.5	4.0	9.9
1968	1.5	2.5	4.0	10.0
1969	1.6	4.6	6.1	13.9
1970	1.7	5.1	6.8	13.7
1971	2.7	5.4	8.1	13.7
1972	3.3	6.6	9.9	15.3
1973	7.0	3.5	10.5	13.1
1974	9.3	4.6	13.9	13.7
1975	9.7	4.8	14.5	11.9
1976	7.0	8.7	15.7	10.4
1977	6.4	10.9	17.3	9.6
1978	6.0	14.3	20.3	13.0
1979	16.4	20.2	36.6	20.1
1980	24.0	33.0	57.0	24.7
1981	41.2	51.9	93.1	36.2
1982	17.8	59.8	77.6	30.3
1983	26.2	55.9	82.2	30.3
1984	52.0	105.6	157.6	35.8
1985	77.6	114.2	191.8	44.6
1986	88.8	119.4	208.2	45.1

Source: Public Sector Financial Statistics, 1973 and 1976 (Ministry of Finance); Economic Report 1986 (Office of the President and Cabinet - Economic Planning and Development).

Table 6.6
Central government finance (Kwacha million)

	Total revenue	Total expenditure	Balance surplus(+) deficit(-)	Deficit as % of GDP
1964	33.7	36.4	-2.7	1.8
1965	40.7	41.7	-1.0	0.6
1966	35.0	48.3	-13.3	6.5
1967	38.9	49.0	-10.1	4.4
1968	40.3	54.3	-14.0	6.2
1969	52.4	73.7	-21.3	8.7
1970	83.7	78.6	5.1	-
1971	76.9	78.5	-1.6	0.5
1972	86.7	84.1	2.6	-
1973	96.3	95.5	0.8	-
1974	100.5	105.4	-4.9	1.1
1975	145.9	137.0	8.9	-
1976	144.8	150.7	-5.9	1.0
1977	154.0	150.7	3.8	-
1978	243.7	248.5	-4.8	0.6
1979	287.1	285.1	2.6	-
1980	306.3	335.2	-28.9	2.9
1981	303.8	368.0	-64.2	5.8
1982	353.0	358.8	-5.8	0.5
1983	387.9	445.0	-57.1	4.0
1984	491.7	493.1	-1.4	0.8
1985	551.0	661.2	-109.4	5.4
1986	681.9	718.8	-36.9	1.6

Source: Monthly Statistical Bulletin, December 1985 and March 1988; and IMF (1995).

As a consequence of these unfavourable developments, and despite the achievements of the first fifteen years of her independence, Malawi remains a very poor country. With a per capita income of US$160 as at 1988, Malawi is one of the 10 poorest nations in the world. About 90 percent of the population still live in rural areas. It has one of the highest child mortality rates in Africa. One child in three dies before the age of five. Life expectancy at birth of 45 years is one of the lowest. School enrolment as a proportion of the relevant age group is still among the lowest, specially at the secondary school and tertiary levels. The literacy rate is among the lowest.

The food self-sufficiency which was achieved quite early after independence no longer seems to be a permanent feature of the economy. This is the situation now facing Malawi, despite having pursued an export-oriented strategy and religiously implemented IMF stabilisation and World Bank structural adjustment programmes for quite a long time. The World Bank attributed Malawi's failure to achieve sustained economic growth to bad luck![8]

From this account of events, one is compelled to ask the questions: what went wrong after doing so well during the first fifteen years of independence when a liberal trade and payments regime was pursued throughout the period? Why did the institution of policy reform measures from 1980 to 1987 which were intended to remove structural constraints to growth not result in lasting restoration of the economy into viability once again?

On the basis of the above discussion, we carried out an econometric test of the export-led growth hypothesis. The analysis in Chapter 4 has suggested that exports and economic growth bear no relationship to each other in the case of Malawi, yet the Malawi authorities pursued an export-led growth strategy. In the event, the development of other economic sectors which would have made an important contribution to economic growth were not given the attention they ought to have received. One such sector is manufacturing. Although it accounted for a small proportion of the GDP, the Granger causality test suggests that the growth of manufacturing led to the growth of GDP. Yet the development of this sector was not given the attention it deserved and instead much more attention was given to the development of exports which had no relationship with the growth of GDP. This partly explains why liberalisation of the economy which was intended to restore economic growth through increased exports only achieved limited results.

The Granger causality test between the growth of GDP and the growth of manufacturing gave the following results:

$$Y_t = -0.126 \ Y_{t-1} + \ 0.193 \ X_{t-1} + 2.05$$
$$\quad \ (-0.786) \qquad (4.164)$$

At_{19} = 2.861 at 1 percent.
= 2.093 at 5 percent.
= 1.729 at 10 percent.
$t_{(b)}$ = 4.164, significant at 1 percent level.
$Ho:d_j$ = 0 is rejected.

This implies that X causes Y or that the growth of manufacturing activity causes the growth of GDP.

F(2, 19) Crit Val = 3.52.

F(2, 19) = 8.22 is significant.

Scaled residuals.

Sample size	= 22.
Mean	= 0.000
Std devn	= 1.023
Skewness	= -0.266
Excess kurtosis	= 0.283
CHI²(2)	= 0.302
DW	= 2.28

$$X_t = -0.031\ X_{t-1} - 0.054\ Y_{t-1} + 10.58$$
$$(-0.147) \qquad (-0.072)$$

$t_{(b)}$ = -0.054, not significant.

$Ho{:}b_j$ = 0 is accepted.

This implies that Y does not cause X or that GDP growth does not cause the growth of manufacturing.

Taking the two equations together, the causality is uni-directional, running from manufacturing to GDP. Since the associated F-test is significant, this suggests that manufacturing is an important causal factor to growth. Therefore, economic development policy should give more attention to the development of this sector. It is, therefore, unfortunate that the Malawi authorities did not accord this sector much priority in the country's development strategy.

However, growth factors must prevail, as stated in the 1965-69 Development Plan and DEVPOL 1971-80 and 1980-90, one of the declared objectives of the Malawi government is the achievement of a high standard of living for the masses. Given this, it is necessary to examine the extent to which the trade regime helped the Government in achieving this cardinal objective.

Table 6.7 contains GDP at current prices, GDP at 1980 prices, population and real GDP per capita at 1980 prices for the period 1964 to 1987. It will be observed from this table that there was no steady growth of real GDP per capita over this period. Real GDP per capita declined in ten of the years. In three of the years, real GDP per capita did not change. There was growth in real GDP per capita in ten of the years. Overall, the performance was not that impressive. In 1987, after 23 years of independence, real GDP per capita was only K19 above the 1964 level or only 15 percent higher than the 1964 real GDP per capita. In other words, real GDP per capita grew by an average rate of only 0.6 percent per year between 1964 and 1987. This result appears to suggest that the liberal trade and payments regime did not help that much in promoting the declared objective of the government, namely to raise the standard of living of the masses.

It is useful, at this point, to relate our econometric results to recent studies in the literature. Mulaga and Weiss (1996) shed further light on the relationship between trade regime and economic growth in Malawi. The pre-reform trade regime is shown to be characterized by controls over imports, foreign exchange allocation, and import tariffs. For the post-reform period, 1970-91, a cross-section regression model is used to test for a relationship at the firm level between increased trade policy reform, as reflected in a decline in the effective rate of protection (ERP), and improved performance of manufacturing firms, measured as a rise in total factor productivity growth (TFP). Forty firms are used, thus representing 85 percent of large-scale manufacturing in Malawi. TFP is measured in the conventional way as follows:

$$TFP = q - (al + bk) \tag{6.1}$$

where q = growth of valued-added in real terms; l - the growth of labour inputs; k = the growth of capital inputs; a and b are shares of factor input costs. Variants of equation (1) are derived and tested. The ERP is measured in the standard manner as follows:

$$ERP_i = \left[t_i - \left(a_{ij} \right)\left(t_j \right) \right] / \left(1 - a_{ij} \right) \tag{6.2}$$

where t_i = the rate of tariff or tariff equivalent on output i; a_{ij} = the share of input j in the value of output i at world prices. The relationship between domestic factory level prices and world prices for commodity i is computed as follows:

$$WP_i = DP_i / (1+t)(1+s) \tag{6.3}$$

Where WP_i = the "cost, insurance, freight" price of i at the Malawi border; DP_i = the domestic ex-factory price; t = the rate of import duty; and s = the rate of import surcharge.

Table 6.7
GDP, population and real GDP per capita

	GDP at current prices (K Mil.)	GDP at 1980 prices (K Mil.)	Population (Mil.)	Real GDP per capita at 1980 prices	% Change
1964	153.4	482.5	3.80	127	n.a
1965	180.2	492.6	3.91	126	-0.8
1966	204.4	541.2	4.02	135	7.1
1967	215.5	571.7	4.12	139	3.0
1968	225.4	570.7	4.23	135	-2.9
1969	244.4	607.1	4.33	140	3.7
1970	267.1	616.2	4.44	139	-0.7
1971	334.9	704.7	4.55	155	11.5
1972	359.1	705.9	4.67	151	-2.6
1973	364.0	717.0	4.79	149	-1.3
1974	461.5	770.4	5.10	151	1.3
1975	529.7	812.9	5.24	155	2.6
1976	612.0	863.6	5.37	161	3.9
1977	728.0	901.0	5.54	163	1.2
1978	800.7	975.9	5.68	172	5.5
1979	857.3	1008.4	5.86	172	0.0
1980	1001.3	1001.3	6.05	165	-4.1
1981	1108.1	948.7	6.23	152	-7.9
1982	1245.1	977.0	6.41	152	0.0
1983	1436.9	1012.1	6.62	153	0.7
1984	1708.5	1045.7	6.84	153	0.0
1985	2023.1	1075.4	7.06	152	-0.7
1986	2301.1	1072.5	7.28	147	-3.3
1987	2865.7	1096.8	7.51	146	-0.7

Source: IMF International Financial Statistics Yearbook 1986 and Financial and Economic Review, Reserve Bank of Malawi, Volume XVIII - No. 4, 1986.

Table 6.8

Manufacturing growth: value-added TFP (% per annum)

Branch	Period 1 (1970-91)		Period 2 (1970-79)		Period 3 (1980-86)		Period 4 (1987-91)	
	VA	TFP	VA	TFP	VA	TFP	VA	TFP
Food products	7.4	3.0	13.5	3.7	1.8	4.6	-4.0	-2.1
Tea manufacturers	4.0	0.2	3.2	-1.0	1.7	-0.1	11.3	6.0
Beverages	8.5	3.6	11.9	5.4	3.5	1.0	5.9	4.5
Tobacco products	11.3	5.1	15.8	9.7	4.9	-3.8	7.6	6.0
Textiles	5.2	-2.3	8.4	-2.6	0.8	-2.8	2.4	-0.6
Leather/footwear	4.4	2.4	6.6	3.3	-0.2	-0.1	4.3	4.2
Wood/paper	3.5	-2.0	8.0	-0.2	-5.8	-6.9	9.7	5.0
Chemical products	5.3	1.4	7.0	2.1	4.1	2.6	1.9	-3.9
Plastic products	10.9	3.4	11.7	0.9	9.7	8.0	10.7	2.5
Metal products	3.7	0.2	2.4	-3.1	3.8	2.8	8.4	8.3
All manufacturing	6.9	1.8	10.1	2.2	2.1	0.7	4.8	2.6

Source: Mulaga and Weiss (1996, p.1272) Table 1.

In terms of exports, the equivalent measure is given by:

$$WP_x = DP_x / (1-t) \tag{6.4}$$

where WP_x = the "free-on-board" price of export x. The link between trade reform and productivity efficiency for the sample of 40 manufacturing firms is thus captured using the following equation:

$$TFP = f(VA, KL, PCM, ERP) \quad f_1, f_2 \rangle 0; \ f_3, f_4 \langle 0 \tag{6.5}$$

where VA = real value-added; KL = capital-labour ratio; and PCM = price-cost margin. The results for value-added and *TFP* are presented in Table 6.8 for four sample periods.

In Table 6.8, period 1 (1970-91) covers the entire sample period; period 2 (1970-79) covers the outward-looking trade regime period; period 3 (1980-86) covers the inward-looking trade-regime period; and period 4 (1987-91) covers the return to an outward-looking trade regime. The results are not entirely conclusive in terms of identifying a trade regime that is directly associated with higher performance in the manufacturing sector of Malawi. The results show that during the outward-looking trade regimes (periods 2 and 4), TFP was negative for tea manufacturers, textiles, wood/paper, metal products, food products, and chemical products. Value-added only fell in the food products branch of manufacturing. Overall, therefore, we cannot conclude that the outward-looking trade regimes in Malawi were associated with growth in the manufacturing sector. Nor do the inward-looking trade regimes offer more conclusive results. TFP was negative for tea-manufactures, tobacco products, textiles, leather and footwear, and wood and paper manufacturing branches. Value-added was negative for the leather and footwear, and wood and paper manufacturing branches.

However, the estimation results for equation (6.5) yield statistically significant results which show that the ERP is negatively associated with TFP; the estimated coefficient is -0.185 in the regression and -0.182 in another. These results suggest that with a fall in the ERP, more foreign exchange is made available in order to enable manufacturing firms to increase their working capacity. This conclusion, though, cannot be taken wholeheartedly given that Table 6.8 indicates that three manufacturing branches (food products, textiles, and chemical products) show negative TFP and one manufacturing branch (food products) show negative value-added, during the period that corresponds to the regression equation results.

It is useful to interpret the findings of Mulaga and Weiss (1996) alongside those of Siggel (1996) on Mexico. Like the former, the latter study investigates manufacturing sector performance under subsequent trade policy regimes. The relationship between growth and various trade regimes is analayzed by decomposing output growth in components attributable to its demand sources. Value-added growth is thus decomposed into four sources, namely growth in domestic demand (*ΔD*) based on constant conditions in the degree of import penetration (*1-μ*) and the value-added/output ratio (*r*); the growth of export demand (*ΔX*); import substitution (*Δμ*, where *μ* = ratio of output to total supply, *S*); and the change in the structure of production (*Δr*):

$$\Delta VA = \mu_1 r_1 \Delta D + \mu_1 r_1 \Delta X + r_1 S_2 \Delta \mu + \mu_2 S_2 \Delta r \qquad (6.6)$$

Where *ΔVA* = value-added growth in the manufacturing sector. The results of the sub-periods for Mexico, obtained by Siggel (1996), are reported in Table 6.9 below. Specifically, the table shows demand sources of growth of value-added in millions of 1980 pesos and in percentage, for Mexico for four sub-periods: 1961-71; 1971-81; 1981-85; and 1985-91.

Table 6.9
Demand sources of value-added growth for Mexico
(millions of 1980 pesos and in percentages)

Period	$\Delta VA/$ VA $(\%)$	ΔVA	$\Delta D.\mu_1.r_1$	$\Delta X.\mu_1.r_1$	$\Delta\mu.r_1.S_1$	$\Delta r.\mu_2.S_2$
1961-71	8.2	60,764 (100%)	52,504 (86.4%)	1,002 (1.6%)	5,252 (8.6%)	2,006 (3.3%)
1971-81	6.9	105,526 (100%)	109,598 (103.9%)	1,907 (1.8%)	-10.131 (-9.6%)	4,151 (3.98%)
1981-85	0.1	781 (100%)	-16,970 (-2172.9%)	3,496 (447.7%)	16,675 (2135.0%)	-2,420 (-309.8%)
1985-91	3.5	207,103 (100%)	217,042 (104.8%)	60,527 (29.2%)	-142,119 (-68.6%)	71,652 (34.6%)

Note: Growth rates of value-added (*VA*) in the first column are annual period averages. *ΔVA*, *ΔD*, *ΔX*, *Δμ* and *Δr* refer to the change of the respective variable from the beginning to the end of each period.
Source: Siggel (1996: p.5421) Table 1.

Overall, the results suggest that manufacturing growth is largely influenced by domestic demand (column 4 for ΔD). During the trade policy reform era, however, foreign demand started to play an important role (column 5 for ΔX); this result reflects the effectws of trade policy reform, and is consistent with the regression results of Mulaga and Weiss (1996).

6.7 Saving and investment performance

This section examines the effect the open trade and payments regime had on the factors directly influencing economic growth. Table 6.10 shows savings, gross fixed capital formation (GFCF), import surplus, stocks, incremental capital-output ratio and the discount rate for the period 1964 to 1987. It will be observed that the import surplus was negative in only two years, i.e. 1977 and 1984. Thus, for the greater part, Malawi imported more than she exported, thereby making it possible for her economy to have adequate supply of resources for domestic use. This partly explains the relatively good savings performance, especially from 1969 to 1987 which saw the savings rate rising to a peak of 20.5 percent of GDP in 1978. Hence, the growth of exports cannot be said to have been behind the good savings performance.

Another phenomenon which requires examination is the structure of protection provided to domestic industry. It has been pointed out in the section on the Development Strategy that the object of tariff policy was only to provide a secure domestic market for internationally competitive producers and manufacturers and not to provide shelter for the inefficient or a stimulus to uneconomic investment. Given this policy stance, it is necessary to examine whether the effective rate of tariff protection was so low that it did not have a significant resource pull away from efficient sectors to inefficient ones. Unfortunately, it is not possible to estimate the rates of effective protection accorded to the domestic industries due to lack of necessary disaggregated data such as would be found in an input-output table which Malawi does not yet have. However, a qualitative indication of the effective protection enjoyed by Malawian industries has been obtained. The United Nations Industrial Development Organisation (UNIDO) report on Malawi *(Industrial Development Review Series, 19 October 1987)* states that the two main features of financial performance of Malawian manufacturing industries are the relatively low value added to gross output ratio, on the one hand, and the relatively high gross profit to value added ratio, on the other (see Table 6.11). This suggests that the effective rate of protection accorded to Malawian industries was significantly important, contrary to the government's objective.

Table 6.10

Savings, gross fixed capital formation, import surplus, stocks (Kwacha million), incremental capital-output ratio and discount rate

	Savings	GFCF	Import surplus	Stocks	ICOR	Discount rate
1964	-5.7	13.2	0.4	-1.2	0.31	4.5
1965	-0.4	19.3	7.6	5.8	0.72	4.5
1966	2.3	29.4	12.6	6.0	1.21	4.5
1967	1.8	25.4	1.9	4.0	2.29	4.5
1968	-0.8	37.4	9.1	-0.7	3.78	5.5
1969	7.4	47.7	8.6	-2.2	2.51	5.5
1970	29.5	61.1	22.0	8.5	2.69	6.0
1971	28.1	54.4	17.1	10.6	0.80	6.0
1972	40.2	72.4	23.5	16.4	2.99	6.0
1973	45.2	74.3	14.1	7.2	15.16	6.0
1974	75.6	87.3	31.5	41.0	0.90	6.0
1975	89.8	131.8	63.3	48.6	1.93	6.0
1976	109.1	135.3	2.9	10.9	1.64	7.0
1977	146.0	161.6	-8.6	18.0	1.39	7.0
1978	164.3	247.1	115.8	60.7	3.40	7.0
1979	90.7	231.9	124.3	11.4	4.10	8.0
1980	108.3	223.1	107.6	25.6	1.55	10.0
1981	131.0	167.8	29.0	27.5	1.57	10.0
1982	186.3	181.7	43.0	84.9	1.32	10.0
1983	230.7	197.3	65.6	130.3	1.03	10.0
1984	249.9	222.7	-96.9	23.8	0.82	10.0
1985	263.9	159.5	38.7	27.7	0.82	11.0
1986	216.1	242.9	15.9	-21.6*	0.87	11.0
1987	337.5	291.2	5.2	34.4*	0.52	14.0

Source: IMF International Financial Statistics Yearbook 1986, and IFS September 1988.

*Provisional - Financial and Economic Review, Volume XVIII No. 4, 1986 and Volume XX No. 1, 1988, Reserve Bank of Malawi; ICOR = incremental capital-output ratio.

6.8   Other responses to the trade and payments regime

It has been pointed out that overbuilding of plant, low capacity utilisation, excessive inventories and limited technical progress are cited as common problems associated with a control system. Since Malawi pursued an open trade and payments regime, there is need to examine whether such problems did not arise. It would have been interesting to look at capacity utilisation rates of Malawian industries. Unfortunately, absence of data makes it impossible for us to do so. However, a look at inventory accumulation enables examination of the question as to whether there was no relationship between inventory building and the trade and payments regime.

Since a restrictive trade regime would normally be expected to be associated with a rising level of inventory accumulation, as a percentage of GDP, the level of inventory holding as a percentage of GDP for each year during the period 1964 to 1987 has been worked out. The results are shown in Table 6.12 below. It will be observed that during the period 1964 to 1979, i.e. the liberal trade period, the trend of inventory holding, as a percentage of GDP, was generally upwards.

During the period of QRs, 1980 to 1981, inventory holding was more or less constant and from 1982 to 1987, the period of QRs with discrete devaluations, the trend was downwards. This seems to suggest that the liberal trade regime contributed to inventory building while QRs had the effect of running down inventory holdings, contrary to expectation.

6.9   Employment effects

This section examines the effect the liberal trade and payments regime had on employment. In analysing this effect, the same methodology used for Zambia has been employed because of the same reasons.   This focuses on manufacturing industry. The data is available from 1970 to 1981.

Between 1970 and 1981, manufacturing accounted for 12.2 percent of formal sector employment. Agriculture, forestry and fishing contributed 38.6 percent; mining and quarrying 0.3 percent; electricity and water 1.1 percent; building and construction 9.9 percent; and the tertiary sector 37.9 percent.

The employment ratios, namely value added per employee, employees per K1 million value added and capital employed per employee are contained in Tables 6.13 and 6.14. The following are observed from these tables:

1. Value added per employee increased from K1074.1 in 1970 to K3927.3 in 1981;

2. The number of employees per K1 million value added decreased from 931 in 1970 to 254.6 in 1981; and

3. Capital employed in constant Kwacha per employee decreased from K4.887.8 in 1970 to K3,284.4 in 1981.

Table 6.11
Share of value-added in gross output and ratio of gross profit to value-added (in percent)

	Share of value-added in gross output		ratio of gross profit to value-added	
	1975	1983	1975	1983
Beverages	21.8	22.4	71.5	76.6
Tobacco	13.2	20.5	33.9	15.4
Textiles	25.4	37.9	56.9	63.7
Wearing apparel (except footwear)	24.9	28.4	58.4	51.8
Wood products (except furniture)	43.5	52.0	61.5	62.2
Furniture (except metal)	16.8	27.7	48.2	54.1
Paper and paper products	18.3	26.5	73.0	82.6
Industrial chemicals Other chemicals	10.9	16.9	85.0	77.8
Rubber products	19.2	24.1	63.0	69.1
Plastic products	20.8	42.0	52.3	72.6
Fabricated Metal products	40.6	35.4	81.9	71.2
Machinery, electrical Transport equipment	27.4	35.2	69.4	60.6
	33.2	16.5	57.0	31.1
	32.3	18.6	71.3	26.6

Source: Table 7, page 20; Industrial Development Review Series Malawi: UNIDO, 19 October 1987.

Table 6.12
Inventory holding as a percentage of GDP

	Inventory (K Mil.)	GDP at current prices	Inventory as % of GDP
1964	-1.2	153.4	-0.8
1965	5.8	180.2	3.2
1966	6.0	204.4	2.9
1967	4.0	215.5	1.9
1968	-0.7	225.4	-0.3
1969	-2.2	244.4	-0.9
1970	8.5	267.1	3.2
1971	10.6	334.9	3.2
1972	16.4	359.1	4.6
1973	7.2	364.0	2.0
1974	41.0	461.5	8.9
1975	48.6	529.7	9.2
1976	10.9	612.0	1.8
1977	18.0	728.0	2.5
1978	60.7	800.7	7.6
1979	11.4	857.3	1.3
1980	25.6	1001.3	2.6
1981	27.5	1108.1	2.5
1982	84.9	1245.1	6.8
1983	130.3	1436.9	9.1
1984	23.8	1708.5	1.4
1985	27.7	2023.1	1.4
1986	-21.6	2301.1	-0.9
1987	34.4	2865.7	1.2

The first two phenomena suggest that the production process became more and more capital-intensive while the last phenomenon suggests that the production process became more and more labour-intensive. Given this contradictory situation, no argument can plausibly be made one way or the other. Therefore, it is not clear how the open trade and payments regime affected employment.

Table 6.13

Labour requirements in manufacturing industry

	Value added (K mil.)	Number of employees	Value added per employee (K)	Number of employees per million value added
1970	20.3	18900	1074.1	931.0
1971	22.8	21100	1080.6	925.4
1972	25.5	24200	1053.7	949.0
1973	23.6	24000	1663.8	1016.9
1974	32.2	26000	1784.1	807.5
1975	40.6	28100	2055.5	692.1
1976	47.0	30200	1813.7	642.6
1977	48.8	31700	1764.2	649.6
1978	59.7	33300	1790.7	557.8
1979	65.3	35900	1785.2	549.8
1980	99.5	39000	2551.3	392.0
1981	135.1	34400	3927.3	254.6

Source: Annual Economic Survey, 1973-79 and 1980-81; May 1983 and June 1985, National Statistical Office, Zomba.

Note: K denotes Zambian Kwacha.

Table 6.14
Capital-labour ratio

	Capital employed per employee (K)	Capital employed GDP deflator (1980 = 100)	in constant Kwacha per employee (K)
1970	2,116.4	43.3	4,887.8
1971	1,919.4	47.5	4,040.8
1972	1,983.5	50.9	3,896.9
1973	4,042.6	50.8	7,957.9
1974	3,331.8	59.9	5,562.3
1975	3,209.6	65.2	4,922.7
1976	3,001.9	70.9	4,234.0
1977	2,994.1	80.8	3,705.6
1978	2,907.4	82.0	3,545.6
1979	2,839.2	85.0	3,340.2
1980	3,143.9	100.0	3,143.6
1981	3,819.8	116.3	3,284.4

Source: Annual Economic Survey, 1973-79 and 1980-81; May 1983 and June 1985, National Statistical Office, Zomba.

6.10   Conclusion

Malawi pursued an open and liberal trade regime and experienced good economic performance in the period 1964 to 1979, which seems to support the thesis that an outward-oriented strategy leads to superior economic performance. However, from 1980 to 1987, the Malawi economy experienced economic downturn. This economic downturn which pervaded all the sectors of the economy, with the exception of the utilities sector, largely emanated from unfavourable developments in the external economic environment, namely, deterioration of the terms of trade, disruption to transport routes carrying the country's imports and exports outside its borders, high debt service payments due to rising interest rates, and adverse weather conditions that considerably reduced agricultural output. Liberalisation measures aimed at opening up the economy even more failed to reverse the process of economic decline which had been set in motion by these unfavourable developments, but instead served to aggravate the situation.

This is because the country lacked a significant industrial or, more specifically, manufacturing sector which would have provided the dynamism for increasing productivity and for sustaining the process of economic growth, once it had been achieved. The virtual absence of this vital sector means that no technological dynamism, through a continual increase in specialisation and the subdivision of productive processes and generation of both static and dynamic economies, was imparted to the economy as a whole. In particular, the economy lacked the existence of a capital and intermediate goods sector necessary for dynamic economies and technological change. Its absence implies that the economy was deprived of a sector which has the potential to expand by feeding upon itself through the growth of demand for its own output and thereby able to provide both the incentives and the means for its own expansion.

The existence of a capital and intermediate goods sector would also have acted as a propelling force pushing the growth of the rest of the sectors and also as a stabilising factor in the event of adverse developments in the external economic environment. In addition, the absence of a significant manufacturing sector means that no linkage was provided between the primary producing sector and the consumer. In short, the absence of a significant industrial sector means that the structure of production of the economy was not transformed from its basic agricultural state and this explains why measures to liberalise the economy even further failed to restore economic growth and why the country still remains among the six poorest countries of the world.

The authorities pursued an export-led development strategy in the belief that exports would play a key role in the growth of the country's GDP. But, as shown by the Granger causality test, exports bear no significant relationship to GDP. This suggests that a lot of development effort and resources were devoted to the development of a sector which could not make much difference to the country's GDP growth. Unfortunately, the development of other sectors, such as manufacturing, which could have made a significant contribution to the growth of the country's GDP were relatively ignored. The Granger causality test carried out between GDP growth of manufacturing suggests that the latter is an important causal factor in GDP growth. However, little attention was paid to the development of this sector which is an important source of growth. Instead, too much attention was devoted to the development of the export sector which has no causal relationship with GDP. This partly explains why further liberalisation of the economy with a view to achieving improved export performance failed to restore economic growth.

The evidence does not suggest that the outward-orientation strategy which the country pursued fostered efficiency on the operation of the economy as a whole. Effective rates of protection appear to have been significant, inventory holding was on an upward trend, and there was no significant difference made to the creation of greater employment opportunities.

In conclusion, the country's economy did well from 1964 to 1979 under export orientation but met with difficulties from 1980 and efforts to liberalise the trade regime failed to restore economic growth partly because exports had no causal relationship with GDP.

Notes

1. For further details, see Economic Planning Division (1981) which details the problems and prospects at the start of the 1980s.

2. The development policies for the period 1971-80 are contained in the Economic Planning Division (1981).

3. A debate in economic reforms in contained in Economic Planning Division (1981). Zomba.

4. See World Bank (1988) for the report to the consultative group for Malawi on the government's medium-term development progam.

5. See World Bank (1988) which describes the promising reforms as well as the bad luck for Malawi.

6. See World Bank (1985) on the resource and policy needs for Malawi's recovery.

7. See World Bank (1988). Report to the Consultative Group for Malawi on the Government's Medium-Term Development Progam. Washington, D.C.

8. World Bank (1988) presents a detailed case study on the issues.

7 Summary and concluding remarks

7.1 Summary

In Chapter 1 the subject of the study, namely, the relationship between trade regime and economic growth was set out. The main analytical methodology for the study was also laid out. In the second chapter, the factors that led a number of developing countries to adopt import-substitution strategies of development and how such strategies eventually turned out as failures in some countries were reviewed. Also reviewed were issues relating to the apparent success of some countries which switched over to export-promotion and the arguments commonly thought to have been behind the success of the outward-oriented strategies. Furthermore, the theoretical and practical arguments for and against import substitution and export promotion strategies of development were discussed.

It was pointed out that the neoclassical view of development policy is that governments should not intervene in their national economies and that their role should simply be to establish an economic environment in which market forces would realize the efficient allocation of resources. The appropriate instruments for creating such an environment are said to be prices and price-denominated policies. Thus, governments of the developing countries are called upon to rationalise and liberalise economic policy around the price system so that they can allow the free play of market forces. In addition, they are advised to eliminate tariffs and quotas, or to reduce them substantially, and to devalue their currencies. It is pointed out that such policies would bring their countries' productive structures in line with comparative advantage which will enable them to achieve fast economic growth. To be able to do this, developing countries are advised to emulate the example of the newly industrialising countries by adopting outward-oriented industrialisation strategies which are said to have been behind the marvellous economic success of these countries. It is pointed out that outward-orientation made these countries pursue rational economic policies by liberalising imports, adopting realistic exchange rates, providing incentives for exports and, above all, getting factor prices right so that their economies could expand in line with their comparative advantage; and reliance on market forces and integration into the world economy yielded results far superior to protection and dissociation from the world economy.

What has been seen is that this is far from the truth. Most of the NICs adopted a system which involved government intervention with some controls and selective protection of some industries; and this system of planning was not abandoned by these countries, even when they turned to export-orientation. In particular, the prior success of import substitution played a crucial role in the success of the outward-orientation strategy of these countries. Furthermore, a favourable international environment, such as easy access to international finance and growing world trade, and re-locational activities of multinational corporations contributed greatly to the success of this strategy.

With regard to the theoretical basis, it has been seen that there are also valid reasons for government intervention and a policy of import substitution. These include the strategic trade theory and the problems of promoting exports due to such factors as the growing protectionism in the developed countries, the problem of shifting comparative advantage, the formation of regional economic blocs in the world economy, the recent market reforms in Eastern Europe, the role of the Bretton Woods institutions in de-industrialising the developing countries and the limited effect of facilitating instruments such as devaluation and countertrade.

There is, thus, no theoretical basis for the view that an "undistorted" price system, which outward-orientation is said to foster, leads to faster economic growth than government intervention or a policy of import substitution. Indeed, the development of the NICs was facilitated by active state intervention. The question of development policy is not simply one of choosing between outward-orientation and import-substitution. The essential aspect of development is structural change, particularly a switch from agriculture to industry. This is what Africa needs most if it is to get out of its abnormally low level of development. African countries need to increase their manufacturing industries and to establish a capital and intermediate goods sector which will act as a propelling force in inducing further industrial growth. The growing importance of the manufacturing industry was an important feature in the development of the now advanced countries and remains so even for the NICs. It matters less whether the process of industrialisation is achieved by import substitution or export promotion.

This is a point which African countries should bear in mind. There is not just one way of achieving industrialisation and African countries should not be misled into the view that this can only be done by adopting a strategy of outward-orientation simply because the Bretton Woods institutions which lend them money say so. Indeed, African countries should exercise care in obtaining financial assistance from the Bretton Woods institutions in support of the so-called structural adjustment programmes. The foreign exchange resources obtained under these programmes are mainly, if not totally, used for import liberalisation which is no more than the financing of consumption with borrowed funds instead of using such resources for upgrading their productive capacities. If this is not watched very carefully, it might lead, in future, to a new economic crisis of far greater proportions with increased debt service difficulties.

In Chapter 3, the various studies that have been undertaken on the relationship between exports and economic growth in an attempt to prove the superiority of export-oriented and free market policies over import-substituting and restrictive trade regimes were reviewed. It was shown that the evidence in support of the superiority of open and free market policies was not conclusive.

The many empirical studies that have been undertaken on the relationship between trade regime and economic growth have not provided conclusive evidence that export-orientation is superior to import-substitution. This is because of flaws in the methodologies they have used. The few recent studies that have tried to correct some of the flaws in the previous studies (i.e. the studies undertaken by Jung and Marshall and Chow) have indicated that no such conclusive evidence can be reached. Indeed, they have pointed to the possibility that import-substitution could very well be superior to outward-orientation. Moreover, we provide insight about the debate on the causal relationship between export promotion and economic growth by looking at the recent literature. As earlier noted, the economic success of the Pacific Basin countries, especially Indonesia, Malaysia, the Philippines, Singapore and Thailand has encouraged other developing countries to adopt aggressive export promotion strategies. A particularly interesting study by Ahman and Harnhirun (1996) provides evidence on cointegration and causality between export promotion and economic growth in the above five member countries of the ASEAN. It is found that exports do not cause the growth of GDP in the Granger sense in any of the countries; however, causality from economic

221

growth to exports is statistically supported in all countries. This evidence, therefore, does not support the export-led growth hypothesis for the most outward-oriented and fastest growth countries in the world. This finding is consistent with an entire body of literaturem and suggests that the answer to the primary question as to whether export promotes catalyses economic growth remains obscure.

In Chapter 4, a more efficient econometric estimating technique, to dispel the doubts that still surround the empirical studies that have so far been undertaken, was employed to study the relationship between trade regime and economic growth for a sample of ten African countries, south of the Sahara so as to contribute meaningfully to the on-going controversy on the subject matter. The econometric technique which was used in this regard is the Granger causality test using the two-stage least squares estimation technique.

It was argued that to prove the superiority of export promotion over import-substitution requires the fulfilment of three conditions: (a) outward orientation should be clearly distinguishable from non-outward orientation; (b) a causal link between outward orientation and export performance should be established; and (c) a causal link between export performance and economic growth should be established. To meet all these conditions, which none of the previous studies has attempted to do with the exception of the Krueger study, the analysis was supplemented by applying the Granger causality test to two countries, one of which has persistently pursued an export oriented strategy and another country which has experimented with both types of trade regimes. This analysis also benefited from the use of long series of observations which most of the previous studies did not have.

The analysis showed that for the ten countries in the sample, export promotion as a development strategy cannot be generalised. Policies of import substitution may be more helpful in bringing about economic growth in some of these countries. The analysis indicated that even for countries in Africa, the export promotion hypothesis is not of general applicability. Some countries would be helped by export promotion to achieve economic growth but other countries would be ill-advised to pursue such a strategy. For some of these countries, a strategy of import substitution would be more helpful in bringing about economic growth.

Chapters 5 and 6 supplemented the analysis of the relationship between trade regime and economic growth using the experiences of Zambia and Malawi, the former country having experimented with the two types of trade regimes at different time periods since independence in 1964 and the latter having essentially pursued an open trade policy since 1964 upon attaining independence. It was found that Zambia achieved better economic performance during periods when her export performance was poor and poor economic performance when her export performance was good. In particular, the country achieved high rates of economic growth when she was pursuing an import substitution industrialisation strategy; and low or negative rates of economic growth when she was having good export performance. This suggests that economic growth and export performance had no relationship with each other and that import subtitution manufacturing had some relationship with GDP. A Granger causality test between exports and GDP showed that the two did not bear any relationship. However, the same test carried out for manufacturing and GDP showed that there was a causal relationship between the two, with the causal relationship being uni-directional and running from manufacturing to GDP. This suggests that manufacturing was an important factor behind GDP growth. Liberalisation efforts implemented with a view to achieving improved export performance failed to restore growth. Instead, these measures destroyed the manufacturing sector which was an important source of the country's GDP growth. Furthermore, these measures failed to boost the performance of other sectors such as savings, investment and employment creation. On the other hand, the pursuit of import substitution did not appear to have led to inefficient methods of production. All in all, import substitution helped the country to achieve better economic performance while trade liberalisation failed to resuscitate the economy from economic collapse and made things even worse.

Malawi pursued an open and liberal trade regime and experienced good economic performance in the period 1964 to 1979, which seems to support the thesis that an outward-oriented strategy leads to superior economic performance. However, from 1980 to 1987, the Malawi economy experienced economic downturn, and further liberalisation of the economy failed to restore economic growth. The authorities pursued an export led development strategy in the belief that exports would play a key role in the growth of the country's GDP. But, as shown by the Granger causality test, exports bear no relationship to GDP. This suggests that a lot of development effort and resources were devoted to the development of a sector which could not make much difference to the country's GDP growth. Unfortunately, the development of other sectors which could have made a significant contribution to the growth of the country's GDP were relatively ignored. One such sector is manufacturing. The Granger causality test carried out between GDP growth and the growth of manufacturing suggests that the latter is an important causal factor in GDP growth. However, little attention was paid to the development of this sector which is an important source of growth. Instead, too much attention was devoted to the development of the export sector which has no causal relationship with GDP.

Further analysis of the country's general economic performance has shown that the liberal trade regime did little to bring about development and enhancement of other growth factors such as savings, investment and the efficiency use of scarce resources and did not help much in facilitating the creation of greater employment opportunities. In conclusion, the Malawi economy did well from 1964 to 1979 but met with difficulties from 1980 and efforts to liberalise the trade regime failed to restore economic growth partly because exports had no causal relationship with GDP.

7.2   Africa's prospects within the WTO

The new international trading system falls under the WTO. The WTO brings under one umbrella all the Uruguay Round Agreements, the GATT 1994 (which includes GATT 1947 and all amendments and protocols to it) and four multilateral agreements (the Agreement on Trade in Civil Aircraft, Agreement on Government Procurement, International Dairy Arrangement, and Arrangement Regarding Bovine Meat). Specifically, the WTO establishes the local framework for the new multilateral trading system as a single, indivisible undertaking. Membership in the WTO is conditional on countries having schedules of concessions and commitments on market access in industrial and agricultural products. Market access also covers the services sector, as reflected in the establishment of the General Agreement on Trade in Services (GATS). Member countries are bound to accept GATT 1994 as well as all of the Uruguay Round Agreements (see Safadi and Laird, 1996). It is expected that the WTO will increase coherence in policy making, through collaboration with the World Bank and the IMF.

For African economies, it would appear that the new WTO will lead to an expansion in trade, mainly due to the reductions in tariff and non-tariff barriers. African countries would thus stand to benefit from liberalization in agriculture and services; and open market access to industrial countries. However, the impact of the WTO (and especially the Uruguay Round 1994) on African countries has been a subject of much controversy.

Table 7.1
Summary of Uruguay round commitments in agriculture and industry, according to Sorsa (1996)

Country	WTO status	Agriculture						Share of lines bound in UR (%)	Industry		
		Ave bound duty (%)	Ave bound ODC (%)	Average rates (%)	Domestic support	Export subsidies	Previous bindings (% of lines)		Ave bound duty (%)	Ave bound ODC (%)	Average rates (%)
Angola	LD	80	0.1		-	-	0	3.8	80	0.1	
Benin	LD	60	18		-	-	29x	1.4	50	19	
Botswana	D	40*	-		-	-	31	68	17°	-	
Burkina Faso	LD	100	50		-	-	29x	1.2	100	50	
Burindi	LD	100	30		-	-	N/A	2.3	100	30	
Cameroon	D	80	24-70	24.5*	-	-	0	0.1	50	22-35	18.5
Ctrl African Rep	LD	30	16		-	-	0	56	38	16	
Chad	LD	80	-		-	-	0	0.0	75	-	
Congo	D	30	0		-	-	0	3.2	15	0	
pCote d'Ivoire	D	15	0-50	20Ω	◆	-	29x	0.4	7	28	
Dijbouti	LD	42	100		-	-	29*	71	40	100	27
Gabon	D	60	19		-	-	0	1.3	59	18	
Gambia	LD	102	10	22*	-	-	0	0.5	56	10	
Ghana	D	98	0.2		-	-	29*	1.1	33	0	
Guinea	LD	38	24		-	-	0	1.3	26	23	16*
Guinea Bissau	LD	40	26	44*	-	-	0	97	50	50	
Kenya	D	100	0		◆	-	0	1.6	54	0	35*
Lesotha	LD	200	-	39Ω	-	-	N/A	100	60	-	
Madagascar	LD	30	250		-	-	N/A	11.1	30	250	41
Malawi	LD	124	20		◆	-	29x	3.6	47	20	
Mali	LD	60	50	52Ω	-	-	29x	2.8	60	50	
Mauritania	LD	37	15		-	-	0	1.3	30	15	63
Mauritius	D	120	17		-	-	0	1.6	65	17	
Mozambique	LD	100	300		-	-	0	1.9	80	300	
Namibia	D	40*	0		-	-	31	68	70°	0	22•

225

Table 7.1 concluded

Country	WTO status	Agriculture					Industry				
		Ave bound duty (%)	Ave bound ODC (%)	Average rates (%)	Domestic support	Export subsidies	Previous bindings (% of lines)	Share of lines bound in UR (%)	Ave bound duty (%)	Ave bound ODC (%)	Average rates (%)
Niger	LD	80	50	-	-	-	29x	65	50	50	-
Nigeria	D	150	80	47*	-	-	0.1	7.0	48	80	36*
Rwanda	LD	80	-	-	-	-	N/A	100	100	-	-
Senegal	D	30	150	44*	◆	-	29x	2	30	44	34*
Sierra Leone	LD	40	20	-	-	-	0	100	49	20-50	-
South Africa	IND	40*	-	7*	by 2000	by 2000	31	68	17°	-	22•
Swaziland	D	40*	-	34Ω	-	-	31	68	17°	-	22•
Tanzania	LD	120	120	-	-	-	0	0.1	120	120	28
Togo	LD	80	7	-	-	-	0	1.0	80	7	
Uganda	LD	80	0	-	-	-	0	2.7	50	-	
Zaire	LD	98	-	-	-	-	N/A	100	96	-	
Zambia	LD	124	0	-	-	-	N/A	4.0	42	-	
Zimbabwe	D	146	15	24*	-	-	8	0.8	38	29	31*

Notes:

■   Simple averages of bound rates as reported in countries' UR schedules

*   From GATT Trade Policy Reviews, latest available

◆   List of domestic programmes permitted, no subsidy commitment

○   Reduced from 24 percent to 17 percent

•   Trade weighted averages

x   Assumes countries with (x) applied same schedule as Senegal as former French colonies

Δ   Assumed same as South Africa

LD = Least developed; D = developing; IND = industrial

Source: Sorsa (1996; p.288-9), Table 1.

Table 7.2

Overview of initial commitments in services by sector (status: 1995)

Country	Total	1 Bus	2 Com	3 Cons	4 Distr	5 Educ	6 Envir	7 Fin	8 Hlth	9 Tour	10 Recr	11 Trans	12 Other	MFN Exem
Angola	2							X		X				X
Benin	3							X		X		X		X
Botswana	3	X	X							X				
Burkina Faso	1									X				
Burindi	5													
Cameroon	2	X								X				X
Ctrl African Rep	5	X	X				X			X	X			
Chad	1									X				
Congo	2									X	X			X
Cote d'Ivoire	4	X		X						X		X		X
Djibouti	3		X							X	X			
Gabon	4	X		X				X		X				
Gambia	12	X	X	X	X	X	X	X	X	X	X	X	X	
Ghana	5			X		X		X		X		X		X
Guinea	5	X					X		X	X		X		
Guinea Bissau	2									X	X			
Kenya	5	X	X					X				X	X	
Lesotha	10	X	X	X	X	X	X	X		X		X	X	
Madagascar	1									X				
Malawi	5	X		X					X	X	X			
Mali	2					X				X				X
Mauritania	2		X							X				
Mauritius	1									X				X
Mozambique	1							X						
Namibia	2	X								X				

Table 7.2 concluded

Country	Total	1 Bus	2 Com	3 Cons	4 Distr	5 Educ	6 Envir	7 Fin	8 Hlth	9 Tour	10 Recr	11 Trans	12 Other	MFN Exem
Niger	2									X		X		X
Nigeria	4		X					X		X		X		
Rwanda	5	X	X	X			X			X	X			
Sierra Leone	10	X	X	X		X	X	X	X	X	X	X		X
South Africa	9	X			X	X	X	X		X		X	X	X
Swaziland	2								X					
Tanzania	1													
Togo	3		X							X	X			
Uganda	1									X				
Zaire	6	X	X	X		X				X	X			
Zambia	4	X		X					X	X				
Zimbabwe	3		X					X		X				X
Total By Sector		19	14	11	5	7	7	12	7	35	11	12	4	12

Source: Sorsa (1996; p.299-300), Table 2.

Note: Bus = Business; Com = Communication; Cons = Construction; Distr = Distribution; Educ = Education; Envir = Environment; Fin = Finance; Hlth = Health; Tour = Tourism; Recr = Recreation; Trans = Transport; MFN Exem = Manufacturing exemption.

While some analysts have raised concerns about the high costs for African countries of complying with the new obligations and the extent these may impede some development strategies, some analysts have pointed out the potential market losses for Africa arising from the possible erosion in the value of its preferences in its export markets following overall cuts in tariffs, and the possible terms-of-trade losses if net importers of food face higher food prices (Sorsa, 1996).

Given that the most recent trade investigations that are bound to influence the behaviour of African countries in the new WTO are contained in the Uruguay Round 1994, it is interesting to highlight the commitments by African countries in the Round. There are three main sectors in which commitments have been made; namely agriculture, industry and services. A summary of the commitments in agriculture and industry, based on Sorsa (1996, Table 1) is given in Table 7.1. An overview of the initial commitments in services by sector, for all the member African countries, is presented in Table 7.2.

The main argument by Sorsa (1996), as contained in Table 7.1 and Table 7.2, is that most African countries did not make substantial liberalization commitments in the Uruguay Round in terms of agriculture, industry and the services sector. However, some of the policies were not directly relevant to most African countries; for example, the Uruguay Round schedules discourage subsidies in agriculture, African countries actually tax (and not subsidise) the agriculture sector. In addition, given that the commitments will hold for the foreseeable future, some African countries have preferred not to lock themselves into non-negotiable commitments. Whether, by so doing, African countries have missed an opportunity to bind themselves to the international trading framework can only be judged in terms of whether or not the countries are losing access to international markets in the long run. As the economies develop, it will become very important to compete in the export market for light industrial goods and agriculture-based manufactured products. Future research should be able to measure the welfare effects and the general benefits that have accrued to two control groups of African countries; those that have undertaken greater commitment within the Uruguay Round vis-à-vis the group of countries that have abstained from any commitment.

7.3   Concluding remarks

This raises the question as to whether we should believe that we must choose rigidly between one trade strategy or the other or whether we should combine both, if the possibilities so suggest. Certainly, whatever is adopted should depend on local circumstances. Outward-looking policies have meant stagnation in some cases, while other economies have grown rapidly under the same policies. The choice of which strategy to choose should depend partly on the circumstances of each individual country. A big country with abundant natural resources, or a common market shared with a number of neighbours, is less dependent on imports from abroad. A period of relative isolation is perhaps necessary to start building up industry until the economy is strong enough to start competing abroad. Countries which are close to the industrial centres and have cheap transport links with them are particularly likely to benefit from access to their markets.

The transition from an inward to an outward-looking policy can involve a country in a painful process of change, especially for a poor country that would in general find it difficult to adapt its economic structure by moving resources from one sector to another. Some countries could find it easier to proceed with a relatively closed economy, perhaps integrated with some other poor countries, and delay its exposure to foreign competition until the process of development has proceeded further. It is also too simple to suggest that less government intervention is all that is required in order to bring about growth and development through an outward-oriented strategy. Detailed planning could well be required if such a strategy is to be pursued successfully, especially if the transition from a highly protected to a more open economy is to be smooth. Unless entrepreneurs respond rapidly to changed circumstances, government intervention might be essential. Nor should the developing countries follow blindly the pattern of industrialization of the rich countries or of the newly industrialised countries. A concentration of efforts in small industry and agriculture could in some cases bring quicker results than an effort to absorb modern technology and break into competitive markets of the rich. All considered, the choice is not simply between an open or a closed economy, it may be possible to combine features of both.

It is, therefore, unfortunate that international financial institutions have given such disproportionately great weight to trade liberalisation in many of their policy reform packages which they often propose to African governments as conditions for obtaining their financial assistance. This stems from a belief that much of the fault for Africa's economic malaise is due to misguided trade policies: high and variable rates of import licences, export taxes, and export marketing boards which pass along few of the benefits of trade to producers. The World Bank's structural adjustment and IMF's stabilisation programmes aim at removing these impediments by liberalising the economic system in order to allow the operation of free market forces. Export promotion policies are believed to assist in bringing about such an environment. The call for liberalisation is based on allocative efficiency: high rates of trade protection distort resource allocation by directing labour, capital, and entrepreneurial talent away from export-oriented sectors and towards import-competing activities and that variable rates of effective protection among the latter introduce further distortions. The proponents of liberalisation argue that trade reform eradicates these biases and raises national income through re-allocation of factors of production to where they are more productive and that these gains can be multiplied many times over if there is also a considerable reduction in the wasteful rent-seeking activities which tend to arise out of protective trade regimes.

The results of this study seem to indicate that to argue that the mere institution of free market forces would direct labour, capital and entrepreneurial talent to where they are more productive, even in cases where such production factors do not exist, is an oversimplification. The process of economic growth is multifaceted. The development literature is full of theories about the necessary ingredients of growth, such as the existence of capital, savings, foreign exchange, entrepreneurship, human skills, technical know-how, etc. It is doubtful that trade reform alone can increase the rate of economic growth, or that it can improve technological performance. Therefore, it might well be prudent not to pin too many hopes on liberalisation and be skeptical about any argument that attempts to draw a causal link between factor productivity and its rate of growth, on the one hand, and trade policy, on the other. Free market forces might not always work.

Import substitution is still a viable option that is available to African countries, which they can also pursue as part of a wider strategy to lay a firm basis for developing exports later on. This is not to say that export promotion is not a viable strategy which can be pursued from the very beginning. Rather, the point is that the promotion of manufacturing by import-substitution via protection can eventually lead to exporting by these same sectors (as it happened in the case of the NICs) and this is an instance of a more general theory about the possible role of trade protection of a temporary nature in economic development, as advanced by the infant industry argument. Indeed, export promotion and import substitution can go hand-in-hand. However, one would like to exercise caution here. As we have seen, the prospects for outward-orientation are not very promising due to various unfavourable factors in the international environment. Given this situation, African countries would probably do better if they paid more attention to import substitution. However, the narrow and fragmented national markets in Africa is a major constraint and they should, therefore, base such import substitution on regional markets within Africa. The African regional economic integration groupings, such as the ECOWAS and the COMESA (formerly PTA), have provided a framework for making this possible. Here is where their opportunity lies to make their import substitution industries succeed based on regional markets where they would not contend with stiff competition from the advanced and the newly industrialising countries, as their products are discriminated against as third country products in these markets. The competition in these markets is among equals with more or less the same level of development and producing products of more or less the same quality. It would be after gaining experience in these markets that they will be able to compete far afield. But by then their countries will have achieved a significant measure of industrialisation and development for the well being of their people. Manufacturing industry holds the key to economic development and African countries should take advantage of the African regional integration groupings to develop their manufacturing industries on the basis of import substitution for national and subregional markets.

To develop manufacturing industry based on national and subregional markets will require African countries to also pay attention to other sectors of the economy. Of particular importance is an increase in agricultural productivity and growth without which industrial development will be difficult to sustain. The expansion of general education is also of critical importance as it is vitally essential to inculcate a scientific and experimental outlook in the population at large so as to internalise the factors necessary for sustained industrial development.

Bibliography

Ambler, S., Cardia, E. and Farazli, J. (1996) On export promotion and growth, *Canadian Journal of Economics*, 29 (2): S366-S370.

Balassa, Bela (1981) *The Newly Industrialising Countries in the World Economy*, New York, Pergamon Press.

Balassa, Bela (1985) Exports, policy choices and economic growth in developing countries. *Journal of Development Economics*, 18: 23-35.

Balasubramanyam, V. N., Salisu, M. and Sapsford, D. (1996) Foreign direct investment and growth in EP and IS countries, *Economic Journal*, 106 (434): 92-105.

Bank of Zambia (1985) *Report and Statement of Accounts for the year ended 31st December*, Lusaka, Zambia.

Banks, Gary (1983) The economics and politics of countertrade, *The World Economy*, 6: 159-182.

Barbone, Luca and Rivera-Batiz, Francisco (1987) Foreign capital and the contractionary impact of currency devaluation, with an application to Jamaica, *Journal of Development Economics*, 26: 1-15.

Barro, R. (1991) Economic growth in a cross section of countries, *Quarterly Journal of Economics*, 106, 2: 407-443.

Bates, Robert H.(1988) Economic Reforms in Africa, a paper presented at a seminar on Economic Reform and Liberalisation in Africa held in Nairobi, Kenya.

Beladi, H. and Marjit, S. (1996) An analysis of rural-urban migration and protection, *Canadian Journal of Economics*, 29 (4): 930-940.

Bhagwati, J and Panagariya, A. (1996) The theory of preferential trade agreements: Historical evolution and current trends, *American Economic Review*, 86 (2): 82-87.

Bhagwati, J. and Rao, M. (1996) The U.S. brain gain - At the expense of Blacks? *Challenge*, 39 (2): 50-54.

Bhagwati, Jagdish (1988) *Protectionism*. Cambridge, Massachusetts: The MIT Press.

Bhagwati, Jagdish (1978) *Foreign Trade Regimes and Economic Development: Anatomy and Consequences of Exchange Control Regimes.* Cambridge, Massachusetts, National Bureau of Economic Research, Ballinger Publishing Company.

Bhagwati, Jagdish (1983) *The Theory of Commercial Policy* edited by Robert C. Feenstra, Cambridge, Massachusetts, Massachusetts Institute of Technology Press.

Bhagwati, Jagdish (1985) *Dependence and Interdependence* edited by Gene Grossman - Essays in Development Economics, Volume 2, The MIT Press, Cambridge, Massachusetts.

Blomstrom, M., Lipsey, R. E. and Zejan, M. (1996) Is fixed investment the key to economic growth? *Quarterly Journal of Economics*, 111 (1): 269-276.

Brownm M. B. and P. Tiffen (1992) *Short Changed: Africa and World Trade*, London and Colorado: Pluto Press with the Transnational Institute.

Bruno, Michael (1979) Classifying Trade Regimes in Trade Policy for Developing Countries, by Donald B. Keesing, *World Bank Staff Working Paper* No. 353.

Campose, C and Luis, S. (1996) Sleeping quotas, pre-emptive quota bidding and monopoly power, *Journal of International Economics*, 40 (1-2): 127-148.

Chenery, Horris B. (1980) Interactions between industrialisation and exports. *American Economic Review: Papers and Proceedings*, 70- 2, 288-292.

Chow, Peter C. Y. (1989) Causality between export growth and industrial development: Empirical evidence from the NICs - Reply. *Journal of Development Economics* 31: 416-417.

Chu, W. (1997) Causes of growth: A study of Taiwan's bicycle industry, *Cambridge Journal of Economics*, 21 (1): 55-72.

Clarete, Ramon L. and Whalley, John (1988) Interactions between trade policies and domestic distortions in a small open developing country. *Journal of International Economics* 24: 345-358.

Bibliography

Czinkota, M. R. (1996) Why national export promotion, *International Trade Forum*, 2: 10-13.

DeRosa, D. (1996) Regionalism and the bias against agriculture in less developed countries, *World Economy*, Global Trade Policy Supplement: 45-66.

Dollar, D. (1991) Outward-oriented developing economies really do grow more rapidly: Evidence from 95 LDCs, 1976-85, *Economic Development and Cultural Change*, 39:220-235.

Doraisami, A. (1996) Export growth and economic growth: A reexamination of some time-series evidence of the Malaysian experience, *Journal of Developing Areas*, 30 (2): 223-230.

Durkin, J. T. Jr (1996) Falling behind and catching up in a model of North-South trade, *Review of International Economics*, 4 (2): 218-233.

Economic Commission for Africa (1989) *African Alternative Framework to Structural Adjustment Programmes for Socio-economic Recovery and Transformation*. Addis Ababa: United Nations.

Edwards, S. (1992) Trade orientation, distortion, and growth in developing countries, *Journal of Development Economics*, 39: 31-57.

El-Osta, B., MacPhee, C. R. and Rosenbaum, D. (1996) International trade, foreign direct investment and domestic market performance, *Eastern Economic Journal*, 22 (1): 63-74.

Esfahani, Hadi S. (1991) Exports, imports, and economic growth in semi-industrialized countries. *Journal of Development Economics*, 35: 93-116.

Evans, David and Alizadeh, Parvin (1984) Trade, industrialisation, and the visible hand, *Journal of Development Studies*, 21 (1): 22-46.

Fajana, Olufemi (1979) Trade and growth: the Nigerian experience, *World Development*, 7 (1): 73-78.

Falvey, R. E. and Gemmell, N. (1996) A formalisation and test of the factor productivity explanation of international differences in service prices, *International Economic Review*, 37, (1): 85-102.

Feder, Gershon (1982) On exports and economic growth, *Journal of Development Economics*, 12: 59-73.

Fischer, R. D. and Serra, P. (1996) Income inequality and choice of free trade in a model of intraindustry trade, *Quarterly Journal of Economics*, 111 (1): 41-64.

Fishlow, Albert (1984) Five stages in my thinking on development by Raul Prebisch: Comment. In Meier, Gerald M. and Seers, Dudley (Eds.) *Pioneers in Development*, Washington, D.C: World Bank.

Francois, J. F. and Kaplan, S. (1996) Aggregate demand shifts, income distribution, and the Linder hypothesis, *Review of Economics and Statistics*, 78 (2): 244-250.

Fransman, Martin (1985) Conceptualising technical change in the Third World in the 1980s: An interpretive survey, The *Journal of Development Studies* 21- 4, 572-652.

Frimpong-Ansah, J.H. (1990) *From Predator to Vampire: The State and the Economy in Ghana*, London, James Currey.

Fujita, Natsuki and James, William E. (1989) Export promotion and the heavy industrialization of Korea, 1973-83, *The Developing Economies*, XXVII (3): 236-249.

Galiani, S and Petrecolla, D. (1996) The changing role of the public sector: An ex-post view of the privatization process in Argentina, *Quarterly Review of Economics and Finance*, 36 (2): 131-152.

Geroski, P. A. (1989) Entry, innovation and productivity growth, *The Review of Economics and Statistics*, 71: 572-578.

Glick, R. and Moreno, R. (1997) The Asian miracle: Growth because of government intervention and protectionism or in spite of it? *Business Economics*, 32 (2): 20-25.

Goldar, Bishwanath (1986) Import substitution, industrial concentration and productivity growth in Indian manufacturing, *Oxford Bulletin of Economics and Statistics*, 48, 2: 143-164.

Gulhati, Ravi, Bose, Swadesh & Atukorala Vimal (1985) Exchange rate policies in Eastern and Southern Africa 1965-1983, *World Bank Staff Working Papers*, No.720 Washington, D.C.

Hare, Paul (1987) Economic reform in Eastern Europe, *Journal of Economic Surveys* 1 (1): 25-58.

Harrison, Ann E. (1994) Productivity, imperfect competion, and trade reform: Theory and evidence, *Journal of International Economics*, 36: 53-73.

Harvey, Andrew (1990) *The Economic Analysis of Time Series*, London: Philip Allan.

Heitger, Bernhard (1986) Import protection and export performance: Their impact on economic growth, *Weltwirtschaftliches Archiv*, 260 (July): 1-19.

Helleiner, G. K. (1996) Why small countries worry: Neglected issues in current analyses of the benefits and costs for small countries of integrating with large ones, *World Economy*, 19 (6): 759-763.

Hiemenz, Ulrich (1988) Expansion of ASEAN-EC trade in manufactures: Pertinent issues and recent developments, *The Developing Economies*, XXVI (4): 341 - 57.

Hirata, Akira (1988) Promotion of manufactured exports in developing countries. *The Developing Economies*, XXVI (4): 422-437.

Hoekman, B. (1996) The European Union's Mediterean free trade initiative, *World Economy*, 19 (4): 387-406.

Hogendon, J. S. (1992) *Economic Development*, London: Harper Collins.

Hsiao, Mei-chu W. (1987) Test of causality and exogeneity between exports and economic growth: The case of the Asian NICs, *Journal of Economic Development*, 12 (2): 143-159.

Imagawa, Takeshi (1985) Export as an additional variable in the income determining function. *Journal of Developing Economies*, XXIII (2): 105-120.

Ingco, M. D. (1996) Tariffication in the Uruguay Road: How much liberalisation? *World Economy*, 19 (4): 425-446.

Ingeue, C. A. and Beladi, H. (1996) Urban unemployment, variable returns to scale and terms of trade, *Managerial and Decision Economics*, 17 (3): 241-442.

Jung, Woo S. and Marshall, Peyton J. (1985) Exports, growth and causality in developing countries, *Journal of Development Economics*, 18: 1-12.

Kaminski, B., Wang, Z. K. and Winters, L. A. (1996) Trade performance - export reorientation in the transition, *Economic Policy*, 23 (October): 421-442.

Kaplinsky, Raphael (1984) The international context for industrialisation in the coming decade, *Journal of Development Studies*, 21 (1): 75-96.

Kaunda, K.D. (1987) Speech on New Economic Recovery Programme, May 1, 1987 released by Cabinet Office on May 2, 1987 in Lusaka.

Kavoussi, Rostam M. (1984) Export expansion and economic growth, *Journal of Development Economics*, 14: 241-250.

Kavoussi, Rostam M. (1985) International trade and economic development: the recent experience of developing countries, *Journal of Developing Areas*, 379-392.

Keesing, Donald B.(1979) Trade policy for developing countries. *World Bank Staff Working Papers*, No. 353, Washington, D.C.

Keller, W. (1996) Absorptive capacity: On the creation and aquisition of technology in development, *Journal of Development Economics*, 49 (1): 199-227.

Kennedy, Peter (1986) *A Guide to Econometrics*, Cambridge, Massachusetts, The MIT Press.

Korhonen, H. Luostarinen, R. and Welch, L. (1996) Internationalization of SMEs: Inward-outward patterns and government policy, *Management International Review*, 36 (4): 315-329.

Krueger, A. O. (1997) Trade policy and economic development: How we learn, *American Economic Review*, 87 (1): 1-22.

Krueger, A.O. (1981) *Trade and Employment in Developing Countries*, Chicago, University of Chicago Press.

Krueger, Anne O. (1978) *Foreign Trade Regimes and Economic Development: Liberalization Attempts and Consequences*, National Bureau of Economic Research 1978, Cambridge, Massachusetts, Ballinger Publishing Company.

Krueger, Anne O. (1980) Trade policy as an input to development, *American Economic Review: Papers and Proceedings*, 70 (2): 288-292.

Krueger, Anne O. and Baran Tuncer (1982) An empirical test of the infant industry argument, *American Economic Review*, 72 (5): 1142-1152.

Krueger, Anne. O. (1985) Import substitution versus export promotion, *Finance and Development*, 22 (2): 20-23.

Krugman, P. (1996) A country is not a company, *Harvard Business Review*, 74 (1): 40-51.

Krugman, P. (1996) The Adam Smith address: What difference does globalization make? *Business Economics*, 31 (1): 7-10.

Krugman, P. (1997) Our misplaced fear of the Third World, *Across the Board*, 34 (3): 11.

Krugman, P. (1997) What should trade negotiators negotiate about? *Journal of Economic Literature*, 35 (1): 113-120.

Krugman, P. and Livas Elizondo, R. (1996) Trade policy and the third world metropolis, *Journal of Development Economics*, 49 (1): 137-150.

Krugman, P. and Venables, A. (1996) Integration, specialization, and adjustment, *European Economic Review*, 40 (3-5): 959-967.

Krugman, Paul R. (1987) Is free trade passe? *Economic Perspectives*, 1 (2): 131-144.

Kunst, Robert M. and Dalia Marin, (1989) On exports and productivity: A causal analysis, *Review of Economic and Statistics*, 71: 699-703.

Kuruvilla, S. (1996) Linkages between industrialization strategies and industrial relations and human resource policies: Singapore, Malaysia, The Phillipines, and India, *Industrial and Labor Relations Review*, 49 (4): 635-657.

Lal, Deepak and Rajapatirana, Sarath (1987) Foreign trade regimes and economic growth in developing countries, *World Bank Research Observer*, 2 (2): 189-217.

Lewis, Arthur W. (1980) The slowing down of the engine of growth. *American Economic Review*, 70: 555-564.

Lewis, Arthur W. (1984) Development economics in the 1950s. In Meier, Gerald M. and Seers, Dudley (Eds.) *Pioneers in Development*, Washington, D.C: World Bank.

Luedde-Neurath, R. (1983) Import controls and export oriented development: A re-examination of the South Korean case 1962-82 Institute of Development Studies, University of Sussex, mimeo.

Malawi Government (1985) *Public Sector Financial Statistics* 1969, 1970, 1973, 1976, 1982 and 1984 - 85

Malawi Government (1986) *Statement of Development Policies*, 1987-1996.

Malawi National Statistical Office: (1985) Annual Economic Survey 1980 - 1981, June (and various issues from 1971).

Malawi (1981) Country Presentation to the United Nations Conference on the Least Developed Countries April 7.

Malawi (1981) *Statement of Development Policies*, 1971-1980.

Malawi (1985) *Economic Report*, Malawi Government.

McKinnon, Ronald I. (1979) Foreign trade regimes and economic development: A review article, *Journal of International Economics* 9: 429-452.

Meier, Gerald M. (1984) The formative period. In Meier, Gerald M. and Seers, Dudley (Eds.) *Pioneers in Development*, Washington, D.C: World Bank.

Meier, Gerald M. (1996) *Leading Issues in Economic Development*, New York, Longmans.

Meijer, Fons (1990) Structural adjustment and diversification in Zambia, *Development and Change*, 21: 657-692.

Menon, J. (1996) The degree and determinants of exchange rate pass-through: Market structure, non-tariff barriers and multinational corporations, *Economic Journal*, 106 (435): 434-444.

Moore, Robert E. (1990) Can trade liberalization lead to an increase in poverty in Central America? *Journal of Economic Development*, 15 (2): 83-91.

Moschos, Demetrios (1989) Export expansion, growth and the level of economic development, *Journal of Development Economics*, 30: 93-102.

Mosley, Paul and Smith, Lawrence (1989) Structural adjustment and agricultural performance in sub-Saharan Africa 1980-87, *Journal of International Development*, 1 (3): 321-355.

Muchelemba, Josephine B. (1988) Employment Prospects In The new Economic Recovery Programme a paper presented at the Tripartite Symposium on The Place of Human Resources and Industrial Relations In the New Economic Recovery Programme, New Fairmount Hotel, Livingstone, 14-16th March, 1988.

Mulaga, G. and J. Weiss (1996) Trade reform and manufacturing performance in Malawi, 1970-91, *World Development*, 24 (7): 1267-1278.

Murinde, V. (1993) *Macroeconomic Policy Modelling for Developing Countries*, Aldershot, Avebury.

Murinde, V. (1996) *Development Banking and Finance*, Aldershot, Avebury.

Mwananshiku, L. (1985) Statement at the Official Opening of the Workshop on the Economic Problems facing Zambia Lusaka, November 26, 1985.

Myles, Gareth D. (1991) Tariff policy and imperfect competition, *The Manchester School*, lix-1, 24-44.

National Commission for Development Planning (1984) Restructuring in the Midst of Crisis, Volume 1: Development Policies and Objectives - Report for the Consultative Group for Zambia; May 22 - 24, 1984.

National Commission for Development Planning (1985): An Action Programme for Economic Restructuring - Report for the Consultative Group for Zambia, June.

National Commission for Development Planning (1988): Report of the Tariff Commission of Inquiry, Volumes I and II, September.

National Commission for Development Planning (1989): Fourth National Development Plan 1989 - 1993, for Zambia.

National Commission for Development Planning (1989): New Economic Recovery Programme: Interim National Development Plan July 1987 - December.

Newbold, P. and Vougas, D. (1996) Drift in the relative price of primary commodities: A case where we care about unit roots, *Applied Economics*, 28 (6): 653-661.

Nishimizu, M. and Sherman Robinson (1984) Trade policies and producivity change in semi-industrialised countries, *Journal of Development Economics*, 16: 177-206.

Nishimizu, Micko and John M. Page, Jr. (1990) Trade Policy, market orientation and productivity change in industry, in J. de Melo and A. Sapir, eds, *Trade Theory and Economic Reform North, South and East*, New York: Oxford University Press.

Nitsch, V. (1996) Do three trade blocs minimise world welfare? *Review of International Economics*, 4 (3): 557-568.

Nixson, Frederick (1989) The less developed countries and the global economy. The *Journal of Development Studies*, 26 (1): 145-156.

Njinkeu, D. (1996) Evaluation of the incentive structure: A survey and application to Cameroon, *World Development*, 24 (3): 557-568.

Nomvete Bax D. (1984) Statement to the Fourth Meeting of the PTA Council of Ministers held in Harare, Zimbabwe, in June, 1984.

Nomvete, Bax D. (1989) Some observations on the issues and potential effects relating to the establishment of a single European market and Lome IV negotiations: implications for the PTA.

Nowak, Michael (1984) Quantitative controls and unofficial markets in foreign exchange: A theoretical framework, *IMF Staff Papers* 404-431.

Ocampo, José Antonio (1986) New developments in trade theory and LDCs, *Journal of Development Economics*, 22 (1): 129-170.

O'Neil, Helen (1987) Transforming a Single - Product Economy: An Examination of the First Stage of Zambia's Economic Reform Program, 1982-86 Economic Development Institute.

Pack, Howard and Westphal, Larry E. (1986) Industrial strategy and technological change: theory versus reality, *Journal of Development Economics*, 22 (1): 87-127.

Palivos, T. and Yip, C. K. (1997) The effects of import quotas on national welfare: Does money matter? *Southern Economic Journal*, 63 (3): 751-760.

Pitt, Mark M. (1981) Smuggling and price disparity, *Journal of International Economics*, 11: 447-458.

Prebisch, Raul (1984) Five stages in my thinking on development. In Meier, Gerald M. and Seers, Dudley (Eds.) *Pioneers in Development*, Washington, D.C: World Bank.

Quibria, M. G. (1989) Neoclassical political economy: Application to trade policies, *Journal of Economic Surveys*, 3 (2): 107-136.

Ram, R. (1985) Exports and economic growth: Some additional evidence, *Economic Development and Cultural Change*, 33 (2): 415-425.

Ram, Rati (1987) Exports and economic growth in developing countries: Evidence from time-series and cross-section data, *Economic Development and Cultural Change*, 36 (1): 51-72.

Ranis, Gustav (1990) Asian and Latin American experience: Lessons for Africa, *Journal of International DevelopmentI*, 2 (2): 151-171.

Rausser, Gordon and Thomas, Scott (1990) Market politics and foreign assistance, *Development Policy Review*, 8 (4): 365-381.

Reserve Bank of Malawi (1987) *Developments in the Currency Pegs of the Malawi Kwacha Exchange Rate and Reasons Behind the Changes*, October 1987.

Reserve Bank of Malawi (1988) *Financial and Economic Review*, Volume 20, No. 1, 1988

Ressler, R. W., Watson, J. K. and Mixon, F. G. Jr (1996) Full wages, part-time employment and the minimum wage, *Applied Economics*, 28 (11): 1415-1419.

Riedel, James (1988) Trade as an engine of growth: Theory and evidence. In Greenaway, David. (Ed.) *Economic Development and International Trade*, London: Macmillan Education Ltd.

Roberts, E. B. and Senturia, T. A. (1996) Globalizing the emerging high-technology company, *Industrial Marketing Management*, 25 (6): 491-506.

Rodrik, Dani (1988) Trade Policy Issues for Sub-Saharan Africa a paper presented at a seminar on Economic Reform and Liberalisation in Africa held in Nairobi, Kenya, organised by CRED (University of Michigan) August, 1988.

Sanderson, Murray (1987) Auctioning of Foreign Exchange: Recent Experiences in Third World Countries - Why Zambia's Auction Failed a paper presented at the Seminar of the Economics Association of Zambia, 29 June - 3 July.

Sanna-Randaccio, F. (1996) New protectionism and multinational companies, *Journal of International Economics*, 41 (1-2): 29-51.

Sarkar, P. (197) Growth and terms of trade: A North-South macroeconomic framework, *Journal of Macroeconomics*, 19 (1): 117-133.

Sarkar, Prabirjit and Singer, H. W. (1991) Manufactured exports of developing countries and their terms of trade since 1965, *World Development*, 19 (4): 333-340.

Schmitz, Hubert (1984) Industrialisation strategies in less developed countries: Some lessons of historical experience, *Journal of Development Studies*, 21 (1): 1-21.

Sephton, Peter S. (1989) Causality between export growth and industrial development: Empirical evidence from the NICs - A comment, *Journal of Development Economics*, 31: 413-15.

Seshamani, V.(1988) Industrial Development in Zambia: Retrospect and Prospect. In Coughlin, P and Gerrishon, K. I.(Eds.) *Industrialisation in Kenya: In Search of a Strategy*, Nairobi: Heinemann.

Sheehey, Edmund J. (1990) Exports and growth: a flawed framework, *Journal of Development Studies*, 27 (1): 111-116.

Shove, C. (1996) A simplified, globally competitive economic development policy framework, *Economic Development Review*, 14 (2): 10-13.

Singer, H. W. (1990) Reading between the lines: a comment on the World Bank Annual Report 1989, *Development Policy Review*, 8: 203-206.

Singer, Hans W. (1988) The World Development Report on the blessings of 'outward orientation': A necessary correction, *Journal of Development Studies*, 24 (2): 233-235.

Singer, Hans W. (1971) The distribution of gains revisited. In Sir Alec Cairncross and Mohinder Puri (Eds.) *The Strategy of International Development*, London: Macmillan Publishing Co.

Singh, Ajit (1979) The 'basic needs' approach to development vs the new international economic order: the significance of Third World industrialization, *World Development*, 7: 585-606.

Singh, Ajit (1982) Industrialization in Africa: A structuralist view. In Fransman, Martin (Ed.) *Industry and Accumulation in Africa*, London: Heinemann.

Siwale, Winston and Ndulo, Manenga (1988) The Foreign Exchange Auction Regime: Zambian Experiences 1985 - 1987.

Sodersten, Bo (1980) International Economics Macmillan, London. Smith, Adam (1776) The Wealth of Nations Penguin English Library (1982), The Chancer Press Ltd, Bungay, Suffolk.

Sorsa, Piritta (1996) Sub-Saharan Africa and the Uruguay Round, The World Economy, pp. 299-300.

Stewart, Frances (1985) The fragile foundations of the neoclassical approach to development, *Journal of Development Studies*, 21 (2): 282-291.

Sutcliffe, Bob (1984) Industry and Underdevelopment Re-examined, *Journal of Development Studies*, 21 (1): 121-133.

Syrquin, Moshe and Hollis Chenery (1989) Three decades of industrialization, *The World Bank Economic Review*, 3 (2): 145-181.

Thomas, V. and J Nash (1992) *Best Practices: Lessons in Trade Policy Reform*, New York: Oxford University Press.

Tybout, J (1992) Researching the trade and productivity link: New directions, *World Bank Economic Review*, 6, 2.

Tyler, William G. (1981) Growth and export expansion in developing countries: Some empirical evidence, *Journal of Development Economics*, 9: 121-30.

United Nations Industrial Organisation (1987) Malawi: *Industrial Development Review Development Series*, October 19,1987.

Valdes-Prieto, Salvador (1990) Drawbacks for indirect exporters and monopoly power, *Journal of Development Economics*, 32: 389-417.

White, Gordon (1984) Developmental states and socialist industrialisation in the Third World, *Journal of Development Studies*, 21 (1): 97-120.

World Bank (1986) *Malawi and the World Bank*, Washington D.C., January 1986.

World Bank (1996) *World Development Report*, Washington D.C.: The World Bank.

World Bank: (1985) *Report to the Consultative Group for Zambia on Progress Towards Economic Restructuring*, Washington, D.C. April 30 .

World Bank: (1988) *Report to the Consultative Group for Malawi on the Government's Medium - Term Development Program*, Washington, D.C., May.

World Bank: (1988) *The Case of Malawi: Promising Reforms and Bad Luck - Preliminary Draft*, October 4.

Yeats, Alexander J. (1989) Developing countries' exports of manufactures: Past and future implications of shifting of comparative advantage, *The Developing Economies*, XXVII (2): 109-135.

Bibliography

Yokoyama, H.(1989) Export-led industrialisation and the Dutch Disease, *The Developing Economies*, XXVII (4): 427-445.

Zambia Cabinet Office (1987) New Economic Recovery Programme (Rules to Govern Applications and Criteria for Allocating Foreign Exchange), May 21.

Zambia Central Statistical Office (GRZ) (1979) *Census of Industrial Production*, 1974, November.

Zambia Central Statistical Office (GRZ) (1981) *Census of Industrial Production*, 1975, November.

Zambia Central Statistical Office (GRZ) (1984) *National Accounts and Input - Output Tables*, 1980, August.

Zambia Central Statistical Office (GRZ) (1986) *Zambia 1985: Country Profile*, September.

Zambia Central Statistical Office (GRZ) (1988) *National Accounts Statistical Bulletin*, No. 2, January.

Index